THE BIG BOOK OF CHICKEN

THE BIG

CHIC

MORE THAN 275 RECIPES FOR THE

BY MARYANA

BOOK OF

CHICKEN

WORLD'S FAVORITE INGREDIENT

VOLLSTEDT

CHRONICLE BOOKS
SAN FRANCISCO

Library of Congress Cataloging-in-Publication Data:

Vollstedt, Maryana.
The big book of chicken: more than 275 recipes for the world's favorite
ingredient / by Maryana Vollstedt.
    p. cm.
ISBN: 9 78-0-8118-5528-0 (alk. paper)
1. Cookery (Chicken)   I. Title.

TX750.5.C45V65 2008
641.6'65—dc22

2007042637

Manufactured in Canada.

Designed by NOON

10 9 8 7 6 5 4 3 2 1

Chronicle Books LLC
680 Second Street
San Francisco, California 94107

www.chroniclebooks.com

Foster Farms chicken is a registered trademark of Foster Farms;
Kamado grill is a registered trademark of L&R Logistics Inc.; Major
Grey's chutney is a registered trademark of J.M. Smucker Company;
Spanek vertical roaster is a registered trademark of Spanek Inc.;
Super Bowl is a registered trademark of the NFL; Tabasco sauce is a
registered trademark of McIlhenny Co.; Ziploc is a registered trademark
of S.C. Johnson Co.

DEDICATION

As always, I dedicate this book to my patient husband, Reed, who is my advisor, agent, tester, shopper, computer person, confidant, and best friend. He has encouraged and supported me throughout my many years of writing cookbooks. It has really been a team effort, and I couldn't have written them without him. Thank you, Reed.

* * *

ACKNOWLEDGMENTS

Thanks again to Bill LeBlond, editorial director of cookbooks at Chronicle Books, for his support and encouragement to continue to write cookbooks. *The Big Book of Chicken* is my ninth cookbook for Chronicle Books, following *Meatloaf, Pacific Fresh,* and *What's for Dinner?* and my best-selling "Big Book" series: *The Big Book of Easy Suppers, The Big Book of Potluck, The Big Book of Breakfast, The Big Book of Soups and Stews,* and *The Big Book of Casseroles.* To Amy Treadwell, project editor at Chronicle Books, for always being available for help and advice during the writing of the book; to Ann Martin Rolke for her expert copyediting, additions, and suggestions; and to all the staff at Chronicle Books. To my daughter Julie Glogau, who tested some of the recipes, and her husband Tom, who was a happy taster. And to Donna Addison, a good cook and friend, for her suggestions and testing.

Thanks to Bob Block and Brian Crow for their professional computer consulting and for their tasting-some-recipes-while-on-the-job consulting.

Special thanks to Foster Farms, who furnished me with more than a year's supply of chicken coupons for testing recipes. All of their quality products are 100 percent natural, with no added salt, chemicals, artificial enhancers, growth hormones, or steroids.

TABLE
OF CONTENTS

198 06_CHICKEN FROM THE OVEN

272 07_CASSEROLES

314 08_CHICKEN ON THE GRILL

INTRODUCTION

Chicken is recognized as the universal food because it appears in almost every civilization and cuisine. Modern-day chickens are the descendants of wild fowl that roamed the dense jungles of primeval Southeast Asia. The domesticated chicken first appeared in about 2000 B.C. in India.

It took centuries for the chicken to eventually become a staple food throughout the world. Each country developed its own poultry cuisine by adding regional ingredients and traditional cooking methods.

Chicken was introduced into the United States when the colonists arrived in 1607. In early times, the eggs were a more important food source than the meat because people had not yet developed a taste for the meat. Chicken has not always been as inexpensive and plentiful as it is today, and it was once considered a delicacy available only to the affluent. It wasn't until after World War II that modern production made it more affordable. Since then, chicken farming has become one of the largest agricultural industries in the United States. It has taken many years of crossbreeding with new chicken strains to develop the plump, meaty, lean bird with a white-fleshed breast characteristic of the chicken that we eat today.

Now chicken is more popular than ever and is the mainstay in many of our diets. It lends itself to almost every method of cooking, and because of its mild and unassertive flavor, it adapts well when combined with vegetables, fruits, pastas, and other ingredients.

In *The Big Book of Chicken,* you will find everything you ever wanted to know about chicken! Tips on how to buy, store, freeze, thaw, prepare, cut up, carve, and most important—HOW TO COOK!

Included are some of your old favorites updated, a few popular classics, many ethnic-inspired recipes, and a variety of new and exciting combinations. All of the recipes have been tested and geared for the home cook, with easy-to-follow directions. There is a recipe for every occasion, from casual and informal for family and friends to sophisticated and elegant for company.

Featured are finger-food appetizers and hors d'oeuvres, healthful soups, imaginative new sandwiches, fresh salads, easy stove-top dishes, hearty dishes from the oven, convenient casseroles, and a complete grilling section. With *The Big Book of Chicken,* this basic protein can always be interesting and exciting.

ALL ABOUT CHICKEN

❋ ADVANTAGES OF CHICKEN

º   It is an excellent source of protein and contains valuable minerals, such as potassium, phosphorus, and some B vitamins.

º   It is low in fat and cholesterol, especially the white meat without skin.

º   It is economical—less expensive than other meats.

º   It is easy to prepare and serve.

º   It lends itself well with other ingredients.

º   It has many uses—in hors d'oeuvres, soups, salads, and main dishes.

º   It is very versatile and can be cooked in many exciting ways.

º   It is readily available.

º   One chicken will easily feed a family of four for a nutritious meal.

º   It freezes well.

º   It adds variety to the menu.

º   It is popular with all ages.

❋ KINDS OF CHICKEN

The consumer today has a wide variety of choices in buying chicken, based on how it is grown, fed, butchered (for kosher), and shipped. However, federal regulations prohibit the use of hormones in all poultry, unlike some other meats.

All Natural
"Natural" chickens have no artificial flavoring, coloring, chemical preservatives, or synthetic ingredients added. They are minimally processed and are shipped fresh, not frozen. All-natural chickens are popular with the conscientious buyer.

Free Range

These are the elite birds because of the higher standards of growing conditions, in contrast to mass-produced poultry. By USDA standards, free-range chickens must have access to the out-of-doors. This does not mean they roam freely; they are still raised in a coop, but with an outside door available. Most are also organically grown, with a vegetarian diet free from antibiotics and growth enhancers. They may be more flavorful because they have been able to exercise. Because of added amenities and specialized growing conditions, they are more expensive.

Organic

Chickens labeled "organic" are raised on certified organically grown food, free from pesticides and antibiotics. They are also more expensive but may be worth it to some consumers.

Kosher

These chickens are produced and slaughtered according to Jewish dietary laws and are said to have more flavor because of strict quality control. They are always shipped frozen and are more expensive.

✳ CLASSIFICATIONS

Chickens are classified and sold by weight.

Cornish game hen	1½ to 2 pounds	roast or broil
Broiler	2½ to 3 pounds	fry, broil, or grill
Fryer	3 to 4 pounds	fry, broil, or grill
Rooster	3 to 5 pounds	have a higher fat content— oven roast or rotisserie
Stewing hen	3 to 6 pounds	an older and tougher chicken— braise or stew
Capon	4 to 10 pounds	a neutered rooster fed a rich diet; full flavored—roast

✳ PARTS OF A CHICKEN

Chicken is available whole, halved, quartered, in various parts, in combination packages, and ground.

Here is a list of standard, packaged chicken products. Some are not always available at all times in all markets.

- Broiler-fryer, cut into serving pieces
- Boneless, skinless breast fillets
- Half breasts with skin and bone
- Boneless, skinless breast halves
- Boneless, skinless breast tenders
- Thin-sliced boneless, skinless breast fillets
- Leg quarters (drumstick and thigh)
- Drumsticks
- Thighs with skin and bone or boneless and skinless
- Wings
- Drummettes (largest wing section)
- Whole chicken
- Roasters (higher fat content and more flavorful)
- Stewing hens (older chickens)
- Cornish game hens (miniature chickens)
- Backs and necks
- Gizzards
- Hearts
- Livers
- Premium parts (breasts, legs, and thighs)
- Grill pack (four large quarters and two breasts with bone)
- Preferred parts (half breasts and thighs)
- Whole, cut up into serving pieces (drumsticks, thighs, wings, breast)
- Ground chicken

✳ CHICKEN BREASTS

Chicken breasts are available halved with bone and skin on, or boned and skinned and in fillets. Boned and skinned chicken breast halves generally weigh between 6 and 8 ounces. They may vary with the producer. They sometimes come with a small extra piece on the side, called a tender. It can be removed and frozen until you get enough to use for a recipe. Tenders work well for stir-fries and sautés. When chicken breasts are uneven (thick on one end), you can flatten them slightly with the palm of your hand. Or, to flatten chicken breasts more completely, place them between two pieces of plastic wrap and pound with the flat side of a meat mallet until they reach the desired thickness.

❋ HOW TO BUY CHICKEN

Always buy from a reputable dealer. The general condition of the market should be clean and fresh, and the chicken attractively arranged in a refrigerated case. Buy chicken that looks fresh and plump without any bruises.

- ° For prepackaged chicken, check the label. It will state the contents, weight, price per pound, price per package, and "sell by" or "use by" date.

- ° Do not buy chicken in a package with bloody liquid in the tray or a package with a leak. Bloody liquid indicates it may have been partially frozen and then thawed.

- ° The color of the skin is determined by the feed and does not indicate freshness or quality.

- ° You can buy chicken by the piece at some markets.

- ° When grocery shopping, buy your chicken last and refrigerate it as soon as possible upon returning home. Do not leave chicken in a warm car. If you are going to be delayed, you can ask for a bag of ice.

- ° Buying family packs of chicken is economical. Wrap individual pieces or combinations in aluminum foil or freezer bags and freeze for later use. Label contents and date.

- ° Premium choice parts (2 breast halves with bone, 2 thighs, and 2 drumsticks) can be purchased in packages in some supermarkets.

- ° Buying a whole chicken to cut up is also economical (see page 21).

❋ HOW TO STORE, FREEZE, AND THAW CHICKEN

To prevent salmonella or food poisoning developing from bacteria found in raw chicken, extra precautions must be taken for proper care and safety. The "danger zone" in which bacteria can quickly reproduce is 40 to 140 degrees F, so it's best to keep chicken below 40 degrees or above 140 degrees.

- Keep store-wrapped chicken in the coolest part of the refrigerator (bottom shelf) and use within 1 or 2 days.

- Follow the safe handling instructions printed on the package. If chicken is wrapped in butcher paper, rewrap or place it in a plastic bag.

- Store raw chicken away from cooked foods, on the lowest shelf possible. Do not let raw chicken drip onto other foods.

- To store chicken leftovers: Cover and refrigerate leftovers as soon as the meal is over. However, some food safety experts recommend that you let the food cool significantly before putting it in the refrigerator and compromising the temperature of the other foods. Do not leave chicken at room temperature longer than 2 hours (preferably 1 hour).

- To freeze fresh chicken: Freeze in the original store wrap for up to 2 months. For a longer period, wrap in foil or place in a freezer bag. Use whole chickens within 12 months and parts within 9 months. Label with contents and date of freezing.

- To freeze cooked chicken: Place in plastic bags. Separate white and dark meat in packets to be used as needed, and label. Use within several months.

- To thaw frozen chicken: Thaw wrapped chicken in the refrigerator on a plate (to catch any drips), never at room temperature on the counter. Allow 5 hours thawing time for each pound of chicken. Always thaw chicken thoroughly before cooking.

- To quick-thaw in the microwave: Remove chicken from the original wrapping and follow the oven manufacturer's directions, using the "thaw" setting.

- To quick-thaw using the cold water method: Place chicken in an airtight bag and then in a bowl or pan of cold water; don't use hot! Change the water every 30 minutes to keep the water cold. Pat the meat dry with paper towels and use immediately.

- Do not cook chicken that is still frozen. It may not heat through to the middle, which could be dangerous.

- Do not refreeze completely thawed chicken unless it has been cooked.

- Transporting chicken: Keep hot chicken hot and cold chicken cold. Return any leftover chicken (and all perishables) to a cooler immediately, especially on a hot day.

✳ HELPFUL EQUIPMENT

º 1 large, heavy skillet with a lid for frying and sautéing (enameled cast iron is preferred, but nonstick can be used)

º 1 medium skillet for smaller quantities

º 1 large Dutch oven for soups, stews, and casseroles, available in stainless steel and enameled cast iron in decorator colors; most popular size is 5-quart

º Stock pot in 8- to 12-quart size with high sides for making stock

º Roasting pan with rack

º Glass baking dishes—from 8-by-8-inch to 9-by-13-inch

º Broiler pan

º Wok or large skillet for stir-fry

º Vertical roaster—the original Spanek is the best, although you can also roast vertically on a beer can (see page 24)

º Grill or barbecue—a covered grill is recommended, but not necessary; use a rotisserie for whole chicken, if available

º Platters and serving pieces, in various sizes and shapes for attractive presentation—always use a clean platter for serving cooked chicken (not the one used for transporting the raw chicken to the grill).

º Crock pot and pressure cooker (follow manufacturer's directions)

º Cutting board—use dishwasher-safe cutting boards or a flexible plastic one reserved for raw meat only

º Accessories—sharp boning knife, chef's knife, cleaver (for hacking whole raw chicken), stainless poultry shears (for cutting up whole chicken), meat thermometer, fork and tongs (for turning when frying, browning, and grilling), pastry brush

✳ PREPARING CHICKEN FOR COOKING

º Wash hands before and after working with chicken, to prevent cross-contamination with other foods.

- Wash all kitchen areas with hot soapy water or a mild bleach solution (1 teaspoon chlorine bleach to 1 quart water) or use disinfecting wipes (available in plastic cartons at most supermarkets) to help sanitize. Rinse with clear water.

- Prepare chicken on a dishwasher-safe plastic cutting board or on a board reserved for raw meat only.

- Trim excess fat and skin with stainless steel kitchen shears and discard scraps and paper towels to outside garbage containers, not in the kitchen. Chicken spoils quickly and will cause an offensive odor.

- To rinse or not to rinse? From a safety standpoint, rinsing is not necessary according to recent studies. In fact, rinsing may potentially spread bacteria to the sink, utensils, and countertops, and onto your hands. Proper cooking will destroy any bacteria present; however, some cooks still prefer to rinse. If rinsing, pat dry thoroughly with paper towels and discard the towels.

- Skin on or skin off? Removing skin reduces the fat by one quarter to one third. On the other hand, cooking chicken with the skin on keeps it moist and adds flavor. If there are health concerns about fat, you can cook the chicken with the skin on and then remove it before serving.

- Boned and skinned chicken breasts and thighs are available in most super-markets. To skin other parts, use a paper towel to gently pull the skin away from the meat in one piece. Wings and drumsticks are not usually skinned.

✳ HOW TO CUT UP A WHOLE CHICKEN

One of the best buys at the supermarket is to purchase a whole bird and cut it up yourself. To cut up a whole chicken, follow these instructions:

1. Place the chicken, breast-side up, on a cutting board. Cut the skin between the thighs and body.

2. Grasping one leg in each hand, lift the chicken and bend back the legs until the bones break at the hip joints.

3. Remove the lower leg and thigh from the body by cutting (from tail toward shoulder) between the joints, close to the bones in back of the bird. Repeat on the other side.

4. To separate the thighs and drumsticks, locate the knee joint by bending the thigh and leg together. With the skin-side down, cut through the joints of each leg.

5. With the chicken on its back, remove the wings by cutting inside of the wings just over the joints. Pull the wings away from the body and cut from the top down, through the joint.

6. Separate the breast and back on each side by placing the chicken on the neck-end or back and cutting (toward the board) through the joints along each side of the rib cage.

7. The breast may be left whole or, to cut into halves, place skin-side down on the board and cut the wishbone in two at the "V" of bone.

❋ BUTTERFLYING A CHICKEN

Butterflying is removing the backbone and flattening the chicken. It speeds up cooking time, ensures a crispy skin, and makes the chicken easy to carve.

1. Lay the chicken, breast-side down, on a cutting board.

2. With poultry shears, starting at the cavity, cut straight back to the neck, keeping just to the right of the backbone. Cut along the left side of the backbone and remove it.

3. Turn the chicken over and spread it open. Flatten with the heels of both hands, pressing on the breastbone and ribs.

4. Freeze the backbone for stock.

❋ WAYS TO COOK CHICKEN

Chicken is so versatile that it can be cooked by almost any method.

Frying
Suitable for a cut-up chicken or chicken parts. Fry in fat, using a heavy skillet, until golden brown and cooked through. (This method is not as popular today, because of diet concerns.)

Sautéing
Cook small cut-up pieces in a small amount of oil, stirring frequently.

Poaching
Gently simmer whole chicken or breasts in flavorful liquid until cooked through.

Deep-Fat Frying
Coat and fry chicken in a large quantity of oil, using a special deep-fry pan.

Stir-Fry
Quickly toss and cook skinless boneless chicken pieces of equal size, often with vegetables, for 3 to 4 minutes in oil. Use a wok or heavy skillet on medium-high heat.

Braising
Brown chicken and vegetables, then slowly cook them in a small amount of liquid, tightly covered for a lengthy time. This can be done on the stove top or in the oven in an ovenproof skillet.

Broiling
Cook chicken directly underneath a heat source. This requires almost constant attention because chicken burns quickly. Broil chicken with the skin on to keep it from drying out.

Microwaving
Follow the oven manufacturer's directions.

Grilling
All parts of the chicken (whole, quartered, or cut up) can be grilled. Heat should be medium direct for parts and indirect for whole. Grilling is popular because little or no oil is added (except for brushing). See grilling section (page 314).

Roasting
Season and bake whole chicken (roaster or broiler) in a roasting pan, uncovered, for about 1¼ hours, depending on the size. A meat thermometer should register 180°F at the thigh; 170°F for breast to prevent drying. (See page 27 for details.)

Vertical roasting
Place a whole chicken on a special vertical roaster, season it with a rub, and set in a shallow pan of water to bake in the oven or cover and grill. The result is a juicy, moist chicken every time.

Beer Can Chicken

This is the same principle as vertical cooking, with the chicken upright. The chicken sits on a half full can of beer inserted in the cavity and is usually done in a covered grill.

❋ HOW TO CHECK WHEN CHICKEN IS DONE

°   Use a meat thermometer for complete accuracy. Insert the thermometer at the thickest part of the meat without touching the bone. Whole chicken should register 180°F at the thigh, boneless breasts 165°F, bone-in breasts 170°F, leg quarters and thighs 180°F, and ground chicken patties 165°F.

°   Cut with a sharp knife in the center; the juices should run clear.

°   Touch the center of the chicken with your finger. It should feel firm and spring back.

°   Bone joints should move easily.

AUTHOR'S NOTE: Concerning temperature control, stoves may vary, with medium on one stove more like medium-high on another. Ovens will also vary. Get to know your own stove and oven and have a reliable oven thermometer.

BASIC POACHED CHICKEN

You can use either boned and skinned chicken breasts or breasts with bone in and skin on. (The bone and skin add extra flavor.) Add the chicken to cold seasoned liquid, then bring it to a simmer and gently simmer the chicken until cooked through.

4	pounds chicken breasts (about 8)
¼	yellow onion, cut up
1	carrot, cut into large pieces
1	celery stalk, cut into large pieces
2	garlic cloves, halved
2 or 3	sprigs fresh parsley
2	sprigs fresh thyme or
	¼ teaspoon dried thyme
2	bay leaves
¼	teaspoon salt
¼	teaspoon peppercorns

In a large pan over high heat, add all the ingredients, cover with about 1 inch of water, and bring to a boil. Immediately skim off any foam that rises to the top. Reduce the heat to low and gently simmer, covered, until the chicken is no longer pink in the center, about 12 minutes, depending on thickness. Remove the chicken from the broth to a plate and cool. Remove the skin and bones and discard. Strain the broth and refrigerate or freeze in cartons for later use. After the broth has cooled in the refrigerator, remove the layer of fat that forms on top.

BASIC COOKED CHICKEN

This explains how to cook a whole chicken or parts, for the meat to be used as a central ingredient for other dishes including salads, soups, sandwiches, and casseroles.

Add a whole chicken to salted water, cover, and gently simmer with several parsley sprigs, a few peppercorns, and half an onion, until the chicken is cooked through and juices run clear, 1 to 1½ hours.

Poach boned and skinned chicken breasts in salted water, covered, until no longer pink in the center, about 12 minutes.

Cool and prepare as called for in the recipe. Refrigerate or freeze until ready to use. Do not overcook, because the chicken will get dried out when cooked again in recipes. Strain and save stock, although it will not be as intense because of the shorter cooking time.

❊ HOW TO ADD FLAVOR TO CHICKEN

Marinades, bastes, rubs, and glazes are used to enhance the flavor of chicken. Other ways to add flavor to chicken are cooking with vegetables—especially garlic and onions—and adding cheeses, herbs, and spices.

Marinades
- A marinade is a seasoned liquid used to add flavor, to keep the chicken moist while cooking, and sometimes to tenderize.

- Marinate in a nonreactive container or a Ziploc bag in the refrigerator for at least 1 to 2 hours (sometimes overnight) to absorb the flavors.

- Bring the chicken to room temperature before cooking.

- Discard leftover marinade, or, if using as a baste during grilling, boil for 1 minute first to kill the bacteria. You could also set aside some marinade before preparing the meat to be used for basting.

Dry Rubs
- Rubs are a combination of dry seasonings used to rub on the inside and outside of the chicken to add a spicy flavor. Rubs are especially popular for grilling.

- Apply the rub and allow it to set for 30 minutes to 1 hour before cooking.

Bastes and Glazes
- Bastes are brushed or spooned on the chicken as it cooks. They add flavor and color.

- Glazes are a form of baste that also add a sheen to the chicken.

Herbs and Spices
- Fresh herbs should be added at the end of the cooking time to avoid over-cooking and loss of flavor.

- Dried herbs can be substituted for fresh herbs and can be added at the beginning of the cooking process. Use about half of the amount of dried herbs as a substitute for fresh herbs. Crumble dried herbs in your fingers to release flavor.

- Spices add pungent and aromatic flavor to chicken and should be used sparingly.

° Fresh parsley is used extensively in cooking chicken. Parsley is a slightly peppery, fresh-flavored herb used for flavoring as well as garnish. There are many varieties of this herb, but the most popular are curly-leaf parsley and the more strongly flavored Italian or flat-leaf parsley. Curly parsley is the most common; it is easily grown in the home garden and is readily available in the market year-round. Flat-leaf parsley has become the parsley preferred by many chefs and gourmet cooks, but is sometimes hard to find. If substituting curly parsley for flat-leaf parsley, increase the amount used slightly.

Cheese

° Cheeses are used in many recipes for added flavor, especially Parmesan cheese. It is a hard, dry cheese made from skimmed or partially skimmed cow's milk. It has a golden rind and straw-colored interior with a rich, sharp flavor. Domestic and imported Parmesans are available, but the primo Parmesan is a Parmigiano-Reggiano made in Italy. It is aged longer and will melt in your mouth. Use a hand grater and do not substitute with the canned variety.

° Almost all cheeses are complementary to chicken. When adding cheeses to cooked chicken dishes, allow time for the cheese to melt and develop flavor.

BASIC ROASTED CHICKEN

Roasting chicken is one of the easiest ways to prepare chicken for a crowd. Leftovers can be used for salads, soups, and sandwiches.

1 chicken (3½ to 4 pounds), excess fat and skin trimmed
Oil or butter
Salt and pepper

Preheat the oven to 350°F. Remove the giblet packet and discard or save it for stock. (Cook the liver separately and not in the stock, since it cooks faster and will make the stock cloudy.)

Rub oil or butter on the outside of the chicken. Salt and pepper it inside and out.

Place the chicken, breast-side up, on a rack in a roasting pan. Roast until a meat thermometer inserted in the thigh registers 180°F, about 1¼ hours, basting the chicken with pan juices several times.

Remove the chicken from the pan and transfer it to a platter. Let it stand for 10 to 15 minutes before carving to redistribute the juices. Tent with aluminum foil to keep warm.

Make gravy, if desired (see page 267). Carve the chicken (see page 28).

✽ HOW TO STUFF A CHICKEN

º Stuffing for whole chicken is usually well seasoned and based on cubed bread, though rice and potatoes can be used. A layer of stuffing can be placed on a flattened, boned, and skinned breast, rolled up, and secured with a toothpick. A small amount of stuffing can also be placed under the skin of a chicken breast with bone and skin on.

º Always stuff a chicken just before cooking, never ahead of time (bacteria may form).

º For safety reasons, pack the stuffing loosely in the body cavity to ensure complete cooking (temperature should read 165°F) or bake separately in a covered casserole.

º Use short skewers to hold together the skin around the cavity to keep stuffing in place.

º Always remove all of the stuffing from the chicken after roasting.

º For an easy, alternative stuffing just for flavoring, add a lemon half or half a dry onion, celery stalks, garlic cloves, and fresh herb sprigs in the cavity.

✽ HOW TO CARVE A WHOLE CHICKEN

º Place the cooked chicken on a cutting board or large platter, breast-side up.

º Grasp the leg (drumstick and thigh) and pull away from the body. Using a sharp knife, cut through the joint and remove the entire leg.

º Cut through the joint to separate the drumstick and thigh. Cut off the meat in thin slices.

º Cut through the skin and joint of the wing and remove.

º To carve the breast, make a deep horizontal cut just above the wing. Carve thin slices vertically, cutting downward. You can use a fork in the opposite hand to stabilize the chicken as you slice. Arrange slices attractively on a clean platter and add garnishes of your choice, such as parsley, cherry tomatoes, fruit rings, etc.

BASIC CHICKEN STOCK

Basic Chicken Stock is the secret to making good homemade soup, especially broth-type soups such as chicken noodle and chicken and rice. It is the base that adds depth to many dishes. Chicken stock is made with whole chicken or with bony parts and giblets (except the liver—it will cloud the broth; cook liver separately). The chicken is covered with water and simmered along with aromatic vegetables and herbs for a long period of time. You can save bony parts that are not called for in many recipes and freeze until you have enough to make stock.

One	3-pound chicken or 3 pounds chicken parts (backs, wings, necks, and giblets)
10	cups water
1	yellow onion, quartered
2	celery stalks, cut into chunks
2	carrots, cut into chunks
½	cup dry white wine (optional)
4	garlic cloves, unpeeled
1	bay leaf
10	peppercorns
3	sprigs fresh parsley
1	teaspoon salt
½	teaspoon dried thyme

In a large soup pot over high heat, combine all the ingredients except the salt and thyme, and bring to a boil. Skim off any foam. Add the salt and thyme (see Note), reduce the heat to low, and simmer, partially covered, for 2½ to 3 hours. Pour the stock through a very fine sieve or a sieve lined with a double thickness of cheesecloth. Discard the solids. (Save chicken meat for another use, if desired.) Degrease the stock with a fat separator or store, covered, in the refrigerator overnight and then remove and discard the layer of fat that forms on the top. Use within 3 days, or freeze in airtight containers for up to 3 months. For a more concentrated stock, cook it again with the bones, uncovered, for about 20 minutes longer.

Makes about 8 cups

NOTE: Some cooks prefer not to season basic stock, depending on its use in future recipes.

QUICK STOCK: To enhance canned broth, boil it with leftover bony chicken parts, ½ onion, and a few parsley sprigs, uncovered, for about 30 minutes, then strain.

ROTISSERIE STOCK: Rotisserie chicken is highly seasoned and makes delicious stock. Cover the carcass with water and add vegetables (see page 350). Cook for about 1 hour and then strain.

BROWNED STOCK: Sear chicken and onions in oil first for a more intense flavor, then proceed as directed.

� STORING CHICKEN

Product	Refrigerator (40°F)	Freezer (0°F)
Raw whole chicken	1 to 2 days	12 months
Raw chicken parts	1 to 2 days	9 months
Raw ground chicken	1 to 2 days	3 to 4 months
Cooked chicken	3 to 4 days	4 months
Cooked chicken with broth	1 to 2 days	6 months

✷ ROASTING CHICKEN

Product	Weight	Temperature	Approximate Time at 350°F
Whole chicken	3- to 5-pound broiler	180°F	1¼ to 1½ hrs
Whole chicken	6- to 8-pound roaster	180°F	1½ to 2¼ hrs
Breast, bone in	6 to 8 ounces	170°F	30 to 40 mins
Breast, boneless	6 to 8 ounces	170°F	25 to 30 mins
Leg quarter, bone in	4 to 8 ounces	180°F	40 to 50 mins
Thigh, bone in	5 to 7 ounces	180°F	40 to 45 mins
Thigh, boneless	3 to 4 ounces	165°F	30 to 35 mins
Wings or drummettes	2 to 3 ounces	180°F	30 to 40 mins

✳ GRILLING CHICKEN

Product	Indirect Heat Internal Temperature (covered grill)	Rotisserie
Roaster, 6 to 8 pounds	2 to 2½ hours	180°F
Whole chicken, 3 to 5 pounds	1 to 1½ hours	180°F
Dark meat, bone in	40 to 45 minutes	180°F
White meat, bone in	30 to 35 minutes	170°F
Boneless chicken parts	10 to 15 minutes	165°F

APPETIZERS & HORS D'OEUVRES

Appetizers are small dishes or bite-size food served before a meal or at a cocktail party with drinks. Hors d'oeuvres are hot or cold savory bites and are also considered party food. Small plates should be provided, along with napkins.

Chicken appetizers are generally hearty and fun to serve. The most popular may be chicken wings. In this chapter you will find several wing recipes, such as Hot and Sweet Chili Wings, Asian Style; Baked Chicken Wings in Honey-Soy Glaze; and Spicy Chicken Wings with Blue Cheese Dressing.

Other delicious chicken appetizers here include Chicken Quesadillas, Easy Grilled Drummettes, and Herbed Chicken Cocktail Bites.

CHICKEN QUESADILLAS

This is a fast way to make quesadillas for a crowd because several can be made at one time by using this broiling method. Chopped chicken, salsa, and cheese make the filling. Use salsa of your choice, purchased or home-made. Serve with the cooling Creamy Avocado Dip.

8 flour tortillas (10-inch)
½ cup Fresh Tomato Salsa (facing page) or purchased salsa, plus extra for serving
2 cups diced cooked chicken breast
8 green onions including some tender green tops, finely chopped
¼ cup chopped fresh cilantro or parsley
1½ to 2 cups (6 to 8 ounces) grated Monterey Jack or Cheddar cheese
Creamy Avocado Dip (facing page), for serving

Preheat the broiler. Lay the tortillas on a flat surface. Spread about 1 table-spoon salsa on one half of each tortilla. Add some chicken, onions, cilantro, and cheese on top. Fold the other halves over and press down to enclose. Place the filled tortillas on a foil-lined broiler pan. Broil until the tortillas begin to brown, about 1 minute. Turn over and broil the other sides until lightly browned, about 40 seconds. Cut each tortilla in half and serve.

Makes 16 wedges

NOTE: These quesadillas can also be baked in a 400°F oven for about 6 minutes.

FRESH TOMATO SALSA

Salsa appears on the Mexican table for every meal, to be served with almost any dish. You can make it as "hot" as you like by varying the amount of chiles that you use. It is best eaten the same day it's prepared.

4   medium tomatoes, seeded, chopped, and drained
¼   cup diced white onion or chopped green onions including some tender green tops
¼   cup chopped fresh cilantro or parsley
1   tablespoon fresh lime juice
1   tablespoon olive oil
1   tablespoon chopped fresh oregano or ¾ teaspoon dried oregano
2   garlic cloves, minced
1   teaspoon minced jalapeño pepper or more to taste
½   teaspoon salt
    Freshly ground pepper

In a medium bowl, stir together all the ingredients, adding pepper to taste. Cover and let stand at room temperature at least 1 hour to allow flavors to blend, then cover and refrigerate until ready to use. Drain, if necessary, before using.

Makes about 3 cups

CREAMY AVOCADO DIP

2   large ripe avocados, peeled, pitted, and mashed
¼   cup sour cream
1   tablespoon fresh lemon juice
¼   teaspoon salt
¼   teaspoon Worcestershire sauce
1 or 2   drops Tabasco sauce

In a medium bowl, mix together all the ingredients.

Makes about 1½ cups

CHICKEN SPREAD

Use a food processor to grind up leftover cooked chicken and make it into a smooth spread for crostini or small open-faced cocktail sandwiches.

2 cups cut-up cooked chicken pieces
2 or 3 mushrooms, cut up
1 shallot, chopped, or 2 green onions including some tender green tops, cut up
1 sprig fresh parsley, cut up
3 to 4 tablespoons mayonnaise
1 teaspoon Dijon mustard
Crostini (toasted baguette) slices for serving (recipe follows)

Place all the ingredients except the baguette slices in a food processor and process until smooth. Scrape down the sides of the bowl as needed. Spread on crostini.

Makes 12 to 14 crostini

CROSTINI

Crostini are thin, toasted baguette slices to serve with soups or as a base for hors d'oeuvre toppings.

¼ cup olive oil
2 large garlic cloves, quartered
1 baguette, cut into ¼- to ⅓-inch slices

In a small jar, combine the oil and garlic. Let stand to allow the oil to absorb flavor, about 30 minutes.

TO BROIL: Preheat the broiler. Arrange the bread slices on a baking sheet and brush them with the garlic oil. Broil on 1 side until toasted, about 1 minute. Turn the slices over and brush with garlic oil. Broil about 40 seconds longer.

TO BAKE: Preheat the oven to 350°F. Arrange the bread slices on a baking sheet and brush both sides with the garlic oil. Bake until lightly browned, about 15 minutes.

Makes about 30 slices

HOT AND SWEET CHILI WINGS, ASIAN STYLE

Enjoy the balance of the sweet and tart flavors of these delicious wings to set the mood for an Asian dinner. Sweet Asian chili sauce can be found in the Asian department in most supermarkets. Provide napkins, as these are sticky.

3 pounds chicken wings (about 12)
½ cup sweet Asian chili sauce, plus extra for dipping
¼ cup soy sauce
¼ cup rice vinegar
1 tablespoon peeled, grated fresh ginger
1 tablespoon honey
1 tablespoon fresh lime juice
2 garlic cloves, minced

Cut off the wing tips with kitchen scissors or a sharp knife and discard or save them for stock. Halve the wings at the joint and trim excess fat and skin. In a large bowl, mix together the remaining ingredients. Add the wings and stir to coat. Cover and refrigerate several hours, stirring once.

Preheat the oven to 375°F. Line a baking sheet with foil. Remove the wings from the marinade and boil the marinade for 1 minute. Place the wings on the baking sheet in a single layer. Bake for 15 minutes. Brush with the boiled marinade and continue to bake until cooked through, about 20 minutes longer.

Makes 24 pieces

SPICY CHICKEN WINGS WITH BLUE CHEESE DRESSING

Pack up these popular wings for your next tailgate party or picnic. They are good hot off the grill or cold along with beer and chips. Serve with Blue Cheese Dressing for dipping.

3 pounds chicken wings (about 12)
½ cup (1 stick) butter, melted
¼ cup fresh lemon juice
2 teaspoons chili powder
1 teaspoon salt
1 teaspoon paprika
1 garlic clove, minced
1 teaspoon prepared mustard
1 teaspoon Worcestershire sauce
Blue Cheese Dressing (page 89) for serving

Cut off the wing tips with kitchen scissors or a sharp knife and discard or save them for stock. Halve the wings at the joint and trim excess fat and skin. In a medium bowl, mix together the remaining ingredients except the dressing. Add the chicken wings and stir to coat. Cover and refrigerate several hours, stirring once. Bring to room temperature before grilling.

Prepare a grill for cooking over indirect medium heat. Remove the wings from the marinade and discard the marinade. Place the wings on a lightly sprayed or oiled grate and grill until lightly browned and cooked through, 30 to 35 minutes, turning several times. Serve with the Blue Cheese Dressing for dipping.

Makes 24 pieces

HERBED CHICKEN COCKTAIL BITES

Meatballs are always a favorite party food and are the first to go. Serve these chicken bites with a tasty mustard dipping sauce for extra flavor. These bites can be baked ahead and frozen, if desired, and then reheated.

1¼ pounds ground chicken
¼ cup mayonnaise
3 tablespoons fine dried bread crumbs
2 tablespoons minced fresh parsley
1 tablespoon finely chopped yellow onion
½ teaspoon celery seed
½ teaspoon salt
¼ teaspoon dried oregano
¼ teaspoon dried basil
   Freshly ground pepper
   Mustard Sauce (recipe follows) for dipping

Preheat the oven to 400ºF. In a medium bowl, mix together all the ingredients except the Mustard Sauce, adding pepper to taste. Form into ¾- to 1-inch balls. Arrange the balls on a lightly sprayed or oiled baking sheet in a single layer and bake until lightly browned, 12 to 15 minutes. Transfer to a serving plate or chafing dish and serve hot with Mustard Sauce and toothpicks for spearing.

Makes about 3 dozen

MUSTARD SAUCE

½ cup mayonnaise
¼ cup plain nonfat yogurt
3 tablespoons Dijon mustard
1 tablespoon white wine vinegar
1 teaspoon ground mustard
1 teaspoon Worcestershire sauce

In a small bowl, whisk together all the ingredients.

Makes about 1 cup

POMEGRANATE-MOLASSES CHICKEN DRUMMETTES

The sweet-tart flavor of pomegranate juice and the caramel flavor of molasses make a complementary marinade for these grilled drummettes. They make a good starter for a barbecue when the grill is fired up. Drummettes are the bony part of the wing and can be purchased in packages at most meat markets.

2 to 2 ½   pounds chicken drummettes (about 20)
½   cup unsulphured molasses
½   cup pomegranate juice

Place the drummettes in a 9-by-13-inch glass baking dish. In a small bowl, mix together the molasses and juice. Pour over the drummettes and marinate several hours in the refrigerator. Bring to room temperature before grilling.

Prepare a grill for cooking over medium indirect heat. Remove the drummettes from the marinade and boil the marinade in a small pan for 1 minute. Place the drummettes on a lightly sprayed or oiled grate and grill until lightly browned and cooked through, about 25 minutes, turning several times and brushing with the boiled marinade.

Makes 20 pieces

CHICKEN CHEESE SWIRLS

This great combination of Tex-Mex ingredients is spread on flour tortillas, then rolled and sliced. They can be made ahead and served at room temperature or warmed in the oven when the guests arrive. They freeze well and are easier to slice when partially frozen.

1   cup shredded cooked chicken
1   cup (4 ounces) shredded Cheddar cheese
½   package (4 ounces) cream cheese, cut into small pieces
1   can (4 ounces) diced green chiles, drained
½   cup finely chopped green onions including some tender green tops
½   cup finely chopped red bell pepper
½   can (2 ounces) chopped black olives
    Four flour tortillas (10-inch)

Preheat the oven to 350°F. In a medium bowl, mix together the chicken, cheeses, chiles, onions, bell pepper, and olives until well blended. Spread the mixture evenly on the tortillas, almost to the edge. Roll up, wrap in plastic wrap, and refrigerate 1 hour or longer. Cut the rolled tortillas into ¾-inch slices and serve at room temperature or place on a baking sheet and bake at 350°F until warmed, about 6 minutes. Serve immediately.

Makes about 24 slices

CHICKEN LIVER–ONION PÂTÉ

Chicken livers are the base for this spread to serve on crackers or cocktail rye bread. It makes a nice addition to a cocktail party during the holidays.

2 tablespoons butter
1 medium sweet white onion, chopped
8 ounces chicken livers, rinsed and dried
1 hard-cooked egg, cut up
2 tablespoons torn fresh parsley

1 teaspoon Worcestershire sauce
½ teaspoon Dijon mustard
¼ teaspoon salt
   Freshly ground pepper

In a medium skillet over medium heat, melt the butter. Add the onions and livers and sauté until the onions are tender and the livers are cooked through, 5 to 6 minutes. Place in a food processor with the remaining ingredients, adding pepper to taste. Process until smooth. Serve in a small bowl.

Makes about 1 cup

CHICKEN SATAY WITH PEANUT DIPPING SAUCE

Satay (or saté) is a favorite Indonesian food consisting of marinated meat, poultry, or fish threaded on skewers, grilled or broiled, and served with a peanut dipping sauce. It can be served as an appetizer or sometimes as a main dish.

MARINADE

2 tablespoons peanut oil
2 tablespoons soy sauce
1 teaspoon honey
1 garlic clove, minced

8 large chicken tenders (about 2 pounds)
8 bamboo skewers, soaked in water for 30 minutes and dried
   Peanut Dipping Sauce (recipe follows)

To make the marinade, in a medium bowl, mix together the oil, soy sauce, honey, and garlic. Add the tenders and mix well. Cover and refrigerate for about 2 hours. Bring to room temperature before grilling.

Prepare a grill for cooking over medium indirect heat. Remove the tenders from the marinade and thread them lengthwise on individual skewers. Discard the marinade. Place the skewers on a lightly sprayed or oiled grate and grill until the chicken is cooked through, 3 to 4 minutes on each side, turning once. Serve with sauce.

Makes 6 to 8 servings

PEANUT DIPPING SAUCE

½ cup chunky peanut butter
4 green onions including some tender green tops, finely chopped
3 tablespoons dry sherry
2 tablespoons honey
2 tablespoons vegetable oil
2 tablespoons peeled, grated fresh ginger or 1 teaspoon ground ginger
1 tablespoon rice vinegar
1 tablespoon soy sauce
1 tablespoon sesame oil
2 teaspoons sweet Asian chili sauce
2 large garlic cloves, minced

In a medium bowl, whisk together all the ingredients. Serve at room temperature.

Makes about 1 cup

EASY GRILLED DRUMMETTES

Drummettes are good to use for an hors d'oeuvre because of their small size. Here, they are marinated in a flavorful marinade, then popped on the grill. They are available in packages at most supermarkets.

MARINADE

4   green onions including some tender green tops, chopped
¼   cup soy sauce
¼   cup dry white wine
2   tablespoons honey
1   garlic clove, minced
1   teaspoon ground ginger

3   pounds chicken drummettes (about 30), excess fat and skin trimmed

In a large bowl, combine all the marinade ingredients and mix well. Add the drummettes and turn to coat. Cover and marinate in the refrigerator several hours or overnight, turning occasionally. Bring to room temperature before grilling.

Prepare a grill for cooking over medium indirect heat. Remove the drummettes from the marinade and place them on a lightly sprayed or oiled grate. Grill until no longer pink on the inside, about 25 minutes, turning once. Serve immediately.

Makes 30 pieces

BAKED CHICKEN WINGS IN HONEY-SOY GLAZE

These wings were voted the best and most flavorful when we had an hors d'oeuvre tasting party. They are good to serve for TV game watching along with other snack food. The recipe can easily be doubled for a crowd.

3 pounds chicken wings (about 12)

½ cup soy sauce

½ cup chopped green onions including some tender green tops

¼ cup rice vinegar

2 tablespoons sesame oil

1 tablespoon honey

1 tablespoon peeled, grated fresh ginger or 1 teaspoon ground ginger

2 garlic cloves, minced

Cut off the wing tips with kitchen scissors or a sharp knife and discard or save them for stock. Halve the wings at the joint and trim excess fat and skin. In a large bowl, mix together the remaining ingredients. Add the wings and stir to coat. Cover and refrigerate several hours, stirring once. Bring to room temperature before grilling.

Prepare a grill for cooking over medium indirect heat. Remove the wings from the marinade and discard the marinade. Place the wings on a lightly sprayed or oiled grate and grill until lightly browned and cooked through, 30 to 35 minutes, turning several times. Serve hot.

Makes 24 pieces

COUNTRY CHICKEN PÂTÉ

Here is a pâté made with a blend of savory meats and herbs, for those who don't like the taste of liver. It should be made several days in advance to allow the flavors to mellow. Serve on baguette slices or crackers with Dijon-Basil Mayonnaise and cornichons for a fancy hors d'oeuvre.

3 slices bacon, diced
1 cup finely chopped yellow onion
1 pound ground chicken
12 ounces ground veal
4 ounces pork sausage
½ cup dried bread crumbs
1 large egg
¼ cup brandy
3 garlic cloves, minced

1 teaspoon dried basil
1 teaspoon salt
½ teaspoon dried thyme
¼ teaspoon ground allspice
½ teaspoon herbes de Provence

Baguette slices for serving
Dijon-Basil Mayonnaise (facing page) for serving
Cornichons (small tart pickles) for serving

Preheat the oven to 350°F. In a small skillet over medium heat, cook the bacon until slightly browned. Remove the bacon to a plate, leaving the drippings in the pan. Add the onions to the skillet and sauté until tender, about 5 minutes. Transfer the onions and bacon to a food processor and add all the remaining pâté ingredients. Process in batches until well blended. Spoon the mixture into a 9-by-5-by-3-inch loaf pan lightly coated with vegetable spray or oil and pat down firmly. Cover with aluminum foil.

Bake for 45 minutes. Remove the foil and bake until the pâté is cooked through and set, at least 30 minutes. Remove the pâté from the oven and pour off any fat that has accumulated. Let it cool completely in the pan. Run a knife around the edges of the pan to loosen the pâté, then invert it onto a plate. Wrap in foil and refrigerate at least 8 hours or overnight before serving. Slice and serve cold on baguette slices with the Dijon-Basil Mayonnaise and cornichons.

Makes 10 to 12 servings

DIJON-BASIL MAYONNAISE

¼ cup mayonnaise
¼ cup plain nonfat yogurt
1 tablespoon Dijon mustard
1 tablespoon chopped fresh basil or
 ½ teaspoon dried basil
1 teaspoon fresh lemon juice

In a small bowl, whisk together all the ingredients until well blended. Cover and refrigerate until ready to use.

Makes about ½ cup

CHICKEN LETTUCE WRAPS

Now you can have a chicken wrap at home similar to the ones served at a popular Chinese bistro. All ingredients must be finely chopped and the lettuce leaves very cold.

1 tablespoon sesame oil	1 large garlic clove, minced
1¼ pounds ground chicken	1 can (15 ounces) water chestnuts, drained and finely chopped
2 celery stalks, finely chopped	½ cup soy sauce
6 green onions including some tender green tops, finely chopped	1 tablespoon sugar
2 ounces mushrooms, finely chopped	⅛ teaspoon cayenne
1 tablespoon peeled, grated fresh ginger or 1 teaspoon ground ginger	8 large leaves iceberg lettuce, chilled

In a large skillet over medium-high heat, warm the oil. Add the chicken and celery and sauté for 2 minutes, breaking up the chicken with a spoon. Add the onions, mushrooms, ginger, and garlic and sauté until the chicken is lightly browned and the vegetables are tender, about 5 minutes. Stir in the water chestnuts, soy sauce, sugar, and cayenne, and simmer, uncovered, until the soy has evaporated and the flavors are blended, about 5 minutes longer.

To serve, spoon the mixture onto the lettuce leaves, roll up, and eat in hand.

Makes 4 servings

BACON-WRAPPED CHICKEN TENDERS WITH ROASTED RED BELL PEPPER DIP

This is a quick hors d'oeuvre to serve at your next party. Chicken tenders are wrapped in bacon for an added salty flavor and baked until crispy. Pass the tasty dip to enjoy.

8 to 10	chicken tenders (about 2 pounds), cut into thirds
24 to 30	pieces bacon (each about 3 inches long) Large toothpicks soaked in water for 30 minutes and drained Roasted Red Bell Pepper Dip (recipe follows)

Preheat the oven to 450°F. Wrap each chicken piece with a bacon strip and secure with toothpicks. Place on a foil-lined rimmed baking sheet and bake until the bacon is crispy and the chicken is cooked through, about 30 minutes. Serve on a platter with the dip in a bowl.

Makes about 24 servings

ROASTED RED BELL PEPPER DIP
This dip is also good on vegetables.

1	cup mayonnaise
⅓	cup chopped roasted red bell pepper (see Note)
5 or 6	fresh basil leaves, torn, or 1 teaspoon dried basil
2	garlic cloves, sliced
1	teaspoon red wine vinegar
¼	teaspoon salt

In a food processor or blender, mix all the ingredients and process until blended. Transfer to a bowl.

Makes about 1 cup

NOTE: Roasted red bell peppers are available in different-sized jars at your supermarket, or you can make your own (see page 159).

CHIPOTLE DEVILED EGGS

Thanks to chickens, we have these spicy deviled eggs. Chipotle chiles add a little heat to this popular appetizer.

10	large eggs, hard-cooked and cooled (see Note)
1/3	cup mayonnaise
1 to 2	teaspoons finely chopped canned chipotle chiles
1/2	teaspoon salt

Cut the hard-cooked eggs lengthwise in half. Remove the yolks to a medium bowl. Lay the whites on a plate. Mash the yolks with a fork. Add the mayonnaise, chiles, and salt and mash until smooth. Fill the whites with the egg yolk mixture.

Makes 20 servings

NOTE: To make hard-cooked eggs, place eggs in a medium, deep pan over medium-high heat and cover with cold water. Bring to a boil. Reduce the heat to low and gently simmer for 10 minutes. Remove the eggs and cool under cold water. Store in the refrigerator until ready to use.

BRUSCHETTA

Bruschetta is a traditional Italian snack of toasted bread topped with cheese, meats, anchovies, or simply brushed with olive oil and garlic. This topping incorporates chicken, tomatoes, cucumber, and onion and is great as an appetizer.

TOPPING

- 1 cup diced cooked chicken breast
- 3 tomatoes, seeded, chopped, and drained
- 1 small cucumber, peeled, seeded, and cut into ¼-inch dice
- ½ red onion, cut into ¼-inch dice
- ½ cup lightly packed fresh basil leaves, chopped
- 2 tablespoons olive oil
- 2 tablespoons red wine vinegar
- 1 garlic clove, minced
  Salt and freshly ground pepper

25 Crostini (page 36)

In a medium bowl, stir together all the topping ingredients, adding salt and pepper to taste. Let stand, covered, at room temperature for 1 hour, stirring occasionally. Drain if necessary.

Top each slice of crostini with about 1 tablespoon of the chicken-vegetable mixture. Serve immediately.

Makes about 25 servings

02

SOUPS

What is more satisfying than a bowl of steaming soup, especially on a cold winter day? Soup is often a "meal in a bowl" to serve as an entrée for a light, wholesome meal.

Today's homemade soups call for fresh ingredients, not just tired leftovers. Homemade stock is best, but good-quality reduced-sodium broth can be used. Most soups can be made ahead and often improve in flavor when reheated. One advantage of soups is that they do not have to be served immediately. They can simmer (but not boil) until ready to eat.

Chicken soups are a combination of chicken with pasta, vegetables, grains, or other meats in a flavorful broth or sauce. This chapter offers a variety of soups to feed a family or a crowd for any occasion or mood.

Try Chicken, Vegetable, and Orzo Soup; Best-Ever Chicken and Mushroom Soup; Chicken Tortellini Soup; Chicken-Vegetable Chowder; Chicken, Corn, and Black Bean Soup; Vegetable Soup with Chicken Meatballs; and many other original creations. A tossed green salad and a loaf of crusty bread are all that you need for a complete meal.

CHICKEN MINESTRONE

This Italian soup, thick with vegetables and chicken, is nourishing and tasty but low in calories and fat. Sprinkle the top generously with freshly grated Parmesan cheese. For convenience and to shorten the cooking time, canned beans are used here. Leftovers are even better the next day.

3 cups tomato juice
2 cups Basic Chicken Stock (page 29) or reduced-sodium chicken broth
2 cups water
1 can (14½ ounces) whole tomatoes, coarsely chopped, including juice
1 small yellow onion, chopped
3 carrots, sliced
2 celery stalks, sliced
¼ cup chopped fresh parsley
1½ teaspoons salt
1 garlic clove, minced
1 teaspoon dried basil

½ teaspoon dried thyme
½ teaspoon dried oregano
Freshly ground pepper
2 cups thinly sliced cabbage
1 medium zucchini, unpeeled, halved lengthwise, and sliced
1 cup 1-inch pieces fresh green beans
¾ cup uncooked macaroni or other small pasta
1 cup shredded cooked chicken
1 can (15 ounces) cannellini beans, drained and rinsed
Freshly grated Parmesan cheese for topping

In a large soup pot over high heat, combine the tomato juice, stock, water, tomatoes, onions, carrots, celery, parsley, salt, garlic, and seasonings. Bring to a boil, reduce the heat to medium-low, and simmer, covered, until the vegetables are tender, 1 hour and 15 minutes. Add the cabbage, zucchini, green beans, and macaroni and cook, covered, until the macaroni and vegetables are tender, about 20 minutes longer. Stir in the chicken and cannellini beans and simmer, uncovered, until heated through. Serve topped with Parmesan cheese.

Makes 8 servings

CHICKEN-VEGETABLE CHOWDER

This hearty, healthful soup full of chunky vegetables and chicken pieces will quickly become everyone's favorite. Include cheese biscuits on the menu for a family meal. If you have any chowder left over, it's even better the next day.

1 tablespoon olive oil

1 cup chopped yellow onion

1 celery stalk, sliced

2 garlic cloves, minced

3 cups Basic Chicken Stock (page 29) or reduced-sodium chicken broth

1½ cups scrubbed, unpeeled, cubed red potatoes (about 2 medium)

2 cups corn kernels, fresh or frozen

3 tablespoons all-purpose flour

3 cups whole milk

2 cups cubed cooked chicken breast

1 tomato, chopped and drained

¾ teaspoon salt

Freshly ground pepper

1½ cups (6 ounces) shredded Cheddar cheese

In a large soup pot over medium heat, warm the oil. Add the onions, celery, and garlic and sauté until tender, about 5 minutes. Add the stock and potatoes and bring to a boil. Reduce the heat to medium-low and simmer, covered, until the potatoes are tender, about 20 minutes. Stir in the corn.

In a medium bowl or pitcher, whisk together the flour and 1 cup of the milk. Add the remaining milk and blend. Stir into the soup, increase the heat to medium-high, and stir until slightly thickened, 3 to 5 minutes. Reduce the heat to medium-low and add the chicken, tomato, salt, and pepper to taste. Simmer, uncovered, until the flavors are blended, about 10 minutes. Remove the pan from the heat, add the cheese, and stir until melted. Do not boil after the cheese is added.

Makes 6 servings

CHICKEN, VEGETABLE, AND RICE SOUP

Here is a standby soup you can always rely on for a wholesome meal. Just the tempting aroma as it simmers on the stove will make you hungry. Homemade stock is the key to this soup.

8 cups Basic Chicken Stock (page 29) or reduced-sodium chicken broth
1 cup chopped yellow onion
1 celery stalk, chopped
2 carrots, chopped
½ red bell pepper, chopped
½ cup uncooked long-grain white rice
1½ teaspoons salt
1 garlic clove, chopped
¼ teaspoon dried marjoram
Freshly ground pepper
2 cups cubed cooked chicken

In a large soup pot over high heat, combine all the ingredients except the chicken. Bring to a boil. Reduce the heat to medium-low and simmer, covered, until the vegetables and rice are tender, about 20 minutes. Add the chicken and simmer, uncovered, until the flavors are blended and the chicken is heated through, about 10 minutes longer.

Makes 6 servings

GOOD FOR YOU
CHICKEN NOODLE SOUP

This soup is known as "soup for the soul." It has a soothing, healing benefit for those down with a cold or the flu, but you don't have to be sick to enjoy this warming soup. Homemade stock makes this soup even better.

1	chicken (3½ to 4 pounds), quartered, excess fat and skin trimmed
10	cups Basic Chicken Stock (page 29) or reduced-sodium chicken broth
1	yellow onion, quartered
2	carrots, scrubbed and cut into 4 chunks
2	celery stalks, including a few tops, cut up
2	garlic cloves, halved
3	sprigs fresh parsley
3 or 4	fresh basil leaves or ½ teaspoon dried basil
¼	cup dry white wine (optional)
2	teaspoons coarse salt
1	teaspoon dried thyme
1	teaspoon black peppercorns
1	bay leaf
4	ounces (2 cups) uncooked egg noodles

In a large soup pot, combine the chicken, stock, onions, carrots, celery, and garlic. Bring to a boil and occasionally skim off any foam that rises to the top. Add the parsley, basil, wine, and seasonings; reduce the heat to medium-low; and simmer, covered, until the chicken is very tender, 1 to 1½ hours. Remove the chicken to a plate to cool. Strain the stock into a large bowl and discard the solids.

Using a fat separator, degrease the stock and return it to the pan or, if time allows, refrigerate it overnight and remove the fat that forms on top. Remove the skin and bones from the chicken and discard. Cut the chicken into bite-size pieces, and add 2 to 3 cups chicken to the stock (use the remainder for other purposes). Add the noodles and bring to a boil. Reduce the heat to medium-low and cook, uncovered, until the noodles are tender, about 10 minutes. Taste for seasoning.

Makes 6 servings

VEGETABLE SOUP WITH CHICKEN MEATBALLS

I made this soup in the morning to serve for a light supper, but it was so good, we ate it all for lunch. It is a "meal-in-a-bowl" soup with tender chicken meatballs, vegetables, and pasta in a flavorful broth with lots of character. This is a good soup to make when family activities often interfere with mealtime, because it can simmer on the stove until ready to serve. Ground chicken is available in most supermarkets.

4 cups Basic Chicken Stock (page 29) or reduced-sodium chicken broth

1 can (14½ ounces) whole tomatoes, including juice, cut up

½ cup chopped yellow onion

1 small zucchini, chopped

1 celery stalk, chopped

1 carrot, peeled and chopped

1 garlic clove, minced

½ teaspoon dried oregano

½ teaspoon salt

Freshly ground pepper

¼ cup uncooked orzo

Chicken Meatballs (facing page)

In a large soup pot over high heat, combine the stock, tomatoes, onions, zucchini, celery, carrot, garlic, oregano, salt, and pepper to taste and bring to a boil. Reduce the heat to medium-low and simmer, covered, for 10 minutes. Add the orzo and meatballs and simmer until the orzo is tender and the flavors are blended, about 10 minutes longer.

Makes 4 to 6 servings

CHICKEN MEATBALLS

1¼ pounds ground chicken
 1 cup dried coarse bread crumbs
 ¼ cup chopped fresh parsley
 2 tablespoons finely chopped yellow onion
 1 garlic clove, minced
 ½ teaspoon salt
 ¼ teaspoon dried allspice
 ¼ teaspoon dried sage
 ⅛ teaspoon freshly ground pepper

In a large bowl, mix together all the ingredients. Cover and refrigerate for 30 minutes for easier handling. Using floured hands, form the mixture into 1½-inch balls.

Preheat the oven to 425°F. Place the meatballs on a lightly sprayed or oiled baking sheet and bake until lightly browned and firm, about 15 minutes.

Makes about 25 meatballs

CHICKEN-VEGETABLE SOUP WITH KIELBASA AND PASTA

Consider this hearty soup filled with robust, heart-warming flavors for a lunch or supper. Kielbasa, a smoked Polish sausage, adds a spicy touch to this thick, chunky soup with vegetables and macaroni.

1 tablespoon vegetable oil

8 ounces kielbasa, halved and cut into ¼-inch slices

1 cup chopped yellow onion

2 garlic cloves, chopped

6 cups Basic Chicken Stock (page 29) or reduced-sodium chicken broth

1 carrot, peeled and chopped

1 celery stalk, chopped

1 zucchini, halved and cut into ½-inch slices

1 teaspoon salt

Freshly ground pepper

1½ cups cubed cooked chicken

½ cup uncooked small (salad) macaroni

In a large soup pot over medium heat, warm the oil. Add the kielbasa, onions, and garlic and sauté until the onions and garlic are tender and the kielbasa is lightly browned, about 5 minutes. Increase the temperature to high. Add the stock, carrots, celery, zucchini, salt, and pepper to taste and bring to a boil. Reduce the heat to medium-low and simmer, covered, until the vegetables are tender, about 20 minutes. Add the chicken and macaroni and simmer, uncovered, until the macaroni is tender and the flavors are blended, about 15 minutes longer.

Makes 4 to 6 servings

CHICKEN, POTATO, AND CHEESE CHOWDER

No fancy ingredients are called for in this substantial, homey soup. Slicing the vegetables in the food processor cuts preparation time considerably.

2   medium russet potatoes (about 1 pound), peeled and sliced
½   yellow onion, sliced
1   celery stalk, sliced
1   can (14½ ounces) reduced-sodium chicken broth
½   teaspoon salt
¼   teaspoon dried marjoram
    Freshly ground pepper
1½ cups whole milk
1   cup cubed cooked chicken
1   cup (4 ounces) shredded Monterey Jack cheese
3   tablespoons chopped fresh parsley
    Paprika for sprinkling on top

In a large soup pot over medium heat, cook the vegetables, broth, and seasonings, covered, until the vegetables are tender, about 20 minutes. With a wire whisk, break up the potatoes until chunky. Stir in the milk, chicken, and cheese and cook until the cheese is melted, about 1 minute. Serve in bowls sprinkled with parsley and paprika.

Makes 4 to 6 servings

VARIATION: Add 3 strips cooked, crumbled bacon with the chicken.

CREAMY MEXICAN CHICKEN-CHEESE SOUP

Hungry folks will love this chicken soup enhanced with Mexican accents and served with warm flour tortillas. Essential ingredients are vegetables, chicken, cilantro, and cheese, but variations can be made.

2 cups Basic Chicken Stock (page 29) or reduced-sodium chicken broth
1 carrot, chopped
1 celery stalk, chopped
1 cup chopped yellow onion
2 garlic cloves, chopped
2 cups whole milk
¼ cup all-purpose flour

1 teaspoon salt
1 teaspoon chili powder or more to taste
½ teaspoon ground cumin
1½ cups cubed cooked chicken
1 cup corn kernels, fresh or frozen
1 cup (4 ounces) shredded Monterey Jack cheese (see Note)
2 tablespoons chopped fresh cilantro or parsley

In a large soup pot over high heat, combine the stock, vegetables, and garlic and bring to a boil. Reduce the heat to medium-low and simmer, covered, until the vegetables are tender, 15 minutes.

In a medium bowl, whisk together the milk, flour, salt, chili powder, and cumin. Increase the heat to high and whisk the milk mixture into the soup. Stir until bubbly and thickened, about 5 minutes. Reduce the heat to low. Add the chicken, corn, cheese, and cilantro and stir until the cheese is melted and the flavors are blended, 5 to 10 minutes. (Do not boil after the cheese has been added.)

Makes 6 servings

NOTE: For a spicier soup, substitute pepper Jack cheese for Monterey Jack cheese.

CHICKEN, VEGETABLE, AND ORZO SOUP

This healthful soup can be made in minutes by chopping the vegetables in a food processor and using canned chicken broth. Orzo is a small, rice-shaped pasta that adds substance to the soup. Serve with fresh fruit for lunch.

2 carrots, peeled and cut up

2 celery stalks, cut up

½ yellow onion, cut up

1 garlic clove

8 cups Basic Chicken Stock (page 29) or reduced-sodium chicken broth

2 boned and skinned chicken breast halves (about 1 pound), cut into bite-sized pieces

⅓ cup uncooked orzo

¾ teaspoon salt

½ teaspoon dried thyme
   Freshly ground pepper

¼ cup chopped fresh flat-leaf parsley

Coarsely chop the carrots, celery, onions, and garlic in a food processor. In a large soup pot over high heat, bring the stock to a boil. Add the vegetables, chicken, orzo, and seasonings. Reduce the heat to medium-low and simmer, covered, until the chicken and vegetables are tender, about 15 minutes. Stir in the parsley.

Makes 8 servings

CHICKEN, LENTIL, AND VEGETABLE SOUP

This soup is full of texture and home-style goodness. Round out the flavors with a sprinkling of feta cheese on top. Lentils are a dried legume used worldwide, especially in the Middle East and India. They are used as a side dish or in salads, soups, and stews. Here they add body to thicken the soup.

4 cups water
2 cups Basic Chicken Stock (page 29) or reduced-sodium chicken broth
1 cup dried brown lentils, sorted and rinsed
1 cup chopped yellow onion
1 celery stalk, diced
2 carrots, diced

1 teaspoon salt
½ teaspoon paprika
¼ teaspoon dried oregano
¼ teaspoon freshly ground pepper
2 cups chopped cooked chicken
1 medium zucchini, cut in half lengthwise and diced
1 tablespoon chopped fresh parsley
Crumbled feta cheese for topping

In a large soup pot over high heat, bring the water, stock, lentils, onions, celery, carrots, salt, paprika, oregano, and pepper to a boil. Reduce the heat to medium-low and simmer, covered, for 45 minutes, stirring occasionally. Add the chicken, zucchini, and parsley and simmer, covered, until the vegetables are tender and the flavors are blended, 15 to 20 minutes longer. Ladle into bowls and sprinkle feta on top.

Makes 4 to 6 servings

PANTRY CHICKEN SOUP

This is a variation on the soup from the famous Pantry Restaurant in Portland, Oregon. Though this restaurant is now closed, you can still enjoy this full-bodied soup at home.

8 cups Basic Chicken Stock (page 29) or reduced-sodium chicken broth
1 yellow onion, chopped
3 celery stalks, chopped
3 carrots, peeled and chopped
½ cup chopped red bell pepper

½ cup (1 stick) butter, softened
1 cup all-purpose flour
2 cups cubed cooked chicken breast
2 teaspoons salt
¼ teaspoon ground white pepper

In a large soup pot over high heat, combine the stock, onions, celery, carrots, and bell pepper. Bring to a boil, then reduce the heat to low and simmer, covered, until the vegetables are tender, about 15 minutes. Strain and set the vegetables aside, and return the stock to the pan. In a small bowl, blend together the butter and flour with a fork. Add 3 tablespoons of hot stock to the flour mixture and mix well. Whisk the mixture back into the stock and simmer until the soup takes on a glaze, about 10 minutes. Add the chicken, salt, and pepper. Add the reserved vegetables, if desired, for a thicker soup. Simmer until the flavors are blended, 5 to 10 minutes.

Makes 6 servings

BEST-EVER CHICKEN AND MUSHROOM SOUP

Mushrooms give an intense flavor to this elegant soup in a rich cream base. Serve it for a first course at a company dinner or for a luncheon with warm homemade rolls.

3 to 4 tablespoons butter
1 cup chopped yellow onion
1 garlic clove, minced
1 pound medium mushrooms, trimmed and sliced
1 tablespoon fresh lemon juice
¼ cup all-purpose flour
3 cups Basic Chicken Stock (page 29) or reduced-sodium chicken broth

1 teaspoon soy sauce
2 cups diced cooked chicken
1¼ to 1½ cups half-and-half or whole milk
¼ cup dry white wine
¾ teaspoon salt
½ teaspoon dried thyme
¼ teaspoon ground white pepper
Sour cream for topping (optional)

In a large soup pot over medium heat, melt 3 tablespoons of the butter. Add the onions and garlic and sauté for 3 minutes. Add the mushrooms and lemon juice and sauté until the vegetables are tender, about 5 minutes longer. (Add more butter now, if desired.) Add the flour and stir until bubbly. Add the stock and soy sauce and bring to a boil over high heat, stirring constantly until thickened, about 2 minutes. Add the chicken, half-and-half, wine, salt, thyme, and pepper. Reduce the heat to low and simmer, uncovered, until the flavors are blended, about 5 minutes. Ladle the soup into bowls and swirl about 1 teaspoon sour cream, if using, into each bowl. Serve immediately.

Makes 4 servings

CREAM OF CHICKEN SOUP

This velvety-smooth soup can be served as a first course or as the main course. For best results, use rich homemade stock, but canned broth can also be used. We served this to our out-of-town guests and they loved it.

6 tablespoons butter

1 cup chopped yellow onion

1 cup thinly sliced baby carrots

2 celery stalks, chopped

½ cup all-purpose flour

6 cups Basic Chicken Stock (page 29) or reduced-sodium chicken broth

¾ teaspoon salt

⅛ teaspoon ground white pepper

1½ to 2 cups diced cooked chicken

½ cup half-and-half

In a large soup pot over medium heat, melt the butter. Add the onions, carrots, and celery and sauté until tender, about 10 minutes. Stir in the flour and blend. Increase the heat to medium-high. Add the stock and bring to a boil, stirring constantly until slightly thickened, 8 to 10 minutes. Season with the salt and pepper. Stir in the chicken and half-and-half. Reduce the heat to low and simmer until the flavors are blended, 5 to 10 minutes longer.

Makes 6 servings

CHICKEN-TOMATO BISQUE

Cook like a pro with this elegant soup to serve as an introduction to a dinner or as a main course. A bisque consists of a rich purée of vegetables, cream, and often seafood. Here chicken is used instead of seafood.

¼ cup (½ stick) butter
1 cup chopped yellow onion
1 celery stalk, chopped
1 carrot, chopped
1 large shallot, chopped
¼ cup all-purpose flour
4 cups Basic Chicken Stock (page 29) or reduced-sodium chicken broth

1 can (28 ounces) whole tomatoes including juice, cut up
4 sprigs fresh parsley, torn
1½ teaspoons salt
½ teaspoon dried thyme
Freshly ground pepper
1 cup whipping cream
2 cups diced cooked chicken

In a large soup pot over medium heat, melt the butter. Add the onions, celery, carrot, and shallot and sauté until tender, 6 to 7 minutes. Stir in the flour and cook until bubbly. Add the stock, tomatoes, parsley, salt, thyme, and pepper to taste. Reduce the heat to medium-low and simmer, uncovered, for about 20 minutes. Cool slightly and, working in batches, transfer to a blender or a food processor and purée until very smooth (a blender works best). Return the pureed soup to the pot and whisk in the cream. Add the chicken and simmer, uncovered, until the flavors are blended, 10 minutes longer.

Makes 4 to 6 servings

ITALIAN CHICKEN AND PASTA SOUP

Wake up the taste buds with this highly seasoned chicken soup with a lot of body and substance. Rotelle is a small, round pasta that resembles a wheel with spokes. Other small pasta can also be used. A tossed green salad with Italian dressing complements the soup.

5   cups Basic Chicken Stock (page 29) or reduced-sodium chicken broth
1   can (14½ ounces) Italian-style tomatoes, lightly puréed in a food processor
1   cup chopped yellow onion
2   carrots, sliced
2   garlic cloves, minced
¾   teaspoon salt
½   teaspoon dried basil

½   teaspoon dried oregano
    Freshly ground pepper
1   zucchini, sliced lengthwise, then quartered and sliced
3   ounces (about 1 cup) uncooked rotelle or other small pasta
2   cups diced cooked chicken
    Freshly grated Parmesan cheese for topping

In a soup pot over medium heat, combine the stock, tomatoes, onions, carrots, garlic, and seasonings. Cover and simmer for 10 minutes. Add the zucchini and rotelle and simmer, covered, until the pasta is cooked and the vegetables are tender, about 10 minutes longer. Stir in the chicken and cook until it is heated through and the flavors are blended, 6 to 7 minutes longer. Serve in bowls and sprinkle with Parmesan cheese.

Makes 4 to 6 servings

CHICKEN TORTILLA SOUP WITH ALL OF THE TRIMMINGS

Escape the chill of winter by serving this party soup with some hot flavors. Guests can customize their soup with the toppings of their choice.

1 tablespoon olive oil

1 cup chopped white onion

4 garlic cloves, minced

5 cups Basic Chicken Stock (page 29) or reduced-sodium chicken broth

1 can (14½ ounces) Mexican-style tomatoes including juice, lightly puréed in a food processor

1 can (4 ounces) diced green chiles, drained

1 tablespoon tomato paste

1 cup corn kernels, fresh or frozen

2 to 3 cups chopped or shredded cooked chicken

¼ cup chopped fresh cilantro

¾ teaspoon salt

½ teaspoon chili powder

½ teaspoon ground cumin

½ teaspoon ground coriander

¼ teaspoon dried oregano

Freshly ground pepper

1 lime, cut into wedges

Toppings: 1½ cups (6 ounces) shredded Monterey Jack cheese, diced avocado, sour cream, 2 cups roughly broken corn tortilla chips

In a large soup pot over medium heat, warm the oil. Add the onions and garlic and sauté until tender, about 5 minutes. Add the stock, tomatoes, chiles, and tomato paste and bring to a boil. Reduce the heat and simmer, uncovered, 5 minutes. Add the corn, chicken, cilantro, and seasonings and simmer until the flavors are blended, about 10 minutes longer. Ladle the soup into bowls and add a squeeze of lime juice to each bowl. Pass the toppings in bowls.

Makes 6 servings

WINTER CHICKEN SOUP WITH TOMATOES AND CANNELLINI BEANS

I made this colorful soup on a cold, snowy day at our cozy cabin on the McKenzie River. It was a perfect winter lunch with garlic bread. The addition of bacon adds a salty taste that complements the other ingredients.

4   bacon slices, diced
1   cup chopped yellow onion
2   garlic cloves, chopped
3½ cups Basic Chicken Stock (page 29) or reduced-sodium chicken broth
2   cans (15 ounces each) cannellini (or other white) beans, drained and rinsed
½   cup diced cooked chicken
1   can (14½ ounces) whole tomatoes including juice, chopped

¼   cup dry red wine
¼   cup chopped fresh flat-leaf parsley
1   teaspoon salt
½   teaspoon dried basil
½   teaspoon dried oregano
    Freshly ground pepper
    Freshly grated Parmesan cheese for topping

In a large soup pot over medium heat, cook the bacon until the fat renders, about 3 minutes. Add the onions and garlic and sauté in the bacon drippings until tender and the bacon is crisp, about 5 minutes longer. Add all of the remaining ingredients except the Parmesan. Reduce the heat to low and simmer, uncovered, until the flavors are blended, 10 to 15 minutes. Serve with Parmesan sprinkled on top.

Makes 4 servings

SOUTHWESTERN CHICKEN AND CORN SOUP

A good choice of nutritional ingredients are included in this appetizing, vegetable-packed chicken soup, offering lots of spicy flavor. Serve for a light supper with cornbread.

4 cups Basic Chicken Stock (page 29) or reduced-sodium chicken broth

1 cup chopped yellow onion

½ cup chopped green bell pepper

1 garlic clove, minced

2 cups cubed cooked chicken breast

1 can (14½ ounces) whole tomatoes including juice, chopped

1 cup corn kernels, fresh or frozen

¼ cup chopped fresh cilantro or parsley

1 tablespoon tomato paste

1 teaspoon chili powder

1 teaspoon salt

½ teaspoon ground cumin

½ teaspoon dried oregano

Freshly ground pepper

Broken tortilla chips for topping

In a large soup pot over medium-high heat, add the stock, onions, bell pepper, and garlic and bring to a boil. Reduce the heat to low and simmer, covered, until the vegetables are tender, about 15 minutes. Add the chicken, tomatoes, corn, cilantro, tomato paste, and seasonings. Bring to a boil, then reduce the heat to medium-low and simmer, uncovered, until the flavors are blended, about 10 minutes longer, or until ready to serve. Serve in bowls and top with a few chips.

Makes 6 servings

CHIPOTLE-CHEDDAR-CHICKEN-CORN CHOWDER

This makes a big pot of chunky soup filled with warming ingredients. Chipotle chile is a smoked jalapeño and can be bought canned in adobo sauce. It gives a little heat and adds a zippy flavor. This makes a good supper soup to serve after a ski trip.

1	tablespoon olive oil
1	cup chopped yellow onion
½	red or green bell pepper, chopped
2	garlic cloves, minced
3	cups Basic Chicken Stock (page 29) or reduced-sodium chicken broth
2	cups scrubbed, unpeeled, cubed new potatoes (about 12 ounces)
1½	cups corn kernels, fresh or frozen
1	chipotle chile in adobo sauce, chopped (about 2 teaspoons)
¼	cup all-purpose flour
3	cups whole milk
1½	cups cubed cooked chicken breast (about 2 large halves)
1	cup seeded, chopped tomato
½	cup (2 ounces) shredded Cheddar cheese
¼	cup chopped fresh parsley
¾	teaspoon salt
	Freshly ground pepper

In a large soup pot over medium heat, warm the oil. Add the onions, bell pepper, and garlic and sauté until tender, about 5 minutes. Add the stock and potatoes and bring to a boil. Reduce the heat to medium-low and simmer, covered, until the potatoes are tender, about 20 minutes. Stir in the corn and chipotle.

In a medium bowl, whisk together the flour and milk and stir it into the soup. Increase the heat to medium-high and stir until thickened, about 5 minutes. Reduce the heat to medium-low, and add the chicken, tomato, cheese, parsley, salt, and pepper to taste. Simmer, uncovered, until the flavors are blended and the cheese is melted, 10 to 15 minutes longer. (Do not boil after the cheese has been added.)

Makes 6 servings

CHICKEN CHILI SOUP

"Wow! This is good," was my husband Reed's first comment on this soup. Serve with avocado halves filled with chopped tomatoes and chopped green onions tossed with a vinaigrette.

1 tablespoon olive oil

1 cup chopped yellow onion

2 garlic cloves, minced

2½ cups Basic Chicken Stock (page 29) or reduced-sodium chicken broth

2 cans (15 ounces each) kidney beans, drained and rinsed

1½ cups diced cooked chicken

1 can (4 ounces) mild diced green chiles, drained

1 teaspoon chili powder

1 teaspoon salt

½ teaspoon ground cumin

Freshly ground pepper

¼ cup fresh cilantro or parsley

1 lime, cut into wedges

In a large soup pot over medium heat, warm the oil. Add the onions and garlic and sauté until the vegetables are tender, about 5 minutes. Add the remaining ingredients except the cilantro and lime wedges. Reduce the heat to low and simmer, uncovered, 15 minutes. Stir in the cilantro just before serving. Serve with lime wedges to squeeze over the soup.

Makes 6 servings

CHICKEN, CORN, AND BLACK BEAN SOUP

This creative, main-course soup is highlighted with traditional Mexican ingredients for a contrast in taste, color, and texture. Salsa and spices add warmth to the soup and toppings can be added. Include a fresh citrus salad and warm breadsticks and you have a lunch or light dinner.

6 cups Basic Chicken Stock (page 29) or reduced-sodium chicken broth

3 boned and skinned chicken breast halves (about 1½ pounds), cut into bite-size pieces

1 white onion, chopped

½ green bell pepper, chopped

½ red bell pepper, chopped

1 garlic clove, minced

1 teaspoon chili powder

1 teaspoon ground cumin

1 teaspoon dried oregano

¾ teaspoon salt

  Freshly ground pepper

2 cans (15 ounces each) black beans, drained and rinsed

1 cup corn kernels, fresh or frozen

1 cup prepared tomato salsa

⅓ cup chopped fresh cilantro or parsley

Toppings: sour cream, chopped green onions, crushed tortilla chips

In a large soup pot over medium heat, add the stock, chicken, onions, bell peppers, garlic, and seasonings and cook for 10 minutes. Reduce the heat to medium-low. Add the beans, corn, and salsa and simmer, covered, until the flavors are blended, stirring occasionally, about 20 minutes longer. Stir in the cilantro and simmer, uncovered, 5 minutes longer. Ladle into bowls and serve with toppings.

Makes 6 to 8 servings

CHICKEN SPAGHETTI SOUP

This is an updated version of an old standby using ground chicken instead of beef. It is just as good as the original and maybe better. Hot cheese bread would make a nice addition.

2 teaspoons vegetable oil
1 pound ground chicken
1 cup chopped yellow onion
½ cup chopped green bell pepper
1 garlic clove, minced
4 cups Basic Chicken Stock (page 29) or reduced-sodium chicken broth
1 can (14½ ounces) Italian-style tomatoes including juice
1¼ cups tomato juice
1 can (8 ounces) tomato sauce
¼ cup chopped fresh parsley
1½ teaspoons salt
½ teaspoon dried basil
¼ teaspoon dried oregano
1 bay leaf
Freshly ground pepper
½ cup uncooked spaghetti, broken into 1- to 1½-inch pieces
Freshly grated Parmesan cheese for sprinkling on top

In a large soup pot over medium heat, warm the oil. Add the chicken, onions, bell pepper, and garlic and sauté, breaking up the chicken with a spoon, until lightly browned and the vegetables are tender, 5 to 6 minutes. Add the remaining ingredients except the spaghetti and cheese and simmer, uncovered, about 10 minutes. Increase the heat to medium-high and add the spaghetti. Cook until the spaghetti is tender and the flavors are blended, about 15 minutes longer. Remove the bay leaf and discard. Serve in bowls and sprinkle with Parmesan cheese.

Makes 4 servings

CHICKEN TORTELLINI SOUP

Here is a soup that is welcome any time of the year. The cheese-filled tortellini add substance and flavor to this easy-to-make soup. Packaged tortellini are found in the refrigerated section of most supermarkets.

2　teaspoons olive oil

1　cup chopped yellow onion

2　garlic cloves, chopped

5　cups Basic Chicken Stock (page 29) or reduced-sodium chicken broth

2　boned and skinned chicken breast halves (about 1 pound), cut into bite-sized pieces

1　can (14½ ounces) whole tomatoes including juice, chopped

½　teaspoon dried basil

½　teaspoon dried thyme

½　teaspoon salt
　　Freshly ground pepper

1　package (9 ounces) cheese-filled tortellini or ravioli

¼　cup chopped fresh parsley
　　Freshly grated Parmesan cheese for topping

In a large soup pot over medium heat, warm the oil. Add the onions and garlic and sauté until tender, about 5 minutes. Add the stock, chicken, tomatoes, and seasonings and simmer, uncovered, about 10 minutes. Add the tortellini and parsley and simmer, uncovered, until the tortellini are tender and the flavors are blended, about 10 minutes longer. Sprinkle with Parmesan cheese.

Makes 6 servings

TUSCAN WHITE BEAN SOUP WITH CHICKEN AND KALE

This Italian soup takes only about 25 minutes to prepare, and it tastes as good as it looks. The kale adds a bright contrasting color and additional flavor. I like to make this to serve for a light supper with rustic bread, and since there are only two of us in our household, we can also have it the next day for lunch.

1 tablespoon olive oil
1 cup chopped yellow onion
1 carrot, peeled and chopped
2 celery stalks, chopped
½ cup chopped red bell pepper
2 garlic cloves, minced
3 cups Basic Chicken Stock (page 29) or reduced-sodium chicken broth
2 cans (15 ounces each) cannellini beans, drained and rinsed
1 can (14½ ounces) Italian-style tomatoes including juice, coarsely chopped

¾ teaspoon salt
½ teaspoon dried rosemary
1 bay leaf
 Freshly ground pepper
3 packed cups sliced kale
1½ cups cubed cooked chicken
1 small zucchini, halved lengthwise and cut into ½-inch slices
 Freshly grated Parmesan cheese for topping

In a large soup pot over medium heat, warm the oil. Add the onions, carrot, celery, bell pepper, and garlic and sauté until tender, about 5 minutes. Add the stock, beans, tomatoes, salt, rosemary, bay leaf, and pepper to taste. Bring to a boil. Reduce the heat to low and simmer, covered, until the flavors are blended, about 15 minutes. Stir in the kale, chicken, and zucchini and simmer 5 to 10 minutes longer. Discard the bay leaf. Ladle into soup bowls and sprinkle with Parmesan.

Makes 6 to 8 servings

WHITE CHILI WITH CHICKEN

Add toppings for extra flavor.

1 pound (2 cups) dry Great Northern white beans, sorted, rinsed, and presoaked (see Note)
6 cups chicken stock
1 large yellow onion, chopped
3 cloves garlic, minced
1 teaspoon ground white pepper
1 teaspoon dried oregano
1 teaspoon ground cumin
1 can (4 ounces) diced green chiles, drained
2 to 3 cups shredded or diced cooked chicken
¼ cup chopped cilantro or parsley
½ teaspoon salt

Toppings: 2 cups shredded Monterey Jack cheese, chopped onions, salsa

In a large soup pot over high heat, combine the presoaked drained beans, 5 cups of the stock, the onion, garlic, white pepper, oregano, and cumin and bring to a boil. Reduce heat to medium-low and simmer, covered, until the beans are tender, about 2 hours, stirring occasionally. Add the chiles, chicken, cilantro, and salt. Simmer, uncovered, 10 minutes longer. Add remaining 1 cup stock if too thick. Serve in large bowls and pass the toppings.

Makes 6 servings

NOTE: To quick-soak dry beans, place beans and cold water to cover in a large soup pot. Bring to a boil over high heat and boil for 2 minutes. Skim off foam and discard. Remove from heat and let stand, covered, 1 hour before using. Drain and proceed with the recipe.

MAIN-COURSE SALADS

Main-course salads are ideal to serve for a luncheon or a light supper. Most prep work can be done ahead and the salad assembled just before serving.

Chicken salads combined with other complementary ingredients are filling and satisfying and add variety to a menu. They are especially popular to serve in the summer when it is too hot to cook, so meals can be served alfresco. Homemade dressings are essential in making good-quality salads. They are more economical, add better flavor, are generally more healthful, and are worth the extra time.

In this chapter, you'll find a wide variety of inviting salads that will please everyone, such as Curried Chicken, Artichoke, and Rice Salad; Spicy Chicken Salad; Chicken, Black Bean, Corn, Tomato, and Rice Salad; Chicken and Pasta Salad with Pesto Mayonnaise; Salad Niçoise with Chicken; and Spinach Salad with Chicken, Bacon, and Blue Cheese.

CHICKEN CAESAR SALAD

When strips of grilled chicken breast are added to this classic Caesar salad, it becomes a main-course salad for an informal supper or luncheon. Crisp romaine, garlicky croutons, and a mild anchovy dressing are the other traditional ingredients in this popular salad.

3   boned and skinned chicken breast halves (about 1½ pounds)
    Vegetable oil for brushing on chicken breasts
    Salt and freshly ground pepper
8   cups chopped hearts of romaine
1   cup Baked Garlic Croutons (facing page)
    Creamy Caesar Dressing (facing page)
12 cherry tomatoes
    Pitted black olives for garnish
    Shaved Parmesan cheese for topping (use a vegetable peeler)

Prepare a grill for cooking over medium indirect heat. Brush the chicken breasts with oil on both sides and season with salt and pepper to taste. Grill until the chicken is no longer pink in the center, about 5 minutes on each side. Remove the chicken from the grill and cool on a plate, then cut into ½-inch strips.

In a large bowl, mix the romaine and croutons with enough dressing to coat. Divide evenly among 6 salad plates. Top with the chicken strips and garnish with cherry tomatoes and olives. Add a few Parmesan shavings on top.

Makes 6 servings

NOTE: Chicken breasts for this can also be broiled or poached.

BAKED GARLIC CROUTONS

2   tablespoons olive oil
3   garlic cloves, minced
¼   teaspoon salt

2   cups ¾-inch cubes Italian bread
1   tablespoon freshly grated Parmesan cheese (optional)

In a medium bowl, mix the oil, garlic, and salt. Let stand 15 minutes. In the meantime, preheat the oven to 350°F. Add the bread cubes to the mixture and toss to coat.

Spread the cubes on a baking sheet and bake until golden, about 12 minutes. Put in a bowl and sprinkle with the cheese, if desired. Cool and store at room temperature in an airtight container for up to 24 hours.

Makes about 2 cups

VARIATION: Sprinkle the croutons with seasoned salt or mixed dried herbs for a more distinct flavor.

CREAMY CAESAR DRESSING

Adjust the amount of anchovies or paste to your taste.

⅓   cup mayonnaise
1   green onion including some tender green tops, cut up
3   tablespoons fresh lemon juice
2   tablespoons olive oil
2   tablespoons freshly grated Parmesan cheese

2 or 3   anchovy fillets, drained and coarsely chopped, or 1 or 2 teaspoons anchovy paste
2   garlic cloves, cut up
1   teaspoon Dijon mustard
1   teaspoon Worcestershire sauce
    Freshly ground pepper

Place all the ingredients in a food processor or blender and process until smooth. Transfer to a bowl, cover, and refrigerate until ready to use.

Makes about 1 cup

SPINACH SALAD WITH CHICKEN, BACON, AND BLUE CHEESE

This combination of favorite ingredients is a winner to serve as a main-course salad with warm French bread.

1   bag (6 ounces) baby spinach, stems removed if desired
2   cups cubed cooked chicken
4   ounces bacon, diced, cooked, and drained
½   red onion, sliced and rings separated
¼   cup crumbled blue cheese
3   tablespoons olive oil
2   tablespoons red wine vinegar
¼   teaspoon salt
    Freshly ground pepper
2   hard-cooked eggs, quartered

In a large salad bowl, mix together the spinach, chicken, bacon, onion rings, and cheese. In a small bowl, whisk together the oil, vinegar, salt, and pepper to taste. Toss with the salad to coat. Arrange the egg wedges around the edge of the salad bowl.

Makes 4 servings

TARRAGON CHICKEN SALAD

This main-course salad is enhanced with a light creamy tarragon dressing and served on crisp, cold greens. Tarragon is an aromatic herb known for its distinctive, anise-like flavor. It is available fresh in the summer or dried year-round. Serve this salad with homemade rolls for an elegant luncheon.

2½   cups cubed cooked chicken
½   cup diced celery
3   ounces mushrooms, coarsely chopped
¼   cup diced red onion
2   tablespoons chopped fresh parsley
     Creamy Tarragon Dressing (recipe follows)
4   cups mixed salad greens

In a medium bowl, combine the chicken, celery, mushrooms, onions, and parsley. Toss with enough dressing to coat. Cover and refrigerate several hours to allow flavors to blend.

To serve, divide mixed greens equally among 4 individual plates and top with the chicken mixture.

Makes 4 servings

CREAMY TARRAGON DRESSING

½   cup mayonnaise
¼   cup sour cream
1   green onion including some tender green tops, sliced
1   sprig fresh parsley
1   tablespoon white wine vinegar
1   tablespoon olive oil
1   teaspoon Dijon mustard
½   teaspoon dried tarragon
½   teaspoon salt
⅛   teaspoon ground white pepper

In a food processor, combine all the ingredients until smooth. .

Makes about 1 cup

AVOCADOS FILLED WITH CHICKEN SALAD

This salad can be made any time of the year because the ingredients are always available. It makes a nice luncheon salad served with warm sourdough rolls. The filling can be made ahead and the avocado prepared just before serving. Allow one avocado per person.

2 cups cubed cooked chicken breast
¾ cup chopped red bell pepper
2 large mushrooms, chopped
1 celery stalk, chopped
½ cup mayonnaise, or more to taste
½ teaspoon dried oregano
½ teaspoon salt
Freshly ground pepper
4 avocados, halved and pitted (leave skin on for serving)
Butter lettuce for lining the plates

In a medium bowl, mix together the chicken, bell pepper, mushrooms, celery, mayonnaise, oregano, salt, and pepper to taste. Arrange 2 avocado halves on each of 4 lettuce-lined plates and fill each half with salad.

Makes 4 servings

TOMATOES STUFFED WITH CHICKEN SALAD

Serve this delicious luncheon salad for your golfing or tennis friends. Lots of tender chicken, eggs, and buttery avocados make a good combination. The mixture can be made ahead but the avocados should be added just before serving. Serve with crusty bread and chilled white wine or iced tea.

6	medium, firm tomatoes, unpeeled
2	cups diced cooked chicken
1	cup diced celery
2	hard-cooked eggs, chopped
¼	cup minced fresh parsley
2 to 3	green onions including some tender green tops, finely chopped
½	cup mayonnaise, plus more to taste
1	teaspoon Dijon mustard
	Salt and freshly ground pepper
1 or 2	avocados, pitted, peeled, and cut into bite-sized pieces
	Large lettuce leaves for lining the plates

With a sharp knife, cut the stem end out of each tomato and discard. Then quarter them about halfway down, keeping the tomatoes intact. Refrigerate until ready to use.

In a medium bowl, combine the chicken, celery, eggs, parsley, and onions. In a small bowl, mix together the mayonnaise, mustard, and salt and pepper to taste. Add to the chicken mixture and mix well. Cover and refrigerate 1 hour. Add the diced avocados to the filling and gently mix. Open the tomatoes slightly and fill them with equal amounts of the salad. Place on 6 individual lettuce-lined plates.

Makes 6 servings

CLASSIC CHEF'S SALAD

Composed salads consist of ingredients arranged in groups, rather than tossed. They can be served in bowls or on individual plates for an impressive presentation. This popular salad is featured in many restaurants, but now you can make it at home with these simple ingredients. Prepare the ingredients ahead and chill before assembling on individual plates.

6   cups shredded iceberg lettuce
6   green onions including some tender green tops, sliced
1   celery stalk, sliced
2   boned and skinned chicken breast halves (about 1 pound), cooked and cut into narrow strips (about 2 cups; see Note)
8   ounces cooked ham, cut into narrow strips (about 1½ cups; see Note)
3   ounces Swiss cheese, cut into narrow strips (see Note)
2   hard-cooked eggs, peeled and cut into wedges
2   tomatoes, cut into wedges
½   cup pitted black olives
    Blue Cheese Dressing (facing page)
    Thousand Island Dressing (facing page)

In a large bowl, toss together the lettuce, onions, and celery. Divide evenly among 4 individual plates. Arrange the chicken, ham, and cheese strips in rows over the top. Garnish with egg wedges, tomato wedges, and olives. Pass the dressings in bowls.

Makes 4 servings

NOTE: To cut chicken, ham, and cheese quickly, stack ¼-inch slices together and cut into 1-by-2-inch strips.

BLUE CHEESE DRESSING

Try this dressing on a chilled wedge of crisp lettuce for a salad. This also makes a good dip (see Note).

1   cup mayonnaise
⅔   cup buttermilk
¼   cup sour cream
2   sprigs fresh parsley, torn up
1   large garlic clove, cut up
1   teaspoon Worcestershire sauce
¼   teaspoon salt
    Freshly ground pepper
1   cup crumbled blue cheese, divided

In a food processor, process the mayonnaise, buttermilk, sour cream, parsley, garlic, Worcestershire sauce, salt, and pepper to taste. Add half of the blue cheese and process until smooth. Transfer to a bowl and fold in the remaining blue cheese.

Makes about 2 cups

NOTE: To make this into a dip, add all of the blue cheese with the other ingredients and process until smooth.

THOUSAND ISLAND DRESSING

1   cup mayonnaise
¼   cup chili sauce or ketchup
2   green onions including some tender green tops, coarsely chopped
1   sprig fresh parsley, torn up
1   tablespoon fresh lemon juice
1   tablespoon sweet pickle relish or 1 sweet pickle, cut up
1   teaspoon prepared horseradish
1   teaspoon Worcestershire sauce
½   teaspoon ground mustard
½   teaspoon salt
2   drops Tabasco sauce

In a food processor, combine all the ingredients and blend until smooth. Cover and refrigerate until ready to use.

Makes about 1 cup

SALAD NIÇOISE WITH CHICKEN

Salad niçoise is a famous composed salad originating in Nice in the south of France. This whole meal on one plate traditionally consists of tuna, but here chicken is used. Other traditional ingredients include potatoes, green beans, onions, and tomatoes, arranged in groups on the plate and garnished with eggs, anchovies, and olives. If possible, use niçoise olives, small oval olives ranging in color from deep purple to brown-black with a rich, nutty flavor. This makes an elegant and impressive salad to serve for a luncheon or light supper.

4 to 5	medium red potatoes (about 2 pounds), unpeeled, scrubbed, and halved
	Red Wine Vinaigrette (facing page)
¼	cup chopped fresh flat-leaf parsley
1	pound green beans, trimmed
10 to 12	cups torn Bibb lettuce
2 to 3	cups cubed cooked chicken breast
3	small tomatoes, cut into wedges
½	red onion, thinly sliced
4	large hard-cooked eggs, quartered
1	cup pitted niçoise, kalamata, or other black olives
2	tablespoons drained capers
	Salt and freshly ground pepper

In a medium saucepan over medium heat, cook the potatoes in salted water to cover, until tender, 15 to 20 minutes. Drain and, while still warm, cut into ½-inch slices and place in a medium bowl. Toss with 2 or 3 tablespoons of the dressing and the parsley. Cover and refrigerate several hours.

In the same pan, cook the beans in salted water to cover until tender-crisp, about 6 minutes. Cool under cold running water and pat dry with a paper towel. In a medium bowl, toss the beans with 2 to 3 tablespoons of the dressing. Cover all the vegetables and refrigerate several hours before assembling.

To assemble, divide the lettuce between 6 individual plates or place on a large platter. Remove the potatoes and beans from the dressing with a slotted spoon. On top of the lettuce, arrange the potatoes on one side, beans on the other side, and chicken in the middle. Add the tomatoes, onion, eggs, and olives around the outside. Scatter the capers on top of the chicken. Sprinkle salt and pepper on the eggs. Pass the remaining dressing in a small pitcher.

Makes 6 servings

RED WINE VINAIGRETTE

½	cup olive oil
¼	cup red wine vinegar
2 or 3	garlic cloves, minced
1	tablespoon Dijon mustard
½	teaspoon dried oregano
¼	teaspoon dried thyme
¼	teaspoon salt
	Freshly ground pepper

In a small bowl, whisk together all the ingredients, adding pepper to taste.

Makes about ¾ cup

SPICY CHICKEN SALAD

This composed salad is arranged on individual plates for interest and eye appeal. Hoisin sauce is a thick, reddish-brown sauce with a sweet and spicy flavor, used extensively in Chinese cooking. It can be found in the Asian section of most supermarkets.

3   cups shredded iceberg lettuce
1   large cucumber, peeled, grated, and blotted dry with paper towels
2   cups shredded cooked chicken
4   green onions including some tender green tops, sliced lengthwise into thin strips
½   cup toasted slivered almonds (see Note)
    Hoisin Dressing (recipe follows)

Divide the lettuce evenly onto 4 plates. Add the cucumber and chicken in groups on top of the lettuce. Sprinkle with the green onions and almonds and drizzle with dressing just before serving.

Makes 4 servings

HOISIN DRESSING

¼   cup hoisin sauce
2   tablespoons rice vinegar
1   tablespoon soy sauce
1   tablespoon water
1   tablespoon toasted sesame seeds
    (see page 95)

In a small bowl, mix together all the ingredients.

Makes about ½ cup

NOTE: To toast the almonds, preheat oven to 350°F. Place almonds on a baking sheet and bake, 5 to 6 minutes. Cool before using.

COMPOSED SALAD OF CHICKEN, HEARTS OF PALM, BELGIAN ENDIVE, AND BUTTER LETTUCE

This is a wonderful combination of textures and flavors and makes an unusual and attractive plate. Serve with olive bread or other artisan bread.

1   jar (14½ ounces) hearts of palm, drained and cut into ½-inch pieces
3   green onions including some tender green tops, finely chopped
3   tablespoons olive oil
2   tablespoons white wine vinegar
2   tablespoons fresh lemon juice
2   tablespoons Dijon mustard
2   teaspoons drained capers
3   cups torn butter lettuce
1   Belgian endive, leaves separated
1   avocado, peeled, pitted, and sliced
2   cups cooked sliced chicken breast
2   hard-cooked eggs, finely chopped

In a medium bowl, mix together the hearts of palm, onions, oil, vinegar, lemon juice, mustard, and capers and let stand for several hours in the refrigerator. To assemble, divide the lettuce between 6 large plates. Remove the hearts of palm from the dressing with a slotted spoon and arrange them around the outside of the lettuce. Add the endive, avocado, and chicken in groups on top of the lettuce with the chicken strips in the center. Drizzle with the dressing and sprinkle the eggs on top.

Makes 6 servings

CHICKEN, GREENS, AND FRUIT SALAD WITH GORGONZOLA

Caramelized almonds add a sweet, nutty taste, and a crunchy texture to this combination of chicken, greens, oranges, apples, avocado, and cheese. Serve with warm croissants for a luncheon your friends will not forget.

5 cups torn green leaf lettuce (about ½ head)
5 cups torn romaine lettuce (about ½ head)
3 cups cubed cooked chicken
1 cup chopped celery
4 green onions including some tender green tops, sliced
1 can (11 ounces) mandarin oranges, drained

1 avocado, peeled, pitted, and chopped
1 red apple, unpeeled, cored, and diced
½ cup crumbled Gorgonzola or other blue cheese
Caramelized Almonds (recipe follows)
Sweet Wine Dressing (recipe follows)

In a large bowl, combine all the ingredients, except the dressing; cover and refrigerate. Just before serving, toss lightly with enough dressing to coat. Serve the salad in a bowl or on individual plates.

Makes 6 to 8 servings

CARAMELIZED ALMONDS

3 tablespoons sugar
½ cup sliced almonds

In a small skillet over medium heat, stir the sugar and almonds together until the sugar melts and coats the nuts, about 2 minutes. Be careful not to burn. Spread the nuts on a piece of foil to cool.

Makes about ½ cup

SWEET WINE DRESSING

¼ cup vegetable oil
2 tablespoons sugar
2 tablespoons dry white wine
1 tablespoon chopped fresh parsley
½ teaspoon salt
Freshly ground pepper

In a small bowl, whisk together all the ingredients.

Makes about ½ cup

CITY SALAD

This salad is similar to one I had at a restaurant overlooking the Bay Bridge in San Francisco, when I had lunch with my editor, Bill LeBlond. Chicken breasts were poached, then marinated in an orange dressing and served on tender butter lettuce surrounded with orange, grapefruit, and avocado slices. The salad, the view, and the company were memorable.

1 cup fresh orange juice
2 tablespoons sesame oil
1 tablespoon honey
1 teaspoon orange zest
¼ teaspoon salt
3 boned and skinned chicken breast halves (about 1½ pounds), poached (see page 25), cooled, and sliced diagonally
1 small head butter lettuce, torn into large pieces
1 grapefruit, peeled, pith removed, and sliced
2 oranges, peeled, pith removed, and sliced
2 avocados, peeled, pitted, and sliced
¼ cup toasted sesame seeds (see Note)

In a shallow medium bowl, whisk together the orange juice, oil, honey, zest, and salt. Remove half of the mixture to another bowl and set aside. Add the chicken slices to the mixture in the bowl. Cover and marinate 30 minutes in the refrigerator, turning once. Divide the lettuce equally among 4 salad plates. Remove the chicken from the dressing and fan it on top of the greens. Arrange the grapefruit, oranges, and avocado around the chicken. Drizzle with the reserved dressing and sprinkle the sesame seeds on top.

Makes 4 servings

NOTE: To toast sesame seeds, stir them constantly in a small nonstick skillet over medium-high heat until golden, about 2 minutes.

CHICKEN NOODLE SALAD WITH SESAME SEED DRESSING

Surprise your guests with this Asian-style salad of chicken, noodles, and vegetables with a sesame-soy dressing. For fun, serve with fortune cookies.

6 ounces chow mein noodles, cooked according to package directions, drained and cooled
2½ cups shredded cooked chicken
8 ounces bean sprouts, washed, drained, and dried
4 ounces mushrooms, sliced
1 can (4 ounces) sliced water chestnuts, drained
⅓ cup chopped fresh cilantro, plus a few sprigs for garnish
6 green onions including some tender green tops, sliced
Sesame Seed Dressing (recipe follows)

In a medium bowl, combine the noodles, chicken, bean sprouts, mushrooms, water chestnuts, chopped cilantro, and onions. Add ¼ cup of the dressing and toss with 2 forks. Let stand at room temperature for 30 minutes. Divide the salad equally among 4 large plates and garnish with cilantro sprigs. Pass the remaining dressing in a small pitcher.

Makes 4 servings

SESAME SEED DRESSING

½ cup rice vinegar
¼ cup soy sauce
3 tablespoons toasted sesame seeds (see Note, page 95)
1 tablespoon sugar
¼ teaspoon salt
¼ teaspoon cayenne pepper

In a small bowl, whisk together all the ingredients.

Makes about ¾ cup

CURRIED CHICKEN, ARTICHOKE, AND RICE SALAD

The light curry dressing binds the ingredients in this simple but elegant main-course supper salad. This was one of the favorites at a tasting party. The fruit adds an exotic touch.

½ cup long-grain white rice, cooked according to package directions (1½ cups cooked)

2 cups cubed cooked chicken

1 jar (6½ ounces) marinated artichoke hearts, drained and cut into bite-size pieces (reserve 2 tablespoons of the marinade for the dressing)

4 green onions including some tender green tops, sliced

¼ cup diced red bell pepper

¼ cup diced celery

Curry Dressing (recipe follows)

Pineapple, kiwi, and papaya slices for serving

In a medium bowl, combine all the ingredients except the dressing and fruit. Toss with enough dressing to coat. Cover and refrigerate several hours to allow the flavors to blend. If the salad seems dry, add a little more dressing or mayonnaise before serving with the fruit for accompaniment.

Makes 4 servings

CURRY DRESSING

¼ cup mayonnaise

¼ cup plain nonfat yogurt

2 tablespoons reserved artichoke marinade

½ to 1 teaspoon curry powder

¼ teaspoon salt

⅛ teaspoon freshly ground pepper

In a small bowl, whisk together all ingredients until smooth, adding the curry powder to taste. Cover and refrigerate until ready to use.

Makes about ⅔ cup

CHICKEN AND PASTA SALAD WITH PESTO MAYONNAISE

Chicken tossed with pasta and a pesto dressing is an appetizing main-course salad for a summer potluck. Prepare this several hours ahead to allow the flavors to mellow. Make the pesto in the summer, when basil is in season, and freeze some for winter use.

6   ounces (2½ cups) rotini, cooked according to package directions, drained
2   teaspoons vegetable oil
2   cups cubed cooked chicken breast
2   celery stalks, chopped
¼   cup chopped green onions including some tender green tops
    Pesto Mayonnaise (recipe follows)
2   hard-cooked eggs, quartered

In a large bowl, toss the cooked pasta with the oil. Add the chicken, celery, and onions and stir gently to combine. Cover and refrigerate several hours. Toss with the dressing 30 minutes before serving. Garnish with the eggs.

Makes 6 servings

PESTO MAYONNAISE

½   cup mayonnaise
3   tablespoons Basil Pesto (facing page) or
    purchased pesto
1   tablespoon fresh lemon juice
¼   teaspoon salt

In a small bowl, mix together all the ingredients. Cover and refrigerate until ready to use.

Makes about ⅔ cup

BASIL PESTO

2 cups firmly packed fresh basil leaves, washed and dried
2 sprigs fresh parsley
2 garlic cloves, coarsely chopped
¼ cup chopped walnuts or pine nuts
¼ cup (1 ounce) freshly grated Parmesan cheese
¼ teaspoon salt
Freshly ground pepper
3 to 4 tablespoons olive oil

Place all the ingredients except the oil in a food processor or blender. Process until minced. With the motor running, slowly pour the oil through the feed tube and blend until a paste forms. Scrape down the sides of the bowl with a spatula. Transfer to a bowl, cover, and refrigerate until ready to use, or freeze in an airtight container for up to 6 months.

Makes about ½ cup

CHICKEN, BLACK BEAN, CORN, TOMATO, AND RICE SALAD

Beans and corn are two major staples in Mexican cooking. Here they are combined with chicken and rice and other tasty ingredients to make a great main-course salad. Serve slightly chilled or at room temperature with a basket of warmed tortillas.

½ cup long-grain white rice, cooked according to package directions (1½ cups cooked), drained

1 can (15 ounces) black beans, drained and rinsed

1 cup cooked corn kernels, fresh or frozen

1 cup shredded cooked chicken

2 small tomatoes, seeded, chopped, and drained

½ cup chopped red bell pepper

¼ cup chopped yellow onion

¼ cup chopped fresh cilantro or parsley, plus a few sprigs for garnish

¼ to ⅓ cup olive oil

¼ cup fresh lime juice

1 teaspoon red wine vinegar

1 teaspoon salt

¼ teaspoon sugar

¼ teaspoon ground cumin

Freshly ground pepper

2 avocados, peeled, pitted, and chopped

In a large bowl, mix together the rice, beans, corn, chicken, tomatoes, bell pepper, onions, and chopped cilantro.

In a small bowl, whisk together the oil, lime juice, vinegar, salt, sugar, cumin, and pepper to taste. Pour over the bean mixture and mix. Cover and refrigerate. Remove from the refrigerator 30 minutes before serving. Just before serving, add the avocados. Garnish with cilantro sprigs.

Makes 6 servings

CHICKEN AND FRUIT SALAD WITH POPPY SEED DRESSING

Leftover rotisserie chicken breast or baked chicken works well in this salad. Chill all fruit before assembling and serve with warm croissants. It is easy to double this recipe if you are serving a large group.

2   cups cubed cooked chicken breast
1   large peach, peeled and cut into chunks
1½ cups pineapple chunks, drained
2   bananas, sliced
½   cup chopped celery
3   tablespoons chopped walnuts (optional)
    Poppy Seed Dressing (recipe follows)
4   large lettuce leaves

In a medium bowl, combine the chicken, fruit, celery, and walnuts. Mix with the dressing and serve on 4 lettuce-lined plates.

Makes 4 servings

POPPY SEED DRESSING

¼   cup mayonnaise
2   tablespoons nonfat plain yogurt
1   tablespoon honey
½   teaspoon poppy seeds
¼   teaspoon salt

In a small bowl, mix together all the ingredients.

Makes about ½ cup

CHICKEN-ARTICHOKE ASPIC

Aspic salads are not as popular today as they were at one time, but this sophisticated salad with a creamy texture and distinctive combination of ingredients still has appeal. Include it at a salad buffet. For convenience, it can be made a day ahead.

1 envelope unflavored gelatin	1 cup shredded cooked chicken breast
1 cup boiling water	1 can (14 ounces) artichoke hearts, drained and cut up
½ cup sour cream	
3 ounces cream cheese, at room temperature, cut up	2 hard-cooked eggs, cut up
¼ cup mayonnaise	3 green onions including some tender green tops, sliced
¼ cup dry white wine	2 or 3 drops Tabasco sauce
1 teaspoon dried marjoram	½ cup chopped pimientos, drained
¼ teaspoon salt	Large lettuce leaves for lining plate
Freshly ground pepper	Cherry tomatoes for garnish

In a glass measuring cup, mix the gelatin with the boiling water. Place the cup in a pan of hot water over medium heat and stir until the gelatin is dissolved, about 2 minutes. Transfer the gelatin to a medium bowl. Beat in the sour cream, cream cheese, mayonnaise, wine, marjoram, salt, and pepper to taste.

In a food processor, combine the chicken, artichoke hearts, eggs, onions, and Tabasco and process until chunky. Stir in the pimientos, fold everything into the gelatin mixture, and mix well.

Spoon into a lightly sprayed or oiled 4-cup mold. Chill until firm, 4 to 5 hours or overnight. Unmold onto a lettuce-lined plate and garnish with tomatoes.

Makes 8 servings

MIXED GREENS WITH CHICKEN, AVOCADO, ORANGE, AND BLUE CHEESE

Don't miss this versatile salad of complementary ingredients with a light orange-flavored dressing. It can be served any time of the year because all of the ingredients are readily available. Rotisserie chicken breast or any cooked chicken can be used.

8 to 10	cups mixed greens
2	avocados, peeled, pitted, and sliced
2	oranges, peeled and cut into bite-size pieces
1	cup cubed cooked chicken
4	green onions including some tender green tops, sliced, or 2 tablespoons chopped red onion
3	tablespoons crumbled blue cheese
	Orange Dressing (recipe follows)

In a large bowl, toss together the ingredients with enough dressing to coat.

Makes 6 to 8 servings

ORANGE DRESSING

½	cup olive oil
2	tablespoons fresh orange juice
1	tablespoon white wine vinegar
1	tablespoon Dijon mustard
1	garlic clove, minced
¼	teaspoon dried thyme
¼	teaspoon salt
	Freshly ground pepper

In a small bowl, whisk together all the ingredients.

Makes about ¾ cup

CHICKEN AND GRAPE SALAD

If you need a salad for a winter luncheon, serve this one of contrasting flavors with a light dressing. Pass a basket of assorted warm artisan breads.

2½	cups cubed cooked chicken breast
1	cup seedless red grapes
½	cup chopped celery
4 to 6	green onions including some tender green tops, chopped
2	tablespoons chopped walnuts
	Honey-Lemon Mayonnaise (page 106)
4	lettuce leaves

In a medium bowl, combine the chicken, grapes, celery, onions, and walnuts. Toss with enough dressing to coat. Cover and refrigerate several hours. Divide the salad evenly onto 4 lettuce-lined plates and serve immediately.

Makes 4 servings

CHICKEN AND PINEAPPLE SALAD

This lovely, light salad was served at a luncheon for my 92-year-old aunt when she came to Eugene for a visit. It was served with a refreshing drink of cranberry juice and a splash of champagne. Everyone had a good time! The ingredients can be prepared ahead, but do not mix until one hour before serving.

1	cup mayonnaise
⅓	cup mango chutney, chopped
¼	cup fresh lime juice
2	teaspoons grated lime zest
½ to 1	teaspoon curry powder
½	teaspoon salt
4	cups diced cooked chicken breast
½	cup fresh pineapple chunks
½	cup thinly sliced green onions including some tender green tops
¼	cup dried cranberries
	Butter lettuce leaves for lining plates
½	cup slivered almonds, toasted (see page 92)

In a medium bowl, mix together the mayonnaise, chutney, lime juice, lime zest, curry powder, and salt.

In the same bowl, mix together the chicken, pineapple, onions, and cranberries with the dressing. Divide the mixture evenly among 6 lettuce-lined plates and sprinkle with the almonds.

Makes 6 servings

OREGON CHICKEN WALDORF SALAD

For this seasonal fall salad, combine cubed chicken, crisp apples, crunchy nuts, and tart cranberries with Honey-Lemon Mayonnaise and serve on butter lettuce. Oregon is the U.S. leader in hazelnut production.

2 cups cubed cooked chicken breast
2 Gravenstein apples, unpeeled, cored, and cut into bite-sized pieces
½ cup chopped celery
½ cup diced red onion
¼ cup dried cranberries
¼ cup chopped toasted Oregon hazelnuts (see Note)
  Honey-Lemon Mayonnaise (recipe follows)
  Butter lettuce for lining plates

In a large bowl, combine the chicken, apples, celery, onions, cranberries, and hazelnuts and toss with dressing to coat. Cover and refrigerate for several hours to allow the flavors to blend. To serve, divide the chicken mixture evenly among 4 lettuce-lined plates.

Makes 4 servings

HONEY-LEMON MAYONNAISE

½ cup mayonnaise
2 tablespoons fresh lemon juice
1 tablespoon honey
1 teaspoon white wine vinegar
¼ teaspoon salt

In a small bowl, whisk together all the ingredients. Cover and refrigerate until ready to use.

Makes about ½ cup

NOTE: To toast the hazelnuts, preheat the oven to 350°F. Spread the hazelnuts on a baking sheet and bake until lightly colored and the skins are blistered, about 10 minutes. Wrap the hot nuts in a clean towel to steam for 1 minute. Then rub the nuts in the towel to remove most of the skins.

CHICKEN AND STRAWBERRY SALAD WITH CHUTNEY DRESSING

You'll enjoy every bite of this salad combining chicken and fresh, juicy strawberries. Make it in the summer when the berries are in season. It goes well with grilled meats for a patio dinner.

2   cups cubed cooked chicken breast

1   cup chopped celery

6   green onions including some tender green tops, sliced

¼   cup chopped walnuts

    Chutney Dressing (recipe follows)

2½   cups hulled, sliced fresh strawberries, plus 8 whole strawberries for garnish

    Lettuce leaves for lining a platter

In a large bowl, mix the chicken, celery, onions, and walnuts with dressing to coat. Cover and refrigerate several hours to allow the flavors to blend. Just before serving, gently fold in the sliced strawberries. Mound the salad on a lettuce-lined platter or divide among 4 individual plates. Garnish with the whole strawberries.

Makes 4 servings

CHUTNEY DRESSING

1   cup mayonnaise

2   tablespoons white wine vinegar

2   tablespoons mango chutney, preferably Major Grey's

½ to 1   teaspoon curry powder

½   teaspoon salt

    Freshly ground pepper

In a medium bowl, whisk together all the ingredients, adjusting the curry powder and pepper to taste.

Makes about 1¼ cups

CHOPPED CHICKEN AND JICAMA SALAD WITH SPICY AVOCADO DRESSING

A combination of colorful ingredients mixed with a spicy avocado dressing has the festive look and taste of Mexico. Jicama is a bulb grown in Mexico and can be purchased at most supermarkets. It gives the salad a crunchy texture and refreshing taste. Serve with a basket of warm tortillas.

2 cups diced cooked chicken
1 cup peeled diced jicama
1 cup diced red bell pepper
1 avocado, peeled, pitted, and diced
6 green onions including some tender green tops, sliced

¼ cup chopped fresh cilantro
   Spicy Avocado Dressing (recipe follows)
   Red leaf lettuce for lining a large platter (decorative if available)
12 cherry tomatoes for garnish

In a large bowl, mix together the chicken, jicama, bell pepper, avocado, onions, and cilantro. Just before serving, mix with enough dressing to coat. Line a large platter with lettuce leaves, mound the salad in the center, and garnish with tomatoes.

Makes 4 servings

SPICY AVOCADO DRESSING
Make only 1 hour ahead or it may discolor.

1 ripe avocado, peeled, pitted, and cut up
½ cup plain nonfat yogurt
½ cup mayonnaise
2 sprigs fresh parsley
1 tablespoon white wine vinegar
1 tablespoon fresh lime juice

1 garlic clove, cut up
1 teaspoon Worcestershire sauce
¼ teaspoon salt
   Freshly ground pepper
2 or 3 drops Tabasco sauce

In a food processor or blender, combine all the ingredients and process until smooth. Cover the surface with plastic wrap to keep it from discoloring.

Makes about 1½ cups

ASIAN-STYLE CHICKEN SALAD

This salad with baby spinach leaves, tender chicken breast pieces, crunchy water chestnuts, and orange segments adds variety to the menu for a company buffet.

6 to 8 cups baby spinach leaves
  1 can (8 ounces) mandarin oranges, drained
  1 cup diced cooked chicken breast
  ¼ red onion, sliced and rings separated
  1 can (4 ounces) sliced water chestnuts, drained
     Asian Vinaigrette (recipe follows)

Mix together the salad ingredients and toss with the dressing to coat.

Makes 4 servings

ASIAN VINAIGRETTE

½ cup vegetable oil
¼ cup rice vinegar
2½ tablespoons soy sauce
1 garlic clove, minced

In a small bowl, whisk together all the ingredients.

Makes about 1 cup

SANDWICHES

You can always rely on a sandwich for a quick and satisfying lunch or light supper. With the wide selection of artisan breads readily available at specialty bakeries, and new creative fillings, sandwiches have taken on a starring role at mealtime. Leftover cooked chicken or purchased rotisserie chicken makes delicious sandwiches with little preparation.

Sandwiches are served hot or cold. Popular today are hot sandwiches made in a panini press—a "state-of-the-art" sandwich toaster with an adjustable lid that makes appealing grid marks. Hot sandwiches can also be made in a traditional sandwich toaster, in a skillet, in a broiler, or on a grill.

In this chapter you will find a wide assortment of sandwiches, such as Chicken and Tomato Panini with Basil Pesto; Tarragon Chicken Croissant Sandwich; Weeknight Wrap-Up; Mediterranean Chicken Sandwich in Pita Bread; and many more exciting combinations.

CHICKEN, AVOCADO, AND SWISS CHEESE PANINI WITH ALMONDS

Panino is Italian for "roll," and refers to a toasted sandwich made in a panini press. In this sandwich, Swiss cheese melts over tender chicken sprinkled with nuts for flavor and crunch.

2	cups shredded cooked chicken
⅓ to ½	cup mayonnaise
1	tablespoon fresh lemon juice
¼	teaspoon salt
8	slices sourdough bread
¼	cup sliced almonds, toasted (see page 92)
1	avocado, peeled, pitted, and sliced
4	slices Swiss cheese

Preheat a panini press or sandwich toaster. In a medium bowl, mix together the chicken, mayonnaise, lemon juice, and salt. Divide the chicken mixture onto 4 slices of bread and sprinkle evenly with the almonds. Add the avocado and cheese slices. Top with the remaining bread slices. Spray the top and bottom of the panini press or sandwich toaster with nonstick cooking spray. Add the sandwiches (working in batches if necessary), close the lid, and toast until golden brown and the cheese is melted, 3 to 4 minutes. Repeat to make remaining sandwiches. Cut each sandwich in half to serve.

Makes 4 servings

CHICKEN, ROASTED RED BELL PEPPER, AND PROVOLONE CHEESE PANINI

As this sandwich toasts, all of the flavors meld together for a unique sandwich treat. Garnish the plate with sliced fresh pears and apples.

3 to 4 tablespoons mayonnaise

1 teaspoon Dijon mustard

1 garlic clove, minced

8 slices Italian bread

2 boned and skinned chicken breast halves (about 1 pound), cooked and sliced

1 jar (7¼ ounces) roasted red bell peppers, drained and cut to fit the bread (you may not use all)

4 slices provolone cheese

Preheat a panini press or sandwich toaster. In a small bowl, mix together the mayonnaise, mustard, and garlic. Spread one side of each slice of bread with the mayonnaise mixture. Layer the chicken, pepper slices, and cheese on 4 slices of bread. Top with the remaining bread slices. Spray the top and bottom of the panini press or sandwich toaster with nonstick cooking spray. Add the sandwiches (working in batches if necessary), close the lid, and toast until golden brown and the cheese has melted, 3 to 4 minutes. Repeat to make remaining sandwiches. Cut each sandwich in half to serve.

Makes 4 servings

CHICKEN AND TOMATO PANINI WITH BASIL PESTO

This irresistible sandwich of chicken, tomato, onion, and cheese is seasoned with a basil pesto mayonnaise. Pesto is a refreshing sauce traditionally made with fresh basil, nuts, cheese, and oil. It can be purchased or homemade.

½ cup mayonnaise
¼ cup Basil Pesto (page 99) or purchased
8 slices crusty Italian bread
2 cooked chicken breasts, sliced
4 thin slices tomato
4 thin slices red onion
4 slices fontina cheese

Preheat a panini press or sandwich toaster. In a small bowl, mix together the mayonnaise and pesto. Spread the mixture on each slice of bread. Layer the chicken, tomato, onion, and cheese onto 4 slices of bread. Top with the remaining bread slices. Spray the top and bottom of the panini press or sandwich toaster with nonstick cooking spray. Add the sandwiches (working in batches if necessary), close the lid, and toast until golden brown and the cheese is melted, 3 to 4 minutes. Repeat to make remaining sandwiches. Cut each sandwich in half to serve.

Makes 4 servings

CHICKEN AND HAM PANINI

Toasted sandwiches are always a good choice for unexpected lunch company. A quick trip to the deli, and the sandwich will be ready when your guests arrive.

8   slices sourdough bread
    Mayonnaise for spreading on bread
    Dijon mustard for spreading on bread
4   thin slices cooked chicken breast
4   thin ham slices
1   large tomato, thinly sliced
4   slices Cheddar cheese

Preheat a panini press or sandwich toaster. Spread 1 side of 4 slices of bread with mayonnaise and 1 side of the other 4 slices with Dijon. Layer the chicken, ham, tomato, and cheese onto the mustard-covered sides of bread. Top with the remaining bread slices. Spray the top and bottom of the panini press or sandwich toaster with nonstick cooking spray. Add the sandwiches (working in batches if necessary), close the lid, and toast until golden brown and the cheese is melted, 3 to 4 minutes. Repeat to make remaining sandwiches. Cut each sandwich in half to serve.

Makes 4 servings

HOT BARBECUED CHICKEN SANDWICH

Prepare this sandwich for a quick supper on a busy night of family activities. Leftover cooked chicken is simmered in a spicy barbecue sauce and served on buns. Serve with crispy coleslaw.

4 hoagie buns, split and warmed (see Note)
   Easy Barbecue Sauce (recipe follows) or
   purchased barbecue sauce, warmed
2 cups cubed cooked chicken

Remove some of the center from each bun (save for crumbs). Warm the chicken in the barbecue sauce, then place it in the buns. Add more sauce on top and serve immediately.

Makes 4 servings

EASY BARBECUE SAUCE

1 cup ketchup
½ cup water
¼ cup chili sauce
2 tablespoons honey
2 teaspoons Worcestershire sauce
2 teaspoons cider vinegar

In a medium saucepan over medium heat, combine all the ingredients and simmer 5 minutes.

Makes about 1 cup

NOTE: To warm buns, wrap them in foil and warm in a 350°F oven for 10 minutes.

CHICKEN BREAST WITH ROASTED RED BELL PEPPER AND AVOCADO ON FOCACCIA

Use leftover or rotisserie chicken in this creative sandwich combination. Focaccia is a large, flat Italian bread brushed with olive oil, salt, and sometimes herbs. It can be eaten as a side bread or used as a base for sandwiches. It comes prebaked and can be purchased in most supermarkets and specialty bakeries.

1   focaccia (11 ounces)
½   cup mayonnaise
2   garlic cloves, minced
    Cooked chicken breast (about 12 ounces), sliced to fit the bread
1   roasted red bell pepper (see page 159), cut into large pieces, or 1 jar (7¼ ounces) roasted red bell peppers, rinsed, drained, dried, and cut into large pieces
1   avocado, peeled, pitted, and cut into strips
2 or 3   slices red onion, separated into rings

Preheat the oven to 350°F. Cut the focaccia in fourths, then cut each piece in half horizontally with a serrated bread knife. (You will have 8 pieces.) In a small bowl, mix together the mayonnaise and garlic. Spread each cut side of bread with the mayonnaise mixture. Layer on the chicken, bell pepper, avocado, and onion rings. Top with the remaining focaccia pieces. Wrap each sandwich in aluminum foil and warm in the oven for 15 to 20 minutes, until heated through.

Makes 4 servings

CHICKEN AND BRIE WITH PESTO SANDWICH

With the delicious artisan breads now available at many bakeries, sandwiches are more popular than ever. Look for ciabatta, a rustic Italian bread with a lot of flavor and texture. Brie is a buttery soft cheese with good melting qualities. Pesto adds a refreshing taste to this open-faced sandwich.

4 slices ciabatta bread
Mayonnaise for spreading on bread
4 thin slices cooked chicken breast
1 tomato, sliced and halved
4 (¾-inch by 3-inch) slices Brie
¼ cup Basil Pesto (page 99) or purchased pesto

Preheat the broiler. Spread the bread with mayonnaise. Layer the chicken slices on the bread. Add the tomato and Brie. Spread a spoonful of pesto over the Brie. Place on a baking sheet and broil until the Brie starts to melt, 3 to 4 minutes. Watch carefully.

Makes 4 servings

WEEKNIGHT WRAP-UP

Chicken, avocado, and red bell pepper make a great filling for tortillas.
Use plain or flavored tortillas. Choose whatever you like for this wrap.

2   cups cubed cooked chicken breast
1   avocado, peeled, pitted, and cut into bite-size pieces
1   roasted red bell pepper (see page 159), cut into strips, or 1 cup purchased roasted red
    bell pepper
¼   cup Creamy Caesar Dressing (page 83)
4   flour tortillas (10-inch; any flavor), warmed (see page 128)

In a small bowl, combine all the ingredients except tortillas. Divide the
mixture down the center of each tortilla. Fold up the bottom one quarter
of the way. Fold in the sides to completely enclose. Place seam-side
down on plates.

Makes 4 servings

TARRAGON CHICKEN CROISSANT SANDWICH

For your next luncheon or shower, serve purchased buttery croissants filled with this savory chicken filling, complemented with a platter of assorted fresh fruit. These sandwiches can be served warm or cold.

2	cups cubed cooked chicken breast
¼	cup chopped celery
¼	cup chopped red onion
¼	cup mayonnaise
1	teaspoon fresh lemon juice
½	teaspoon dried tarragon
¼	teaspoon salt
	Dash ground white pepper
4	large croissants, split

In a medium bowl, mix together the chicken, celery, onion, mayonnaise, lemon juice, tarragon, salt, and pepper. Fill the croissants with the chicken mixture and serve cold or wrap in foil and warm in a 350°F oven for 15 minutes.

Makes 4 servings

CHICKEN SANDWICH WITH CRANBERRIES AND HAZELNUTS

I was served this sandwich at a small bakery café on the Oregon coast, and it was so good, I included it in this book. Roasted turkey was originally used, but chicken gives the same delicious taste.

2 cups chopped cooked chicken breast
3 tablespoons dried cranberries
¼ cup chopped toasted hazelnuts (see page 106)
¼ cup chopped green onion including some tender green tops
¼ cup mayonnaise plus extra to spread on rolls
1 tablespoon Dijon mustard
¼ teaspoon salt
Freshly ground pepper
4 ciabatta rolls, split
Lettuce leaves (optional)

In a medium bowl, mix together the chicken, cranberries, nuts, and onions. In a small bowl, mix together the ¼ cup mayonnaise, the mustard, salt, and pepper to taste. Add to the chicken mixture and mix well. Spread the rolls with additional mayonnaise and add the filling and a lettuce leaf, if using. Add the roll tops and cut the sandwiches in half to serve.

Makes 4 servings

CHICKEN AND EGG SANDWICH

A mixture of diced chicken and hard-cooked eggs is a good way to use leftover eggs from Easter. Serve as a sandwich filling or on spinach leaves as a salad.

2	cups diced cooked chicken breast
2 or 3	hard-cooked eggs, chopped
⅓	cup finely chopped celery
2	tablespoons drained capers
½	cup mayonnaise or more to taste
1	teaspoon fresh lemon juice
¼	teaspoon salt
	Freshly ground pepper
8	slices bread

In a medium bowl, stir together the chicken, eggs, celery, and capers.
In a small bowl, mix together the mayonnaise, lemon juice, salt, and pepper to taste. Spread the mayonnaise mixture on all of the bread, add filling on 4 slices, and top with the remaining bread. Cut in half to serve.

Makes 4 servings

BROWN BAG SPECIAL

This is a good sandwich to pack for a picnic lunch. It can be made ahead and the sandwich stays moist. Wrap crisp lettuce leaves in foil and add just before eating. Include some raw vegetables, pickles, and chips for a fun outing.

3 cups diced cooked chicken
1 celery stalk, finely chopped
½ red bell pepper, finely chopped
4 green onions including some tender green tops, finely chopped
½ cup mayonnaise or more to taste, plus extra for spreading on the bread
¼ teaspoon salt
   Freshly ground pepper
8 slices pumpernickel bread or other brown bread

In a medium bowl, mix together all the ingredients except the bread. Spread mayonnaise on all of the bread. Divide the mixture evenly between 4 slices. Top with the remaining bread. Cut in half to serve.

Makes 4 servings

CHICKEN IN A BAGEL

Flavored bagels of your choice can be used for this quick sandwich of chicken breast topped with onion and a tart, creamy cranberry sauce.

¼   cup cream cheese, softened
1   tablespoon cranberry sauce
4   plain, garlic, or onion bagels, split and toasted
4   thin slices cooked chicken breast
½   red onion, sliced and separated into rings
    Lettuce leaves
    Sweet pickles for serving

In a small bowl, blend together the cream cheese and cranberry sauce. Spread it on the cut side of each bagel. Layer on the chicken slices, onion rings, and lettuce leaves. Add the bagel tops and cut in half. Serve with sweet pickles.

Makes 4 servings

HOT OPEN-FACED CHOPPED CHICKEN SANDWICH

When you want a light snack for lunch or supper, serve this robust baked sandwich of chopped chicken, vegetables, and salami topped with cheese.

1 tomato, seeded, diced, and drained
1 avocado, peeled, pitted, and diced
8 green onions including some tender green tops, sliced
1 cup diced cooked chicken breast
4 slices salami, diced
½ cup Vinaigrette Dressing (recipe follows)
1 long loaf French sourdough bread, sliced lengthwise
4 ounces thinly sliced Swiss cheese

Preheat the oven to 350°F. In a medium bowl, combine the tomato, avocado, onions, chicken, and salami with enough dressing to moisten. Remove some bread from the center of the loaf (save for crumbs), leaving a thick crust. Brush the cut sides of the bread with dressing. Spoon the chicken mixture onto both pieces of bread and top with the cheese slices. Bake until warmed and the cheese is melted, about 15 minutes. Cut each half into 6 slices.

Makes 12 servings

VINAIGRETTE DRESSING

½ cup olive oil
¼ cup red wine vinegar
1 garlic clove, minced
1 tablespoon Dijon mustard
¼ teaspoon salt
  Freshly ground pepper

In a small cup or bowl, whisk together all the ingredients.

Makes about ¾ cup

CHICKEN-GUACAMOLE ROLL-UPS

Everyone will love this sandwich with a Mexican twist. Diced cooked chicken is wrapped in a tortilla with guacamole and salsa and eaten out of hand. Lay out the ingredients and let everyone assemble their own. Serve extra warm tortillas in a basket.

4 flour tortillas (10-inch), warmed (see page 128)
Guacamole (recipe follows)
2 cups diced cooked chicken breast
½ cup Fresh Tomato Salsa (page 35) or purchased salsa
2 cups shredded iceberg lettuce
Sour cream for serving

Place the tortillas on a flat surface and spread them with guacamole. Top with the chicken, a spoonful of salsa, and lettuce. Fold up the bottom one quarter of the way. Fold in the sides to completely enclose. Place seam-side down on plates and serve with sour cream.

Makes 4 servings

GUACAMOLE

3 medium avocados, peeled, pitted, and coarsely mashed
½ small tomato, chopped and drained
2 tablespoons chopped fresh cilantro or parsley
2 tablespoons fresh lime juice or lemon juice
1 teaspoon chopped red onion
1 to 2 drops Tabasco sauce
½ teaspoon salt
Freshly ground pepper

In a medium bowl, stir together all the ingredients until blended, adding pepper to taste.

Makes about 2 cups

CHICKEN TOSTADAS

Tostadas are open-faced, crisp tortillas with good stuff on top. In Mexico they are eaten as a snack for lunch or a light supper. Here they are served as a sandwich. For convenience, use ready-fried tostada shells, available at most supermarkets.

8	tostada shells
1	can (14½ ounces) refried beans (vegetarian preferred)
4	cups shredded or diced cooked chicken
1½	cups (6 ounces) shredded Monterey Jack cheese
½	cup sliced pitted olives
2	cups shredded lettuce
2	avocados, peeled, pitted, and sliced
	Salsa for serving
	Sour cream for serving

Preheat the oven to 350°F. Place the tostada shells on a baking sheet. Spread about ¼ cup beans on each tostada. Add ½ cup chicken. Sprinkle with the cheese and olives. Bake until heated through and the cheese melts, 10 to 12 minutes. Top with the lettuce and avocado slices and pass the salsa and sour cream in separate bowls.

Makes 8 servings

CHICKEN AND PINTO BEAN BURRITOS

A burrito is a tortilla filled with savory ingredients, then folded, rolled, and eaten out of hand. Mexicans eat them as a snack any time of the day, so why shouldn't we? Leftover rotisserie chicken works well for this Mexican-style sandwich.

1 cup (4 ounces) shredded Monterey Jack cheese
1 cup Fresh Tomato Salsa (page 35) or purchased salsa
1 cup sour cream
6 green onions including some tender green tops, diced
1 can (15 ounces) pinto beans, drained and rinsed
8 flour tortillas (10-inch), warmed (see Note)
3 cups shredded cooked chicken
2 avocados, peeled, pitted, and sliced

In a medium bowl, mix together the cheese, salsa, sour cream, and onions and set aside. In a microwave-safe bowl, microwave the beans until warm, about 2 minutes, and keep warm. To assemble, lay the tortillas on a flat surface. Divide the chicken, beans, and cheese mixture evenly down the center in a wide strip leaving a 2-inch margin at the bottom. Add a few slices of avocado. Fold up the bottom one quarter of the way. Fold in the sides to completely enclose. Place seam-side down on plates or eat out of hand.

Makes 6 servings

NOTE: To warm tortillas, preheat the oven to 325°F. Wrap tortillas in aluminum foil in 2 packages and bake for about 15 minutes. Or, wrap tortillas in paper towels or a clean dampened towel and microwave 40 to 50 seconds on high.

CHICKEN TACOS

Ground chicken is readily available in most supermarkets and makes a good substitute for ground beef in tacos. This is a fun supper that will appeal to kids because everyone assembles their own taco. Serve toppings in bowls.

2   teaspoons vegetable oil
2   pounds ground chicken
½   teaspoon chili powder
½   teaspoon ground cumin
1   teaspoon salt
    Freshly ground pepper
¾   cup Fresh Tomato Salsa (page 35)
    or purchased salsa
3   tablespoons chopped fresh cilantro (optional)
12 corn tortillas (8-inch), warmed (see page 128)

Toppings: Sour cream; 1 can (16 ounces) fat-free refried beans, warmed; 1 cup (4 ounces) shredded Cheddar or Monterey Jack cheese; ½ cup chopped green onions including some tender green tops; additional salsa; shredded iceberg lettuce; ripe olives; 1 avocado, peeled, pitted, and sliced

In a medium skillet over medium heat, warm the oil. Add the chicken and sauté, breaking it up with a wooden spoon until the chicken is no longer pink, about 5 minutes. Season with the chili powder, cumin, salt, and pepper to taste. Stir in the salsa and cilantro and mix well. Add about ¼ cup meat mixture down the center of each tortilla. Fold up the sides and add the toppings.

Makes 12 servings

CHICKEN, APPLE, AND CHUTNEY SANDWICH

Chutney is an East Indian condiment that includes fruit, vinegar, sugar, and spices. Here it adds exotic flavors in this enticing sandwich of chicken, crisp apples, and sharp Cheddar cheese.

½ cup mayonnaise
½ cup mango chutney, chopped
¼ teaspoon curry powder
8 slices cracked wheat bread
2 boned and skinned chicken breast halves (about 1 pound), cooked and sliced
1 Granny Smith apple, unpeeled and thinly sliced
Sharp Cheddar cheese, sliced to fit the bread
Large spinach leaves or 4 lettuce leaves

In a small bowl, mix together the mayonnaise, chutney, and curry powder. Spread the mixture on each slice of bread. Divide the chicken, apple slices, cheese, and spinach equally among 4 slices of bread. Top with the remaining bread slices. Cut in half to serve.

Makes 4 servings

MEDITERRANEAN CHICKEN SANDWICH IN PITA BREAD

Chopped olives and salty capers add variety to this chicken-filled pita bread sandwich. Pita, also called pocket bread, is a Middle Eastern flat bread. When split horizontally, it forms a pocket that lends itself well to a variety of fillings. It is available in most supermarkets.

3   cups diced cooked chicken breast
½   cup chopped, roasted red bell pepper
    (see page 159) or purchased, drained
½   cup diced red onion
½   cup diced celery
¼   cup chopped black olives
1   tablespoon capers, drained
    Basil Mayonnaise (recipe follows)
2   medium pita breads, halved

In a medium bowl, mix together the chicken, bell pepper, onions, celery, olives, and capers with just enough Basil Mayonnaise to coat. Cover and refrigerate several hours. To assemble, open up the pita bread halves and spoon the filling into the pockets.

Makes 4 servings

BASIL MAYONNAISE

1   cup mayonnaise
2   garlic cloves, minced
1   tablespoon red wine vinegar
1   tablespoon chopped fresh basil or
    1 teaspoon dried basil
½   teaspoon salt
    Freshly ground pepper

In a medium bowl, mix together all the ingredients. Cover and refrigerate until ready to use.

Makes about 1 cup

05

STOVE-TOP
CHICKEN

Stove-top cooking includes skillet dishes, sautés, stir-fries, and braises. These dishes are convenient to make because they are cooked in one skillet or pot, with very little clean-up required. Many stove-top dishes are quick to make, which appeals to people on the go.

Chicken stove-top dishes are unlimited in possibilities for creative combinations, such as Stir-Fried Hoisin Chicken; Chicken and Pasta with Creamy Tomato-Wine Sauce; Chicken and Orzo with Spinach and Gorgonzola; Chicken, Sausage, and Shrimp Gumbo; Chicken Meatballs in Tomato-Mushroom Sauce with Angel Hair Pasta; Arroz con Pollo; Chicken Fettuccine with Spinach and Cheese Sauce; and many others to discover in this chapter.

CHICKEN MEATBALLS IN TOMATO-MUSHROOM SAUCE WITH ANGEL HAIR PASTA

For a delightful dinner, tender chicken meatballs are simmered in a rich tomato sauce and served over pasta. Any long-strand pasta can be used. Add a tossed green salad and garlic bread to round out the menu.

1¼   pounds ground chicken

1   cup dried bread crumbs

2   shallots, finely chopped, or 2 tablespoons finely chopped yellow onion

2   tablespoons freshly grated Parmesan cheese, plus additional for topping

2   tablespoons chopped fresh basil or ½ teaspoon dried basil

½   teaspoon dried oregano

½   teaspoon salt

    Freshly ground pepper

    Tomato-Mushroom Sauce with Basil (facing page)

8   ounces angel hair pasta, cooked according to package directions, drained

Preheat the oven to 425°F. In a medium bowl, mix together the ground chicken, bread crumbs, shallots, 2 tablespoons Parmesan cheese, the basil, oregano, salt, and pepper to taste. Cover and refrigerate for 30 minutes for easier handling. Form the mixture into 1½-inch balls (use floured hands). Place the meatballs on a lightly sprayed or oiled baking sheet and bake until lightly browned and firm, about 15 minutes. Meanwhile, prepare the sauce. Add the meatballs to the sauce and simmer, covered, until the flavors are blended, about 10 minutes longer. Serve with the pasta and sprinkle with more Parmesan.

Makes 4 to 6 servings

TOMATO-MUSHROOM SAUCE WITH BASIL

1 tablespoon vegetable oil
½ cup chopped yellow onion
4 ounces mushrooms, sliced
1 garlic clove, chopped
1 can (14½ ounces) Italian-style tomatoes including juice, cut up
1 can (16 ounces) tomato sauce
¼ cup fresh chopped basil or 1 teaspoon dried basil
¼ cup chopped fresh parsley
1 teaspoon salt
¼ teaspoon sugar
    Freshly ground pepper

In a large Dutch oven over medium heat, warm the oil. Add the onions, mushrooms, and garlic and sauté until tender, about 5 minutes. Add the tomatoes, tomato sauce, and seasonings. Simmer, uncovered, 5 to 10 minutes longer.

Makes about 4 cups

CHICKEN TENDERS AND VEGETABLE SAUTÉ

For a quick fix, this easy dish can be prepared in minutes on top of the stove. Chicken tenders are the small, narrow pieces found on chicken breasts. They are available in packages at most supermarkets, or you can remove them from breasts and freeze until you have accumulated enough for a recipe. They work well in sautés and stir-fry dishes.

1 to 2	tablespoons vegetable oil, divided
1	pound chicken tenders, cut into bite-size pieces
1	cup chopped yellow onion
½	cup chopped green bell pepper
4	ounces mushrooms, sliced
1	can (15 ounces) Italian-style tomatoes, slightly puréed in food processor
½	teaspoon dried basil
½	teaspoon dried oregano
½	teaspoon salt
	Freshly ground pepper
4	ounces (2 cups) rigatoni, cooked according to package directions, drained
	Freshly grated Parmesan cheese

In a large skillet over medium heat, warm 1 tablespoon of the oil. Sauté the chicken until lightly browned, about 5 minutes. Transfer it to a plate. Add the onions, bell pepper, and mushrooms and sauté until tender, about 5 minutes. Add more oil, if needed. Return the chicken to the pan. Add the tomatoes, basil, oregano, salt, and pepper to taste and simmer, uncovered, until the chicken is cooked through and the flavors are blended, about 10 minutes longer. Add rigatoni to the pan and stir until pasta is coated with sauce. Sprinkle with Parmesan cheese and serve immediately.

Makes 4 servings

BREADED CHICKEN BREASTS AND CAPERS

A Dijon-mayonnaise coating adds an interesting flavor to these chicken breasts topped with crispy fried capers. Frying capers brings out their flavor for a new taste treat!

¼   cup Dijon mustard
¼   cup mayonnaise
½   cup dried bread crumbs
¼   teaspoon salt
    Freshly ground pepper
4   boned and skinned chicken breast halves (about 2 pounds)
2 to 3   tablespoons olive oil
½   cup drained and rinsed capers

In a shallow bowl, mix together the mustard and mayonnaise. On a piece of waxed paper, mix the bread crumbs, salt, and pepper to taste. Dip the chicken breasts in the Dijon mixture on both sides and then roll in the crumbs to coat.

In a large skillet over medium heat, warm 2 tablespoons of the oil. Add the chicken and cook until lightly browned, about 5 minutes on each side. Reduce the heat to low, cover, and cook until the chicken is opaque through, about 10 minutes longer. Add more oil, if needed. Transfer the chicken to a warm platter and keep warm. Add the capers to the pan and fry about 1 minute. Sprinkle on top of the chicken and serve immediately.

Makes 4 servings

CHICKEN BREASTS AND FENNEL SAUTÉ

A mixture of red and green bell peppers, fennel, and mushrooms makes a colorful topping for these chicken breasts. Fennel is a bulb with a stem and feathery foliage (fronds). It is often mislabeled as "sweet anise," but fennel has a lighter licorice flavor. Some of the fennel fronds can be used for garnish.

3 to 4 tablespoons vegetable oil, divided
1 small red bell pepper, sliced lengthwise into ⅜-inch strips
1 small green bell pepper, sliced lengthwise into ⅜-inch strips
1 yellow onion, thickly sliced and separated into rings
1 small bulb fennel, stems and fronds removed and bulb sliced lengthwise

8 ounces mushrooms, sliced
2 garlic cloves, chopped
2 tablespoons capers, drained and rinsed
1 tablespoon balsamic vinegar
½ teaspoon dried thyme
6 boned and skinned chicken breast halves (about 3 pounds)
Salt and freshly ground pepper

In a large skillet over medium heat, warm 2 tablespoons of the oil. Add the bell peppers, onion rings, fennel, mushrooms, and garlic and sauté until tender, about 10 minutes. Add more oil if needed. Stir in the capers, vinegar, and thyme and mix well. Transfer to a plate.

In the same skillet, add 1 more tablespoon oil. Add the chicken breasts and cook until lightly browned, about 5 minutes on each side. Reduce the heat to low, cover, and cook until the chicken is opaque through, about 10 minutes longer. Season with salt and pepper to taste. Return the vegetables to the pan to reheat. Arrange the chicken breasts on a platter and top with the vegetables.

Makes 6 servings

HERBED CHICKEN AND VEGETABLE SAUTÉ

This sauté dish delivers a lot of flavor without a lot of work. Chicken tenders work well for this dish accented with green bell pepper strips. Serve with rice or pasta.

½ cup water
2 tablespoons all-purpose flour
½ teaspoon dried basil
½ teaspoon dried oregano
½ teaspoon salt
Freshly ground pepper
3 tablespoons vegetable oil
1 pound chicken tenders, cut into strips
1 yellow onion, cut into ½-inch strips
1 small green bell pepper, cut into ½-inch strips
1 small red bell pepper, cut into ½-inch strips
1 garlic clove, minced

In a small bowl, mix together the water, flour, basil, oregano, salt, and pepper to taste. Set aside.

In a large skillet over medium-high heat, warm the oil. Add the chicken and vegetables and sauté until the chicken is cooked through and the vegetables are tender, about 10 minutes. Add the flour mixture and stir until thickened, about 1 minute.

Makes 4 to 6 servings

CHICKEN À LA KING

You don't have to be a candidate to enjoy this dish typically served at political luncheons. Now, you can make it at home in this updated version, with mushrooms and peas added. It can be served over biscuits, rice, English muffins, or in individual pastry shells.

3	tablespoons butter
4	ounces mushrooms, sliced
1	large shallot, finely chopped
¼	cup all-purpose flour
1½	cups Basic Chicken Stock (page 29) or reduced-sodium chicken broth
1	cup whole milk
2	tablespoons dry white wine (optional)
½	teaspoon salt
⅛	teaspoon ground white pepper
2½	cups diced cooked chicken (use both white and dark meat)
1	cup peas, fresh or frozen
½	jar (2 ounces) drained, chopped pimientos

In a large saucepan over medium heat, melt the butter. Add the mushrooms and shallots and sauté until tender, about 5 minutes. Add the flour and stir until bubbly. Gradually add the stock, milk, wine, and seasonings and whisk until thickened, about 2 minutes. Add the chicken, peas, and pimientos. Reduce the heat to medium-low and cook until the flavors are blended, about 2 minutes.

Makes 4 servings

CHICKEN CHARISMA

Wonderful flavors come through in this elegant dish of sautéed chicken and mushrooms with a wine and sour cream sauce. It will become one of your favorite dishes to serve for a company dinner.

2½ tablespoons butter, divided
8 ounces mushrooms, sliced
4 green onions including some tender green tops, sliced
4 boned and skinned chicken breast halves (about 2 pounds)
1 teaspoon dried tarragon
Salt and freshly ground pepper
1 cup dry white wine
½ cup sour cream
1 teaspoon cornstarch

In a large skillet over medium heat, melt 1½ tablespoons of the butter. Add the mushrooms and onions and sauté until tender, about 5 minutes. With a slotted spoon, transfer them to a plate. Add the remaining 1 tablespoon butter and cook the chicken until lightly browned, about 5 minutes on each side. Season with the tarragon and salt and pepper to taste on both sides. Pour the wine over the top. Reduce the heat to low, cover, and cook until the chicken is opaque through, about 10 minutes longer. Transfer the chicken to a serving plate and keep warm.

In a small bowl, mix together the sour cream and cornstarch. Raise the heat to medium and return the mushrooms and onions to the pan. Add the sour cream mixture to the pan juices and whisk until smooth and slightly thickened, 1 to 2 minutes. Pour the sauce over the chicken and serve immediately.

Makes 4 servings

SAUTÉED CHICKEN BREASTS WITH PINE NUTS AND TOMATOES

Mediterranean flavors highlight this dish with chicken and prosciutto in a subtle tomato-wine sauce. Serve with sautéed summer squash, orzo, and cracker bread.

½ cup pine nuts
2 tablespoons olive oil, divided
4 boned and skinned chicken breast halves (about 2 pounds)
1 cup chopped yellow onion
1 garlic clove, minced
1 can (14½ ounces) whole Italian-style tomatoes including juice, lightly puréed in a food processor

¼ cup dry white wine
2 ounces prosciutto, chopped
1 teaspoon dried oregano
½ teaspoon salt
Freshly ground pepper

In a large, dry skillet over medium-high heat, add the pine nuts and stir constantly until toasted, about 2 minutes. Set aside. Add 1 tablespoon of the oil to the skillet and cook the chicken until lightly browned, about 5 minutes on each side. Transfer the chicken to a plate. Add the remaining oil and sauté the onions and garlic until tender, about 5 minutes. Stir in the tomatoes, wine, prosciutto, and seasonings and mix well. Return the chicken breasts and nuts to the pan. Reduce the heat to medium-low and simmer until the flavors are blended and the chicken is cooked through, about 10 minutes.

Makes 4 servings

CHICKEN WITH CRANBERRY-HORSERADISH SAUCE

Here, sautéed chicken is simmered with an interesting blend of cranberries and horseradish added for extra punch. Serve with baked sweet potatoes and additional cranberry sauce.

1½ tablespoons vegetable oil
 4 boned and skinned chicken breast halves (about 2 pounds)
    Salt and freshly ground pepper
 ½ cup Basic Chicken Stock (page 29) or reduced-sodium chicken broth
 ½ cup fresh orange juice
 ½ cup whole cranberry sauce, homemade or canned
 1 tablespoon prepared horseradish
 1 tablespoon Dijon mustard

In a large skillet over medium-high heat, warm the oil. Add the chicken breasts and cook until lightly browned, about 5 minutes on each side. Season with salt and pepper to taste and transfer the chicken to a plate. Remove the skillet from the heat and whisk in the stock, juice, cranberry sauce, horseradish, and mustard. Return the chicken to the skillet and mix with the sauce. Simmer on medium-low until the sauce thickens and the chicken is cooked through, about 10 minutes, turning several times. Transfer to a platter and spoon the sauce over top.

Makes 4 servings

CHICKEN BREASTS WITH OLIVE TAPENADE

Tapenade is a thick, earthy paste made with olives, capers, anchovies, olive oil, and lemon juice, originating in the Provence region of France and used as a condiment. Here it makes a great topping for chicken breasts. Serve with a fresh green vegetable.

4   boned and skinned chicken breast halves (about
    2 pounds)
    Salt and freshly ground pepper
2   tablespoons olive oil
    Triple-Olive Tapenade (facing page; see Note)

Place the chicken breasts between 2 pieces of plastic wrap and pound with the flat side of a meat mallet to ⅜ inch thick. Season with salt and pepper to taste. In a large skillet over medium heat, warm the oil. Add the chicken and cook until lightly browned on both sides and cooked through, about 15 minutes. Transfer to a plate and keep warm. Add the tapenade to the drippings and stir until warm, about 30 seconds. Spoon the mixture on top of the chicken.

Makes 4 servings

NOTE: Prepared tapenade can be purchased in some delis. You will need about 1 cup.

TRIPLE-OLIVE TAPENADE

This tangy blend of three olives is also good spread on crostini for an hors d'oeuvre.

½ cup pitted ripe black olives, drained
½ cup pimiento-stuffed green olives, drained
¼ cup pitted kalamata olives, drained
1 tablespoon fresh lemon juice
1 large garlic clove, cut up
1 anchovy fillet, cut up, or 1 teaspoon anchovy paste (optional)
1 teaspoon capers, drained
2 leaves fresh basil or ½ teaspoon dried basil
   Freshly ground pepper
1 tablespoon olive oil

In a food processor, combine all the ingredients except the oil. With on/off pulses, process until coarsely chopped. Scrape down the sides of the bowl as needed. Add the oil in a steady stream until blended.

Makes about 1 cup

STOVE-TOP CHICKEN STEW

Everyday food can be tasty and special with this combination of chicken thighs and a variety of vegetables. Once the vegetables are prepared and in the pot, it needs very little attention for a complete one-pot meal.

¼ cup all-purpose flour
1 teaspoon dried rosemary
1 teaspoon salt
  Freshly ground pepper
6 bone-in chicken thighs (about 2¾ pounds), skin and excess fat trimmed
1 tablespoon vegetable oil
3 medium new red potatoes (about 1 pound), unpeeled and quartered

1 yellow onion, quartered
2 carrots, sliced
1½ cups Basic Chicken Stock (page 29) or reduced-sodium chicken broth
1 can (14 ounces) quartered water-packed artichoke hearts, drained
8 ounces medium mushrooms, halved
1 cup peas, fresh or frozen, rinsed under cold water

On a piece of waxed paper, combine the flour, rosemary, salt, and pepper to taste. Roll the chicken in the mixture to coat. Reserve any remaining flour mixture. In a Dutch oven over medium-high heat, warm the oil. Add the chicken and cook until lightly browned, about 5 minutes on each side.

Add the potatoes, onions, carrots, and stock. Reduce the heat to medium-low and simmer, covered, 30 minutes. Add the artichokes and mushrooms and simmer, covered, until the vegetables are tender and the chicken is cooked through, 10 minutes longer. Add the peas and cook, uncovered, 5 minutes longer.

To thicken the sauce, blend ¼ cup of the leftover flour mixture with ¼ cup water and stir into the stew until bubbly and thickened, 2 to 3 minutes. Add more salt, if needed.

Makes 4 to 6 servings

NOTE: If making ahead, add the peas during the last 5 minutes while reheating, to preserve their bright green color and plump texture.

SAUCY CHICKEN WITH MUSHROOMS IN TOMATO SAUCE

For a quick supper that bursts with flavor, try these chicken tenders in a spicy tomato sauce with mushrooms and olives, served on rice. A Caesar salad is a complementary side.

2 tablespoons olive oil, divided

1½ pounds chicken tenders

Salt and freshly ground pepper

8 ounces mushrooms, sliced

½ cup chopped yellow onion

1 garlic clove, minced

1 can (14½ ounces) diced tomatoes with juice

¼ cup dry red wine

1 tablespoon tomato paste

1 teaspoon dried basil

1 teaspoon dried oregano

½ teaspoon ground cumin

⅛ teaspoon cayenne

12 pimiento-stuffed green olives, sliced

1 cup long-grain white rice, cooked according to package directions (3 cups cooked)

¼ cup chopped fresh flat-leaf parsley

In a large skillet over medium-high heat, warm 1 tablespoon of the oil. Add the chicken and sauté until it turns white, 2 to 3 minutes. Season with salt and pepper to taste. Transfer to a plate. Add the remaining oil and sauté the mushrooms, onions, and garlic until tender, about 5 minutes. Add the tomatoes, wine, tomato paste, basil, oregano, cumin, and cayenne. Reduce the heat to medium and simmer 5 minutes. Return the chicken to the pan and add the olives. Cover and simmer until the flavors are blended, 5 to 10 minutes longer. Serve over the rice with a sprinkling of the parsley on top.

Makes 4 servings

BRAISED ROSEMARY CHICKEN BREASTS ON ONIONS

Serve this dish with style and ease. Chicken breasts cook on a bed of sweet, buttery onions until tender, then they are topped with a lemon-rosemary sauce.

2 cups Basic Chicken Stock (page 29) or reduced-sodium chicken broth
2 large sweet white onions, sliced
4 tablespoons (½ stick) butter, divided
4 boned and skinned chicken breast halves (about 2 pounds)
2 tablespoons chopped fresh rosemary or 2 teaspoons dried rosemary, divided
1 teaspoon salt
Freshly ground pepper
1 tablespoon fresh lemon juice
Parsley sprigs for garnish

In a large skillet over medium heat, add the stock, onions, and 2 tablespoons of the butter. Cook, uncovered, until the onions are tender and the liquid is reduced, about 10 minutes. Sprinkle both sides of the chicken breasts with half of the rosemary, the salt, and pepper to taste. Place the chicken breasts on top of the onions. Reduce the heat to low, cover, and simmer until the chicken is cooked through, about 15 minutes. To serve, arrange the chicken breasts on the onions on a large platter. Increase the heat to high and, in the same pan, add the lemon juice, the remaining 2 tablespoons butter, and the remaining rosemary and bring to a boil. Pour over the chicken breasts. Garnish with parsley sprigs.

Makes 4 servings

SPICY BOUILLABAISSE WITH CHICKEN

Here, chicken is added to this famous French seafood stew enhanced with spices. To serve, bring the pot to the table and ladle it over thick slices of French bread in large bowls. This is a fun dish to serve company and will get you raves. Just add a tossed green salad with a vinaigrette dressing to complete the meal.

3   tablespoons butter
1   cup chopped yellow onion
3   garlic cloves, minced
3   tablespoons all-purpose flour
2   tablespoons brown sugar
1   teaspoon salt
½   teaspoon curry powder
½   teaspoon ground cloves
⅛   teaspoon crumbled saffron
    Freshly ground pepper

1   can (46 ounces) tomato juice
¼   teaspoon Tabasco sauce
8   ounces crabmeat, flaked
8   ounces sea scallops (cut in half if large)
2   cups chopped cooked chicken
1   can (6½ ounces) minced clams, including juice
¼   cup dry white wine
¼   cup chopped fresh parsley
8   ounces large shrimp, peeled and deveined

In a Dutch oven over medium heat, melt the butter. Add the onions and garlic and sauté until tender, about 5 minutes. Stir in the flour and blend. Add the sugar, salt, curry powder, cloves, saffron, and pepper to taste and mix well. Whisk in the tomato juice, add the Tabasco, and bring to a boil, stirring constantly until thickened.

Reduce the heat to medium-low and add the crabmeat, scallops, chicken, clams and juice, wine, and parsley. Simmer, uncovered, until the flavors are blended, about 10 minutes. Add the shrimp and cook until it turns pink, 3 to 4 minutes longer. Serve in bowls.

Makes 6 to 8 servings

CHICKEN BREASTS AND SHRIMP

The mild flavor of chicken breasts adapts well to a variety of other ingredients, including some seafood. Here they are paired with shrimp in a velvety tomato-cream sauce. Serve with white rice.

1½ tablespoons olive oil, divided

4 boned and skinned chicken breast halves (about 2 pounds)

1 teaspoon salt

Freshly ground pepper

6 green onions including some tender green tops, sliced

1 garlic clove, minced

12 ounces medium shrimp, peeled and deveined

¾ cup dry white wine

¼ cup sour cream

2 tablespoons tomato paste

1 cup long-grain white rice, cooked according to package directions (3 cups cooked)

¼ cup chopped fresh flat-leaf parsley

In a large skillet over medium-high heat, warm 1 tablespoon of the oil. Add the chicken and cook until lightly browned, about 5 minutes on each side. Season with the salt and pepper to taste. Reduce the heat to low, cover, and cook until the chicken is opaque through, about 10 minutes. Transfer it to a plate, cover, and keep warm in a 250°F oven. Raise the heat under the skillet to medium. Add the remaining oil and sauté the onions and garlic, about 2 minutes. Add the shrimp and sauté until it turns pink, 3 to 4 minutes. Stir in the wine, sour cream, and tomato paste and blend. Place the rice on a platter and add the chicken breasts. Top with the shrimp sauce and sprinkle with the parsley.

Makes 4 to 6 servings

PENNE WITH CHICKEN, ZUCCHINI, MUSHROOMS, AND TOMATO SAUCE

Looking for a weeknight inspiration? Pasta dishes are always welcome for a satisfying meal. This pasta entrée with chicken and vegetables is healthful as well as delicious.

1 large zucchini, halved lengthwise and cut horizontally into ¼-inch slices
3 ounces mushrooms, quartered
2 cups cubed cooked chicken breast
2 cups Quick Tomato Sauce (recipe follows)
8 ounces (2½ cups) penne, cooked according to package directions, drained
  Salt and freshly ground pepper
  Freshly grated Parmesan cheese for topping

Place the zucchini and mushrooms in a pan with a steamer rack over gently boiling water, and steam, covered, until tender-crisp, 6 to 7 minutes.

Remove the rack and pour off the water. In the same pan, combine the vegetables with the chicken and tomato sauce. Simmer to blend the flavors, about 5 minutes. Add the penne, salt, and pepper to taste and toss gently to mix well.

Transfer to a warmed bowl, sprinkle with the Parmesan cheese, and serve immediately.

Makes 4 servings

QUICK TOMATO SAUCE
A great tomato sauce made from ingredients you can keep in the pantry.

1 can (16 ounces) tomato sauce
¼ teaspoon dried oregano
¼ teaspoon dried basil
¼ teaspoon salt
  Freshly ground pepper

In a saucepan, combine all the ingredients over medium heat and simmer, about 10 minutes.

Makes 2 cups

CHICKEN PAPRIKA WITH CARAWAY NOODLES

In this classic Hungarian dish, the directions have been streamlined, but you achieve the same authentic flavor. Paprika is the traditional spice, providing a sweet, rich, earthy flavor and color. It is a powder made from grinding aromatic sweet red pepper pods several times. Paprika is available in most supermarkets, but Hungarian paprika is considered superior and can be found in ethnic food stores. Store in the refrigerator to ensure freshness. Sour cream is added at the last minute, creating a pretty pink sauce. Serve this dish with Caraway Noodles.

1 tablespoon butter
1 tablespoon vegetable oil
1 chicken (3½ to 4 pounds), cut into serving pieces, excess fat and skin trimmed
1 cup chopped yellow onion
1 green bell pepper, chopped
1 garlic clove, minced
1 tablespoon paprika (preferably sweet Hungarian)
1 cup Basic Chicken Stock (page 29) or reduced-sodium chicken broth
½ teaspoon salt
  Freshly ground pepper
2 tablespoons all-purpose flour
1 cup light sour cream
  Caraway Noodles (facing page)

In a Dutch oven over medium-high heat, melt the butter with the oil. Cook the chicken pieces until lightly browned on all sides, about 15 minutes. Transfer them to a plate. Reduce the heat to medium. Add the onion, bell pepper, and garlic and sauté until the vegetables are tender, about 5 minutes. Stir in the paprika and mix well. Add the stock, salt, and pepper to taste and bring to a boil.

Return the chicken to the Dutch oven. Reduce the heat to low, cover, and simmer until the chicken is opaque through, about 1 hour. (This dish can be made ahead up to this point and finished at serving time.) In a small bowl, blend the flour with the sour cream. Transfer the chicken to a warmed platter. Add the sour cream mixture to the pan juices and whisk until heated and slightly thickened. Pour over the chicken and serve immediately with the noodles.

Makes 4 servings

CARAWAY NOODLES

4 ounces (2 cups) egg noodles, cooked
    according to package directions, drained
1 tablespoon butter
1 tablespoon fresh lemon juice
2 teaspoons caraway seeds
1 teaspoon salt
    Freshly ground pepper

Return the noodles to the pan in which they were cooked and mix with the butter, lemon juice, caraway seeds, salt, and pepper to taste.

Makes about 3 cups

CHICKEN WITH ZUCCHINI, MUSHROOMS, AND PASTA

For everyday cooking, this dish with ground chicken, vegetables, and pasta is packed with flavor. It comes together fast for a quick stove-top entrée. Ground chicken is available at most supermarkets.

1½ tablespoons olive oil
1 pound ground chicken
½ cup chopped yellow onion
1 zucchini, thinly sliced
4 ounces mushrooms, thinly sliced
2 garlic cloves, minced
2 tablespoons chopped fresh basil or
1 teaspoon dried basil

½ teaspoon salt
Freshly ground pepper
6 ounces (about 2 cups) rigatoni, cooked according to package directions, drained
1 large tomato, seeded, chopped, and drained
1 can (8 ounces) tomato sauce
Freshly grated Parmesan cheese for sprinkling on top

In a large skillet over medium heat, warm the oil. Add the chicken, onions, zucchini, mushrooms, garlic, basil, salt, and pepper to taste and sauté, breaking up the chicken with a spoon, until it turns white and the vegetables are tender-crisp, 8 to 10 minutes. Add the rigatoni, tomato, and tomato sauce, and mix well. Cook until the flavors are blended, 5 to 10 minutes longer, stirring several times. Sprinkle with Parmesan cheese.

Makes 4 servings

CHICKEN AND PASTA WITH CREAMY TOMATO-WINE SAUCE

| Here is a satisfying solution for a quick, one-pot meal with little effort.

1 tablespoon vegetable oil

½ cup chopped yellow onion

2 garlic cloves, minced

1 can (28 ounces) whole tomatoes including juice, cut up

¼ cup dry white wine

½ teaspoon paprika

½ teaspoon salt

Freshly ground pepper

2 or 3 drops Tabasco sauce

¼ cup sour cream

2 tablespoons chopped fresh parsley

½ cup (2 ounces) freshly grated Parmesan cheese, divided

10 ounces (3 cups) ziti, cooked according to package directions, drained

2 cups diced cooked chicken

In a large skillet over medium heat, warm the oil. Add the onions and garlic and sauté until tender, about 5 minutes. Add the tomatoes, wine, paprika, salt, pepper to taste, and Tabasco. Increase the heat to high and bring to a boil. Reduce the heat to low and simmer, uncovered, to develop the flavors and reduce the sauce, about 10 minutes longer. Transfer to a food processor and purée. Return the sauce to the pan and add the sour cream, parsley, and ¼ cup of the Parmesan. Add the ziti and chicken and mix well. Sprinkle with the remaining Parmesan.

Makes 4 servings

CREAMY CHICKEN-PESTO FETTUCCINE

Just a quick toss of chicken and pasta in a creamy pesto sauce and dinner is ready in minutes. If you don't have any pesto in your freezer, it can be found in the refrigerated section of most supermarkets.

½ cup Basil Pesto (page 99) or purchased pesto
½ cup half-and-half
2 cups cubed cooked chicken breast
9 ounces fettuccine, cooked according to package directions, drained
  Freshly grated Parmesan cheese for serving

In a large saucepan over medium heat, warm the pesto and cream. Add the chicken and pasta and toss until well mixed and heated through, about 5 minutes. Serve in a large bowl and pass the Parmesan.

Makes 4 servings

CHICKEN, SAUSAGE, AND TOMATOES WITH RIGATONI

An advantage to this stove-top dish is that you can make the sauce ahead and then add the pasta just before serving. Serve with a spinach salad and crusty bread.

2   tablespoons olive oil
8   ounces chicken tenders, cut into
     bite-sized pieces
8   ounces bulk mild Italian sausage
1   cup chopped yellow onion
2   garlic cloves, minced
1   can (14½ ounces) crushed tomatoes
1   can (14½ ounces) Italian-style tomatoes
     including juice, chopped
½   cup chopped fresh basil or 1 teaspoon
     dried basil
¼   cup dry red wine
½   teaspoon salt
     Freshly ground pepper
6   ounces (2 cups) rigatoni, cooked according to
     package directions, drained
½   cup (2 ounces) freshly grated Parmesan cheese

In a large skillet over medium-heat, warm the oil. Add the chicken, sausage, onions, and garlic and sauté, breaking up the sausage with a spoon, until the chicken and sausage are no longer pink and the onions and garlic are tender, about 10 minutes. Add the tomatoes, basil, wine, salt, and pepper to taste. Reduce the heat to low and simmer, uncovered, until the flavors are blended, 10 to 15 minutes longer. Stir in the rigatoni and mix well. Pass the cheese in a bowl.

Makes 4 to 6 servings

CHICKEN ON PASTA WITH PUTTANESCA SAUCE

This spicy tomato sauce gets its name from the Italian word *puttana,* or "lady of the night." According to one story, the tantalizing aroma from the sauce was an invitation for men to come visit! You can have a lot of fun with this alleged tale with friends. Here, chicken is added to the sauce and served on spaghetti for a great company dish. Serve with a mixed green salad and crusty bread.

2 tablespoons olive oil

1 cup chopped yellow onion

4 ounces mushrooms, coarsely chopped

2 garlic cloves, chopped

3 cups cubed cooked chicken

2 cans (15 ounces each) Italian-style tomatoes including juice, slightly puréed in a food processor

1 cup pitted kalamata or ripe black olives, halved

1 cup chopped roasted red bell pepper (see Note, facing page) or purchased

¼ cup chopped fresh flat-leaf parsley

2 tablespoons capers, drained and rinsed

2 teaspoons anchovy paste (optional)

¾ teaspoon dried oregano

¾ teaspoon dried basil

⅛ teaspoon red pepper flakes

½ teaspoon salt
Freshly ground pepper

10 ounces (2½ cups) ziti or other short pasta, cooked according to package directions, drained

1 cup shredded Asiago cheese

In a large skillet over medium heat, warm the oil. Add the onions, mushrooms, and garlic and sauté until tender, about 5 minutes. Add the chicken, tomatoes, olives, bell pepper, parsley, capers, anchovy paste, and seasonings. Reduce the heat and simmer, uncovered, until thickened, about 15 minutes. Serve on the ziti and sprinkle with the cheese.

Makes 8 servings

NOTE: To roast a bell pepper, preheat the broiler. Halve the pepper lengthwise and remove the seeds and ribs. Make several 1-inch slits around the edges in each pepper half. Place them, skin-side up, on an aluminum foil–lined baking sheet. Press the pepper halves down with the palm of your hand to flatten. Broil 4 inches from the heat until the skin is charred, about 10 minutes. Remove from the broiler, fold the foil tightly over the peppers, and let steam for 10 to 15 minutes. Unwrap the peppers and peel off the skin. A whole pepper can also be roasted over a gas flame by spearing it with a long-handled fork and turning as it becomes charred, or placed on a grill and turned with tongs as it chars. Proceed with steaming and peeling as directed.

CHICKEN AND MUSHROOM FONDUE

In this fondue, chicken pieces and mushrooms are cooked in a fondue pot at the table in a low-fat cooking broth and served with a tarragon dipping sauce. I prefer this broth to the usual oil because it eliminates the fat. Other vegetables can be used, such as zucchini slices, onion pieces, and bell pepper chunks. This is a fun way to entertain, especially during the holidays.

White Wine–Chicken Broth (facing page) for cooking
4 boned and skinned chicken breast halves (about 2 pounds),
    cut into bite-sized pieces
1 pound medium mushrooms, stems trimmed (use the caps only)
    Tarragon Sauce (facing page) for dipping

In a medium saucepan over medium heat, warm the broth. Transfer it to a fondue pot on the table over an alcohol burner. Place the chicken and mushrooms in individual bowls. Using cooking forks, have each guest cook chicken and mushrooms in the broth to the desired doneness. The broth must be kept hot. If it cools, transfer it to a pan and reheat on top of the stove and then return to the fondue pot. Serve with Tarragon Sauce.

Makes 4 to 6 servings

WHITE WINE–CHICKEN BROTH

This broth can also be used for seafood fondue. Substitute beef broth for beef fondue.

1½ cups Basic Chicken Stock (page 29) or reduced-sodium chicken broth
1 cup dry white wine
3 or 4 green onions including some tender green tops, sliced
2 sprigs fresh parsley
1 garlic clove, split
1 teaspoon dried thyme

In a medium saucepan over medium heat, combine all the ingredients and heat until almost boiling, about 5 minutes.

Makes about 3 cups

TARRAGON SAUCE

½ cup mayonnaise
¼ cup sour cream
1 tablespoon minced green onion
2 teaspoons chopped fresh tarragon or ½ teaspoon dried tarragon
2 teaspoons white wine vinegar

In a small bowl, mix together all the ingredients.

Makes about ¾ cup

CHICKEN CHILI

Using ground chicken instead of ground beef makes a lighter and leaner chili. This is a perfect winter meal to serve while sitting around a cozy fire watching a sporting event on TV. Pass the toppings separately in small bowls and serve with garlic bread. Pour your favorite drink.

1	tablespoon vegetable oil
1¼	pounds ground chicken
1	yellow onion, chopped
3	cans (15 ounces each) kidney beans, drained and rinsed
1	can (28 ounces) whole tomatoes including juice, chopped
1	can (15 ounces) tomato sauce
1	tablespoon chili powder or more to taste
¾	teaspoon salt
½	teaspoon ground cumin
¼	teaspoon freshly ground pepper
2 to 3	drops Tabasco sauce

Toppings: Shredded Cheddar cheese, chopped green onions, sour cream, crushed tortilla chips

In a Dutch oven or large pot over medium heat, warm the oil. Add the chicken and onions, breaking up the chicken with a spoon, and cook until the chicken is no longer pink and the onions are tender, about 10 minutes. Reduce the heat to medium-low and add the remaining ingredients except the toppings. Simmer, uncovered, until the flavors are blended, 20 to 30 minutes, stirring occasionally. Ladle into bowls and pass the toppings.

Makes 4 to 6 servings

MACARONI AND CHEESE WITH CHICKEN

Here is a familiar dish with a delicious update. Mac' and cheese has always been popular with kids, and now, with chicken added, it will become a family favorite. For variation, add chiles, either mild or hot.

8 ounces (2 cups) elbow macaroni, cooked according to package directions, drained

1 tablespoon all-purpose flour

½ cup whole milk

½ teaspoon salt
Freshly ground pepper

2 cups (8 ounces) shredded sharp Cheddar cheese

2 tablespoons freshly grated Parmesan cheese

1 cup diced cooked chicken

1 can (4 ounces) chopped green chiles, drained (optional)

Put the cooked macaroni in a pot over medium heat. Stir in the flour. Add the milk, salt, and pepper to taste and mix well. Add the cheeses and chicken and stir until the cheese is melted and the chicken is warmed, about 2 minutes. Add the chiles, if using, and mix well. Serve immediately.

Makes 4 servings

CHICKEN FETTUCCINE WITH SPINACH AND CHEESE SAUCE

Here fettuccine is combined with cooked chicken and fresh spinach, then finished with a rich, creamy cheese sauce. Fettuccine is a flat-strand pasta that takes just minutes to cook.

8 ounces fettuccine, cooked according to package directions, drained
2 cups cubed cooked chicken breast
6 ounces fresh baby spinach, stems removed if desired

Cheese Sauce (recipe follows)
Salt and freshly ground pepper

Put the fettuccine in a pot over low heat. Stir in the chicken and spinach. Add the cheese sauce and toss for 2 to 3 minutes until the spinach is wilted and combined with the pasta. Season with salt and pepper to taste and serve immediately.

Makes 4 servings

CHEESE SAUCE
If made ahead, add the sour cream when rewarming.

2 tablespoons butter
2 tablespoons all-purpose flour
1 cup whole milk
¼ cup Basic Chicken Stock (page 29) or reduced-sodium chicken broth
¼ cup (1 ounce) freshly grated Parmesan cheese
2 tablespoons dry white wine
¼ teaspoon salt
  Pinch ground white pepper
½ cup sour cream

In a medium saucepan over medium heat, melt the butter. Add the flour and stir until bubbly. Add the milk and stock and stir until smooth and thickened, about 2 minutes. Add the Parmesan, wine, salt, and pepper and stir until the cheese is melted, about 1 minute longer. Remove from the heat and stir in the sour cream.

Makes about 1½ cups

CHICKEN AND CHEESE RAVIOLI WITH TOMATO SAUCE

When it comes to weeknight meals, most cooks want fast and easy recipes. This sauce with ground chicken can be prepared in just minutes. Ravioli is an Italian specialty of little noodle squares filled with various food mixtures. It is found in the refrigerated section of most supermarkets. For variation, tortellini can be substituted for the ravioli.

1   tablespoon vegetable oil
1¼ pounds ground chicken
½   cup chopped yellow onion
1   garlic clove, minced
1   can (14½ ounces) whole tomatoes with juice, puréed in a food processor
1   can (8 ounces) tomato sauce
½   teaspoon dried basil

½   teaspoon dried oregano
¼   teaspoon sugar
¼   teaspoon salt
    Freshly ground pepper
1   package (9 ounces) cheese ravioli, cooked according to package directions, drained
    Freshly grated Parmesan cheese

In a large skillet over medium heat, warm the oil. Add the chicken, onions, and garlic and sauté, breaking up the chicken with a spoon, until it turns white and the vegetables are tender, about 5 minutes. Stir in the tomatoes, tomato sauce, basil, oregano, sugar, salt, and pepper to taste. Reduce the temperature to low and simmer, uncovered, until the flavors are blended, about 10 minutes. Serve over the ravioli and sprinkle with Parmesan cheese.

Makes 4 servings

HURRY UP CHICKEN SPAGHETTI

These days, with many couples both working, fast skillet dishes are more popular than ever. Here is an easy way to make spaghetti with ground chicken when time is limited. Just thirty minutes and dinner is on the table. Serve with garlic bread.

1	teaspoon vegetable oil
1¼	pounds ground chicken
½	cup chopped yellow onion
	Salt and freshly ground pepper
1	can (15 ounces) crushed tomatoes
1	can (8 ounces) tomato sauce
¼	cup dry red wine
¼	cup chopped fresh parsley

¼	teaspoon dried thyme
¼	teaspoon dried basil
¼	teaspoon dried oregano
10	ounces spaghetti, cooked according to package directions, drained
¼	cup (1 ounce) freshly grated Parmesan cheese

In a large skillet over medium heat, warm the oil. Add the chicken and onions, and sauté until the chicken is lightly browned and the onions are tender, about 10 minutes. Season with salt and pepper to taste. Add the tomatoes, tomato sauce, wine, parsley, and seasonings. Reduce the heat and simmer, covered, until the chicken is no longer pink in the center, about 20 minutes. Serve over the hot spaghetti and sprinkle with the Parmesan cheese.

Makes 4 servings

CHICKEN MARINARA SAUCE ON PASTA

For a leisurely meal, here is a highly seasoned tomato sauce with chicken added, to serve on spaghetti or any thin pasta. Toss a crisp green salad with Italian dressing and serve along with crusty bread and a hearty dry red wine. The sauce can be made ahead and frozen and used when needed.

1 tablespoon olive oil
½ cup chopped yellow onion
2 large garlic cloves, chopped
1 can (28 ounces) whole tomatoes including juice, coarsely chopped
1 can (8 ounces) tomato sauce
⅓ cup dry red wine or reduced-sodium chicken broth
¼ cup slivered fresh basil or ½ teaspoon dried basil
1 tablespoon coarsely chopped fresh parsley

½ teaspoon dried oregano
½ teaspoon sugar
½ teaspoon salt
Freshly ground pepper
2 cups cubed cooked chicken
10 to 12 ounces linguine or spaghetti, cooked according to package directions, drained
Freshly grated Parmesan cheese for sprinkling on top

In a large skillet over medium heat, warm the oil. Add the onions and garlic and sauté until tender, about 5 minutes. Stir in the tomatoes, tomato sauce, wine, basil, parsley, oregano, sugar, salt, and pepper to taste. Reduce the heat to medium-low and simmer, uncovered, until the sauce is slightly thickened, about 15 minutes.

Stir in the chicken and simmer, covered, until the flavors are blended, about 10 minutes longer. Serve over the spaghetti and sprinkle with Parmesan cheese.

Makes 6 servings

CHICKEN AND ORZO WITH SPINACH AND GORGONZOLA

Orzo is a tiny oval pasta that can be used instead of rice. It makes a good base for this "no fuss" quick and easy skillet dish. Serve with a hearty red wine. Gorgonzola, the famous cheese from Italy, has many uses in salads and as a topping on pasta, vegetables, and some meats, and is complementary to red wine.

1 tablespoon olive oil

½ cup chopped red bell pepper

2 shallots, chopped

1 garlic clove, minced

1 package (10 ounces) frozen spinach, thawed and squeezed dry

1 cup chopped cooked chicken

½ teaspoon salt
Freshly ground pepper

8 ounces (about 1 cup) orzo, cooked according to package directions, drained

¼ cup Basic Chicken Stock (page 29) or reduced-sodium chicken broth

½ cup crumbled Gorgonzola

In a medium skillet over medium heat, warm the oil. Add the bell pepper, shallots, and garlic and sauté until tender, about 5 minutes. Add the spinach and chicken and mix well. Season with the salt and pepper to taste. Toss with the orzo and stock and sprinkle with the Gorgonzola. Serve immediately.

Makes 4 servings

CHICKEN, TOMATO, ZUCCHINI, AND ORZO

Weeknight cooking will not get boring with this combination dish of chicken, vegetables, and orzo. Dinner is just thirty minutes away!

1 can (14½ ounces) whole tomatoes including juice, chopped
1½ cups Basic Chicken Stock (page 29) or reduced-sodium chicken broth
2 garlic cloves, minced
1 teaspoon dried basil
½ teaspoon dried thyme
½ teaspoon dried marjoram
1 teaspoon salt
Freshly ground pepper
2 boned and skinned chicken breast halves (about 1 pound), cut into bite-sized pieces
6 ounces (¾ cup) uncooked orzo
1 small zucchini, cut into ½-inch slices

In a large Dutch oven over medium heat, combine the tomatoes, stock, garlic, and seasonings. Bring to a boil. Stir in the chicken, orzo, and zucchini. Reduce the heat to medium-low and simmer, covered, until the chicken is no longer pink and the orzo is tender, 20 to 25 minutes.

Makes 4 servings

CHICKEN TENDERS, ANDOUILLE SAUSAGE, AND RICE

This stove-top entrée consists of chicken and rice with andouille sausage added for a spicy flavor and peas for color.

1 tablespoon olive oil

1 pound chicken tenders, cut into 1-inch pieces

2 fully cooked Cajun-style andouille sausage links (8 ounces) cut into ¼-inch slices

½ cup chopped yellow onion

1 garlic clove, minced

1 cup uncooked long-grain white rice

2 cups Basic Chicken Stock (see page 29), or reduced-sodium chicken broth

1 tomato, chopped and drained

½ teaspoon salt

Freshly ground pepper

1 cup frozen peas

In a Dutch oven over medium heat, warm the oil. Add the chicken tenders, sausage, onions, and garlic and sauté until the chicken is lightly browned and the vegetables are tender, 6 to 7 minutes. Stir in the rice. Add the stock, tomato, salt, and pepper to taste. Reduce the heat to low, cover, and cook until the liquid is absorbed and the rice is tender, about 20 minutes. Stir in the peas and cook about 1 minute longer. Serve immediately.

Makes 4 servings

CHICKEN IN A POT, CHINESE STYLE

This chicken gains a wonderful mahogany color and unique flavor from slow simmering in the honey–soy sauce on top of the stove. It is carved Chinese-style and served with rice or noodles. Star anise is a star-shaped pod native to China and used for flavoring. You can buy a small amount in bulk.

HONEY–SOY SAUCE

½	cup soy sauce
¼	cup packed brown sugar
2	tablespoons dry sherry or white wine
1	tablespoon honey
1	tablespoon peeled, grated fresh ginger or 1 teaspoon ground ginger
2	garlic cloves, minced
1	whole star anise
1	chicken (3½ to 4 pounds), giblets removed, excess fat and skin trimmed, wings tucked under the back
6 to 8	green onions including some tender green tops, 1 onion cut into 1-inch pieces and the remaining onions sliced

Rice or Chinese noodles for serving, cooked according to package directions, drained

In a small pan over high heat, stir together all the ingredients for the Honey–Soy Sauce, and bring to a boil. Place the chicken in a Dutch oven, pour the sauce over it, and turn to coat. Cover and bake for 35 minutes. Turn the chicken over and baste it with sauce. Cook, covered, until the chicken is very tender and no longer pink in the center or a meat thermometer inserted in the thigh registers 180°F, about 30 minutes longer. Remove the chicken to a cutting board. To carve, cut off the drumsticks, thighs, and wings and arrange them around the outside of a platter. Quickly bone the rest of the chicken as much as possible and arrange it in the center of the platter. Sprinkle with the sliced onions. Degrease the sauce and mix some with the noodles or rice to coat. Serve the remaining sauce in a small pitcher.

Makes 4 servings

CHICKEN FAJITAS

My grandson Cameron, a student at Oregon State University, fixed this recipe at his co-op house for more than twenty-five students and guests, and it was a big hit. Warmed tortillas are filled with the chicken-vegetable mixture along with a selection of toppings.

Fajita Marinade (facing page)

4 boned and skinned chicken breast halves (about 2 pounds), cut into long, ½-inch strips

3 tablespoons vegetable oil, divided

1 red bell pepper, cut into long, ½-inch strips

1 green bell pepper, cut into long, ½-inch strips

1 yellow bell pepper, cut into long, ½-inch strips

1 yellow onion, sliced

12 flour tortillas (10-inch), warmed (see page 128)

Toppings: Chunky Guacamole (facing page), sour cream, chopped black olives, chopped tomatoes, Black Bean Salsa (page 295)

Make the marinade. Reserve 2 tablespoons in a small dish. Add the chicken to the remaining marinade and toss to coat. Cover and refrigerate 2 to 3 hours.

Preheat the oven to 300°F. Remove the chicken from the marinade and discard it. In a large skillet over medium heat, warm 2 tablespoons of the oil. Add the chicken and sauté until no longer pink, about 6 minutes. Transfer it to a plate and keep warm in the oven. Discard any juices that accumulate in the pan and wipe it out with a paper towel.

Add the remaining 1 tablespoon oil to the same pan over medium heat. Add the bell peppers and onions and sauté until the vegetables are tender-crisp, 6 to 8 minutes, adding more oil if needed. Add the reserved 2 tablespoons marinade to the pan and mix with the vegetables.

Serve the warmed tortillas in a basket. Serve the chicken and vegetables on large, individual, warmed plates. Pass the toppings in separate bowls. Let guests assemble their own fajitas by placing some chicken and vegetables in the center of each tortilla, adding toppings as desired, rolling up, and eating out of hand or with a fork.

Makes 4 to 6 servings

NOTE: Chicken breasts can be grilled for this instead of sautéed. Prepare a grill for cooking over medium indirect heat. Marinate the chicken breasts whole, then remove them from the marinade and grill until cooked through, about 5 minutes on each side. Cut the chicken breasts into strips and transfer them to a plate to keep warm in the oven until ready to serve.

FAJITA MARINADE

¼ cup dry white wine
     Juice of 1 lime
1 tablespoon vegetable oil
2 garlic cloves, minced
1 teaspoon ground cumin
¼ teaspoon dried oregano
¼ teaspoon salt
     Freshly ground pepper

In a medium bowl, stir together all the ingredients.

Makes about ½ cup

CHUNKY GUACAMOLE

3 ripe avocados, peeled, pitted, and cut up
1 small tomato, seeded, chopped, and drained (optional)
2 tablespoons fresh lemon juice
2 drops Tabasco sauce
¼ teaspoon Worcestershire sauce
¼ teaspoon chili powder
¼ teaspoon salt

In a medium bowl, mash the avocados slightly with a fork. Add all the remaining ingredients and mix well. Place in a bowl and put plastic wrap directly on the surface of the guacamole to prevent browning, then refrigerate until serving time. Serve at room temperature.

Makes about 1½ cups

SANTA FE CHICKEN STEW

Hominy is added to this stew for a regional touch and a different flavor. Hominy is dried white or yellow corn kernels with the hull and germ removed, and it has a chewy texture. Cornbread and honey are often served with this stew.

1   tablespoon olive oil
4   boned and skinned chicken thighs (about 1½ pounds)
1   teaspoon ground cumin
     Salt and freshly ground pepper
½   cup chopped green onions including some tender green tops
2   large garlic cloves, chopped
1   can (14½ ounces) Mexican-style tomatoes including juice, cut up
1   cup canned white or yellow hominy, drained and rinsed
½   can (2 ounces) diced green chiles, drained
¼   cup chopped fresh cilantro, divided

In a large skillet over medium-high heat, warm the oil. Add the chicken thighs and cook until lightly browned, about 5 minutes on each side. Season with the cumin and salt and pepper to taste. Transfer the chicken to a plate. Reduce the heat to medium. Add the onions and garlic and sauté until tender, about 5 minutes. Add the tomatoes, hominy, chiles, and 2 tablespoons of the cilantro. Return the chicken to the pan and simmer, uncovered, turning it several times until the chicken is no longer pink in the center and the sauce is slightly thickened, 15 to 20 minutes. Transfer the chicken to a platter and spoon the sauce over. Sprinkle with the remaining cilantro.

Makes 4 servings

CHICKEN AND FRIED RICE

When chicken is added to fried rice, it serves as a main course. This is a good way to use leftover cooked chicken or rotisserie chicken.

1½ tablespoons vegetable oil, divided

1 cup chopped green bell pepper

½ cup chopped yellow onion

½ cup chopped celery

2 large eggs, lightly beaten

1 cup long-grain white rice, cooked according to package directions (3 cups cooked)

1½ cups cubed cooked chicken

½ cup soy sauce or more to taste, plus extra for serving

In a large skillet over medium heat, warm 1 tablespoon of the oil. Add the bell pepper, onions, and celery and sauté until tender-crisp, 6 to 7 minutes. Push the vegetables to the sides of the skillet, leaving a space in the center. Increase the heat to medium-high. Add the remaining ½ tablespoon oil to the center of the skillet. When hot, add the eggs and scramble fast until dry. Then mix the vegetables with the eggs in the pan. Stir in the rice, chicken, and soy sauce and mix well. Reduce the heat to medium and cook several minutes longer, until heated through, stirring occasionally. Pass extra soy sauce.

Makes 4 to 6 servings

STIR-FRIED HOISIN CHICKEN

An intriguing combination of chicken, onions, water chestnuts, and red bell peppers is served on rice in this stir-fry dish. The flavor comes from bottled hoisin sauce, a sweet, spicy sauce of soybeans, garlic, chile peppers, and spices. It can be found in the Asian section of most supermarkets.

1 tablespoon vegetable oil

3 tablespoons sesame seeds

1 tablespoon peeled, chopped fresh ginger

1 pound chicken tenders, cut into bite-sized pieces

½ cup chopped yellow onion

½ cup chopped red bell pepper

½ teaspoon salt

½ can (4 ounces) sliced water chestnuts, drained and coarsely chopped

⅓ cup hoisin sauce

1 tablespoon soy sauce

2 teaspoons rice vinegar

1 teaspoon Worcestershire sauce

1 cup long-grain white rice, cooked according to package directions (3 cups cooked), drained

¼ cup sliced green onions including some tender green tops

In a large skillet over medium-high heat, warm the oil. Add the sesame seeds and ginger and sauté until the ginger is fragrant and the seeds are golden, about 2 minutes. Add the chicken, onions, bell pepper, and salt and sauté until the chicken is cooked through and the vegetables are tender, 5 to 6 minutes. Stir in the water chestnuts, hoisin sauce, soy sauce, vinegar, and Worcestershire and cook until the flavors are blended, 2 to 3 minutes longer. Serve on the rice and sprinkle with the green onions.

Makes 6 servings

CHICKEN, MUSHROOM, SUGAR SNAP PEAS, AND RED BELL PEPPER STIR-FRY

Stir-fry is a convenient and quick way to prepare a healthful dinner because very little oil is called for. All of the ingredients should be prepared and ready to use before starting to cook. The contrasting colors of the chicken and vegetables add eye appeal to this dish. Serve over rice or Chinese noodles.

2 tablespoons soy sauce, plus extra for serving

2 tablespoons dry white wine

2 teaspoons cornstarch

1 teaspoon peeled, grated fresh ginger or ¼ teaspoon ground ginger

1 large garlic clove, minced

1 pound chicken tenders, cut into bite-size pieces

3 tablespoons peanut oil or vegetable oil, divided

4 ounces mushrooms, sliced

1 celery stalk, sliced diagonally into 1-inch slices

1 cup sugar snap peas, trimmed

½ red bell pepper, cut into ½-inch pieces

6 green onions including some tender green tops, sliced, plus finely chopped green tops for sprinkling on top

1 cup long-grain white rice, cooked according to package directions (3 cups cooked)

In a large bowl, whisk together the soy sauce, wine, cornstarch, ginger, and garlic. Stir in the chicken and let it stand at room temperature for 10 minutes.

In a wok or large skillet over medium-high heat, add 1½ tablespoons of the oil. When the oil is hot, remove the chicken from the marinade with a slotted spoon and add it to the wok. Reserve the marinade. Stir-fry until the chicken is cooked through, 3 to 4 minutes. Transfer the chicken to a plate.

Add the remaining 1½ tablespoons oil to the wok. When the oil is hot, add the mushrooms, celery, sugar snap peas, bell pepper, and sliced onions and stir-fry until the vegetables are tender-crisp, about 5 minutes. Return the chicken to the wok along with the reserved marinade and stir-fry until heated through and the sauce is thickened, 2 to 3 minutes longer. Sprinkle with chopped green onions. Serve immediately with the rice and additional soy sauce.

Makes 4 servings

CHICKEN AND VEGETABLE STIR-FRY WITH ASIAN SAUCE

In this colorful dish, chicken tenders are stir-fried with onions, green and red bell peppers, and zucchini in an all-purpose sauce. Serve with rice and Asian Sauce as a side dish.

Asian Sauce (recipe follows), divided
2 teaspoons cornstarch
1 pound chicken tenders, cut into bite-size pieces
4 tablespoons peanut oil or vegetable oil, divided
1 white onion, sliced and rings separated

1 red bell pepper, cut into ½-inch strips
1 green bell pepper, cut into ½-inch strips
1 zucchini, cut into ⅜-inch slices
1 cup long-grain white rice, cooked according to package directions (3 cups cooked)

In a medium bowl, blend ½ cup of the Asian Sauce with the cornstarch and stir until blended. Stir in the chicken and let it stand at room temperature for 10 minutes.

In a wok or large skillet over medium-high heat, add 2 tablespoons of the oil. When the oil is hot, add the vegetables and stir-fry until they are tender-crisp, about 5 minutes. Transfer to a plate. Add the remaining 2 tablespoons oil. With a slotted spoon, remove the chicken from the marinade and stir-fry until cooked through, 3 to 4 minutes. Reserve the marinade. Return the vegetables to the pan along with the marinade and stir until thickened. Mix the rice with the remaining Asian Sauce to coat. Serve the chicken and vegetables over the rice.

Makes 4 to 6 servings

ASIAN SAUCE

½ cup water
¼ cup soy sauce
¼ cup hoisin sauce
2 garlic cloves, minced
1 tablespoon rice vinegar

In a small bowl, mix together all the ingredients.

Makes about 2 cups

CHICKEN, MUSHROOM, AND WALNUT STIR-FRY

Stir-fried walnuts impart a nutty taste to the oil, adding a distinctive flavor to the chicken. Serve with white rice and additional soy sauce.

¼ cup vegetable oil
½ cup walnut pieces
2 boned and skinned chicken breast halves (about 1 pound), cut into bite-sized pieces
8 ounces mushrooms, thinly sliced
   Freshly ground pepper
2 teaspoons cornstarch
3 tablespoons soy sauce, plus more for serving
¾ cup long-grain white rice, cooked according to package directions (2¼ cups cooked)

In a wok or large skillet over medium-high heat, add the oil. When the oil is hot, add the walnuts and stir-fry until lightly browned, 2 to 3 minutes. With a slotted spoon, remove the walnuts and set aside. Add the chicken and mushrooms to the skillet, and stir-fry until the chicken is cooked through and the mushrooms are tender, about 5 minutes. Add the pepper to taste.

In a small bowl, blend together the cornstarch and soy sauce. Add to the chicken and mushroom mixture and stir constantly until thickened, about 1 minute. Remove from the heat and stir in the walnuts. Serve over the rice.

Makes 4 servings

CHICKEN PICCATA

In this version of the famous Italian dish, chicken is called for instead of veal, but with similar flavor. Thinly sliced chicken breast fillets are available in packages and are convenient to use for this recipe because they do not need to be flattened. Round out the meal with fluffy rice and a green vegetable.

3 tablespoons all-purpose flour
1 teaspoon salt
Freshly ground pepper
4 boned and skinned, thinly sliced chicken breast fillets (about 2 pounds)
1½ tablespoons butter
1 tablespoon olive oil
6 ounces mushrooms, sliced
½ cup Basic Chicken Stock (page 29) or reduced-sodium chicken broth
¼ cup fresh lemon juice
¼ cup dry white wine
1 tablespoon drained capers
¼ cup chopped fresh flat-leaf parsley

On a piece of waxed paper, mix together the flour, salt, and pepper to taste. Add the chicken and turn to coat.

In a large skillet over medium-high heat, melt the butter with the oil. Add the chicken and mushrooms and sauté until the chicken is lightly browned, 5 to 6 minutes on each side. Remove to a platter. Add the stock, lemon juice, wine, and capers to the skillet and bring to a boil, scraping up any browned bits in the bottom of the pan. Return the chicken to the skillet and add the parsley. Reduce the heat to medium-low and simmer until the flavors are blended and the chicken is cooked through, about 10 minutes, turning once. Spoon the sauce over the chicken and serve immediately.

Makes 4 servings

CHICKEN MARSALA

This recipe is traditionally made with veal, but here it is adapted for chicken. Marsala is Italy's most famous fortified wine, and it adds a rich, slightly sweet, smoky flavor to the chicken. Rice or pasta is a good accompaniment for this special dish.

4 boned and skinned chicken breast halves (about 2 pounds)
⅓ cup all-purpose flour
½ teaspoon salt
    Freshly ground pepper
2 tablespoons olive oil, divided
8 ounces mushrooms, sliced
2 shallots, chopped
1 cup Basic Chicken Stock (see page 29) or reduced-sodium chicken broth
½ cup Marsala wine
1 tablespoon fresh lemon juice
½ cup half-and-half
1 teaspoon ground sage

Place the chicken breasts between 2 sheets of plastic wrap and pound with the flat side of a meat mallet, to ⅜ inch thick. On a piece of waxed paper, mix the flour, salt, and pepper to taste. Add the chicken breasts and turn to coat.

In a large skillet over medium-high heat, warm 1 tablespoon of the oil. Add the chicken and cook until lightly browned, about 5 minutes on each side, then transfer to a plate. In the same skillet over medium heat, warm the remaining oil. Add the mushrooms and shallots and sauté until tender, about 5 minutes. Add the stock, wine, and lemon juice to the skillet and boil, about 1 minute, scraping up the browned bits with a spoon. Reduce the heat to medium. Add the half-and-half and sage and mix well. Do not boil. Return the chicken to the pan and cook until the sauce is thickened and the chicken is reheated, about 2 minutes.

Makes 4 servings

CHICKEN STROGANOFF

This classic dish gets its name from the nineteenth-century Russian diplomat Paul Stroganoff. It originally called for beef, but this recipe uses chicken breasts for a lighter version. For a company dinner, it can be made ahead, then reheated and sour cream added just before serving. Serve over parsleyed rice or egg noodles.

6 tablespoons all-purpose flour

1 teaspoon salt

¼ teaspoon freshly ground pepper

4 boned and skinned chicken breast halves (about 2 pounds), cut into ¾-inch cubes

4½ tablespoons butter, divided

6 to 8 green onions including some tender green tops, sliced

8 ounces medium mushrooms, sliced

2 garlic cloves, minced

2 cups Basic Chicken Stock (page 29) or reduced-sodium chicken broth

¼ cup dry white wine

2 tablespoons chopped fresh parsley

2 teaspoons Dijon mustard

½ cup light sour cream

On a piece of waxed paper, mix together the flour, salt, and pepper. Add the chicken and coat with the mixture. Reserve the remaining flour mixture.

In a large Dutch oven over medium heat, melt 2 tablespoons of the butter. Add the chicken and sauté until lightly browned, about 5 minutes. Remove to a plate. Add the remaining 2½ tablespoons butter and sauté the onions, mushrooms, and garlic until tender, about 5 minutes.

Stir in the reserved flour. Add the stock and stir until thickened, about 2 minutes. Add the wine, parsley, and mustard. Return the chicken to the pan. Reduce the heat to medium-low and simmer, uncovered, until the flavors are blended and the chicken is cooked through, about 10 minutes. Just before serving, add the sour cream and stir until heated through, about 3 minutes. Serve immediately.

Makes 4 to 6 servings

ITALIAN CHICKEN

Of the many chicken recipes I have tested for this book, this turned out to be one of the best for an all-around dish. Your family will love it and so will company. Fresh greens from the garden or farmer's market make a complementary salad.

1½ tablespoons olive oil, divided

3 drumsticks (about 12 ounces), excess fat and skin trimmed

3 thighs (about 1¼ pounds), excess fat and skin trimmed

1 cup chopped yellow onion

1 cup chopped red bell pepper

3 garlic cloves, chopped

1 can (14½ ounces) Italian-style tomatoes including juice, slightly puréed

1 can (8 ounces) tomato sauce

¼ cup dry red wine

1 teaspoon salt

½ teaspoon dried thyme

½ teaspoon dried basil

½ teaspoon dried oregano

1 bay leaf
  Freshly ground pepper

¼ cup chopped fresh flat-leaf parsley

6 ounces spaghetti, cooked according to package directions and drained
  Freshly grated Parmesan cheese for sprinkling on top

In a Dutch oven over medium heat, warm 1 tablespoon of the oil. Add the chicken and cook until lightly browned, about 5 minutes on each side. Transfer it to a plate. Add the remaining ½ tablespoon oil. Add the onions, bell pepper, and garlic and sauté until tender, about 5 minutes. Add the tomatoes, tomato sauce, wine, salt, thyme, basil, oregano, bay leaf, and pepper to taste and mix well. Reduce the heat to medium-low and simmer, covered, until the chicken is cooked through, about 45 minutes. Discard the bay leaf and stir in the parsley. Serve on top of the spaghetti and sprinkle with Parmesan cheese.

Makes 4 to 6 servings

CHICKEN TAGINE

A tagine is a flavorful Moroccan stew consisting of meat, vegetables, and spices gently simmered until the meat is tender and the flavors are mellow. It is traditionally served with couscous. Tagine is also the name of the Moroccan cooking pot shaped like a cone, originally made of earthenware. Today's tagine pot is available in a combination of enameled cast iron and earthenware and can be used on the stove top as well as in the oven. A Dutch oven will also work for this recipe.

1	small globe eggplant, cut into ½-inch slices
2½	tablespoons olive oil, divided
6	boned and skinned chicken thighs (about 2 pounds), cut into large bite-size pieces
2	cups chopped yellow onions
2 or 3	large garlic cloves, chopped
1	teaspoon paprika
1	teaspoon ground coriander
1	teaspoon ground cumin
1	teaspoon turmeric
1	teaspoon coarse salt
½	teaspoon ground ginger
¼	teaspoon cinnamon
⅛	teaspoon saffron threads
	Freshly ground pepper
1	can (14½ ounces) diced tomatoes with juice
1	cup Basic Chicken Stock (page 29) or reduced-sodium chicken broth
1	tablespoon fresh lemon juice
3	tablespoons chopped fresh flat-leaf parsley
¼	cup pitted kalamata olives
	Couscous (facing page)
¼	cup toasted slivered almonds (see page 92)

Preheat the oven to 400°F. Place the eggplant on a baking sheet and brush both sides with 1½ tablespoons of the oil. Bake for 20 minutes. Turn over and cook until tender, about 5 minutes longer. Remove to a plate and cool, then cut into cubes and set aside.

In a Dutch oven over medium-high heat, warm the remaining 2 tablespoons oil. Add the chicken thighs and sauté until lightly browned on all sides, 6 to 7 minutes. Reduce the heat to medium. Add the onions and garlic and sauté until tender, about 5 minutes. Stir in the seasonings, adding pepper to taste, and cook for 1 minute. Add the tomatoes, stock, and lemon juice and bring to a boil on high heat. Reduce the heat to low and cook, covered, until the flavors are blended, about 25 minutes. Add the parsley and eggplant and cook, uncovered, to heat through, 10 minutes longer. Stir in the olives. Serve in large bowls over a scoop of couscous and sprinkle with the almonds.

Makes 6 servings

COUSCOUS

1 cup water
¼ teaspoon salt
1 cup couscous
1 teaspoon butter

In a medium saucepan over medium-high heat, bring the water and salt to a boil. Quickly stir in the couscous. Remove from the heat. Stir in the butter. Cover and let stand for 5 minutes. Fluff with a fork.

Makes about 2 cups

CHICKEN, SAUSAGE, AND SHRIMP GUMBO

This Creole specialty is a mainstay of New Orleans. It is a stewlike dish that includes a variety of ingredients such as okra, onions, celery, tomatoes, chicken, sausage or ham, and often shellfish. A good gumbo begins with a roux, which involves browning the flour and oil for extra flavor and color. This version has it all—chicken, vegetables, sausage, and shrimp. Serve over rice and turn on the jazz.

½ cup vegetable oil

½ cup all-purpose flour

2 cups sliced frozen okra, rinsed, stem ends trimmed, cut into ½-inch slices

1 cup chopped yellow onion

1 cup chopped celery

1 cup chopped green bell pepper

2 garlic cloves, minced

1 teaspoon dried thyme

1 teaspoon dried oregano

1 teaspoon paprika

1 teaspoon salt

¼ teaspoon cayenne

¼ teaspoon ground mustard

1 bay leaf

5 cups Basic Chicken Stock (page 29) or reduced-sodium chicken broth

1 can (15 ounces) whole tomatoes including juice, chopped

3 andouille sausages, cut into ½-inch slices

3 boned and skinned chicken breast halves (about 1½ pounds), cut into bite-size pieces

1 pound medium shrimp, shelled and deveined

1 cup long-grain white rice, cooked according to package directions (3 cups cooked)

¼ cup chopped green onions including some tender green tops

In a Dutch oven over high heat, add the oil and heat until very hot. Add the flour and whisk constantly until it is a dark reddish brown in color, 3 to 4 minutes. Do not allow it to burn. Reduce the heat to medium-high. Add the okra, yellow onions, celery, bell pepper, and garlic and mix well. Stir in the seasonings. Slowly add the stock to the mixture and stir until blended. Stir in the tomatoes. Reduce the heat to medium-low and simmer, covered, for 1 hour. Add the sausage and chicken and simmer until the chicken is cooked through, about 20 minutes longer. Add the shrimp and simmer just until the shrimp turns pink, about 5 minutes longer. Discard the bay leaf. Serve in large bowls with 2 large spoonfuls of rice on top. Sprinkle with the green onions.

Makes 8 servings

STOVE-TOP CHICKEN AND SHRIMP PAELLA

This shortcut recipe for paella is one of the best. It is made in a Dutch oven on top of the stove, but it can be transferred to a warmed paella pan for serving for an authentic look, if you wish. This only serves four, but can be doubled.

1   tablespoon olive oil
1   large yellow onion, chopped
1   cup chopped green bell pepper
1   cup cubed ham (about 8 ounces)
1   garlic clove, minced
1   cup uncooked short-grain Arborio rice
½   teaspoon paprika
½   teaspoon salt
¼   teaspoon saffron threads, crumbled
    Freshly ground pepper
2¼ cups Basic Chicken Stock (page 29) or
    reduced-sodium chicken broth
1   cup cubed cooked chicken breast
½   cup pimiento-stuffed green olives, halved
1   tomato, cut into bite-size pieces
8   ounces large shrimp, peeled and deveined

In a Dutch oven over medium heat, warm the oil. Add the onions, bell pepper, ham, and garlic and sauté until the vegetables are tender, about 5 minutes. Stir in the rice. Add the paprika, salt, saffron, and pepper to taste and mix well. Add the stock, chicken, olives, and tomato and bring to a boil. Reduce the heat to low and cook, covered, until the rice is tender and the liquid is absorbed, about 20 minutes. Nestle the shrimp into the rice and cook, covered, just until the shrimp turns pink, about 5 minutes.

Makes 4 servings

CHICKEN AND POTATOES, GREEK STYLE

This quick and easy chicken-potato dish has all of the classic Greek flavors of olives, lemon, and feta cheese. Serve with a green vegetable for color contrast.

4   medium potatoes (about 2 pounds), peeled and quartered
2   tablespoons olive oil, divided
2   boned and skinned chicken breast halves (about 1 pound), cut into bite-size pieces
¼   cup pitted kalamata olives
1   tablespoon fresh lemon juice
1   tablespoon chopped fresh oregano or 1 teaspoon dried oregano
½   teaspoon coarse salt
    Freshly ground pepper
½   cup crumbled feta cheese

In a medium saucepan over high heat, cover the potatoes with salted water and bring to a boil. Reduce the heat to medium-low and cook until they are almost tender, about 15 minutes. (Do not overcook, as they will also be cooked with the chicken.) Drain and, when slightly cool, cut into ¾-inch cubes and set aside.

In a large skillet over medium-high heat, warm 1 tablespoon of the oil. Add the chicken and sauté until lightly browned, about 5 minutes. Add the remaining oil and the potatoes and stir until the potatoes are lightly browned and the chicken is cooked through, 5 to 6 minutes longer. Add the olives, lemon juice, oregano, salt, and pepper to taste and mix well. Sprinkle with the feta and serve immediately.

Makes 4 servings

CHICKEN CURRY

When friends from India, Gopal and Asha Dutia, came to visit my son and daughter-in-law for an extended stay, they volunteered to teach us how to make an authentic chicken curry. Asha says the proper ingredients must be used—fresh curry powder and garam masala, a mixture of Indian spices. Also the onions and butter must be stirred constantly for about 15 minutes, until thoroughly cooked and almost broken down. Then the other ingredients are added and slowly cooked to blend flavors. The combination of white and dark meat adds complexity and depth to the dish. Cooked white rice is the traditional accompaniment. The condiments served on the side for toppings are an American custom and not part of the native dish. Indians would traditionally serve a salad of chopped tomatoes, green onions, and cucumber tossed with lime juice and served with a glass of buttermilk.

⅓ cup butter

3 medium yellow onions, very thinly sliced

3 garlic cloves, minced

One ½-inch piece fresh ginger, peeled and chopped

1¾ cups Basic Chicken Stock (page 29) or reduced-sodium chicken broth, divided

6 boned and skinned chicken thighs (about 1¾ pounds), cut into bite-size pieces

2 boned and skinned chicken breast halves (about 1 pound), cut into bite-size pieces

2 tomatoes, chopped and drained

1½ to 2 tablespoons curry powder

2 teaspoons garam masala (see Note, facing page)

1 teaspoon salt or more to taste

½ teaspoon turmeric

½ teaspoon paprika

¼ teaspoon cayenne

1 tablespoon fresh lime juice

¼ cup chopped fresh cilantro

1 cup basmati rice, cooked according to package directions (3 cups cooked)

Toppings: Chopped hard-cooked eggs, purchased mango chutney, raisins, chopped green onions, sliced bananas, chopped peanuts

Lime slices for garnish

In a large pot over medium heat, melt the butter. Add the onions and stir constantly for 10 minutes. Reduce the heat to medium-low if they start to brown. Add the garlic, ginger, and ½ cup of the stock. Stir 5 minutes longer. Stir in both types of chicken. Add the remaining 1¼ cups stock and reduce the heat to low. Add the tomatoes and seasonings. Cover and simmer until the flavors are blended, about 30 minutes. Add the lime juice and cilantro and mix well. Serve in bowls with rice. Place the toppings in small bowls. Garnish with lime slices.

Makes 6 servings

NOTE: Garam masala can be found in bulk in some specialty stores and in the spice section of some supermarkets.

ARROZ CON POLLO

This popular Spanish dish of contrasting flavors and colors includes chicken, rice, onions, green bell pepper, tomatoes, spices, and peas. It is slowly simmered on top of the stove to develop all of the authentic flavors.

2½ tablespoons vegetable oil

2 boned and skinned chicken breast halves (about 1 pound), cut into large bite-size pieces

1 cup chopped yellow onion

1 cup chopped green bell pepper

2 garlic cloves, minced

1 cup long-grain white rice, cooked according to package directions (3 cups cooked), drained

2¼ cups Basic Chicken Stock (page 29) or reduced-sodium chicken broth

1 teaspoon ground cumin

1 teaspoon dried oregano

1 teaspoon paprika

1 teaspoon salt

½ teaspoon chili powder

¼ teaspoon freshly ground pepper

1 bay leaf

1 cup chopped tomatoes, drained

1 cup green peas, fresh or frozen, rinsed (see Note)

½ cup small pimiento-stuffed green olives

2 tablespoons chopped fresh parsley

In a Dutch oven over medium heat, warm the oil. Add the chicken, onions, bell pepper, and garlic and sauté until the chicken is lightly browned and the vegetables are tender, about 5 minutes. Stir in the rice, stock, and seasonings and bring to a boil.

Reduce the heat to low and simmer, covered, for 20 minutes. Stir in the tomatoes, peas, and olives. Cover and simmer until the flavors are blended, about 10 minutes longer. Discard the bay leaf. Sprinkle with the parsley before serving.

Makes 6 servings

NOTE: If making ahead, do not add the peas until warming time, to ensure bright, plump peas.

CLASSIC FRIED CHICKEN

If you are hungry for some good, old-fashioned fried chicken, here it is. Soaking the chicken in buttermilk adds a tangy flavor and produces a crispier crust. Choice parts do not include bony parts such as wings, backs, and neck (see page 18).

1	cup well-shaken buttermilk	
1	teaspoon paprika	
1	teaspoon salt, divided	
2 to 3	drops Tabasco sauce	
1	package premium chicken parts (about 3 pounds) or a 3½- to 4-pound chicken, cut up (use choice parts)	

1   cup all-purpose flour
Freshly ground pepper
Canola oil for frying

In a large bowl, mix together the buttermilk, paprika, ½ teaspoon of the salt, and the Tabasco. Add the chicken and turn to coat. Let stand in the refrigerator for 1 hour. Bring to room temperature before cooking.

On a piece of waxed paper, mix the flour, the remaining ½ teaspoon salt, and pepper to taste. Remove the chicken from the buttermilk mixture and shake off the excess. Roll the chicken in the flour mixture and set on a cooling rack. Repeat with all of the chicken.

In a large skillet over medium-high heat, heat about ¼ inch of oil to very hot. Add the chicken and cook it, turning several times with tongs, until lightly browned on all sides, 10 to 15 minutes. Do not crowd; cook in batches, if necessary. Add more oil, as needed. Reduce the heat to low. Cover tightly and cook until the chicken is no longer pink in the center, 40 to 45 minutes, turning once. Remove the lid and cook until crispy, 5 to 10 minutes longer. Drain on paper towels.

Makes 4 servings

VARIATION: After browning, transfer the chicken to a 2-quart casserole, cover, and bake in a 350°F oven until the chicken is no longer pink in the center, about 45 minutes. Remove the lid for the last 5 minutes of cooking time to crisp up the chicken.

CRUST VARIATION: Add 1 teaspoon chili powder to the flour. Reduce the flour to ½ cup and add ½ cup (2 ounces) freshly grated Parmesan cheese. Add 1 or 2 large cloves garlic, minced, to the buttermilk. Use self-rising flour for a crispier crust. Add dried herbs to the flour.

QUICK CHICKEN MOLE

If you like it hot, you will like this famous Mexican dish using prepared mole sauce in this shortcut version. It has all of the same flavors as the long-cooking sauce and takes just minutes to make. Mole sauce is available in Mexican grocery stores and some supermarkets.

¾ cup Basic Chicken Stock (page 29) or reduced-sodium chicken broth
¼ cup prepared mole sauce (stir before measuring)
4 boned and skinned chicken breast halves (about 2 pounds), poached (see page 25)
Cilantro sprigs for garnish

In a small pan over medium heat, stir together the stock and mole sauce until slightly thickened and heated through, about 2 minutes.

Slice each chicken breast diagonally and arrange slightly overlapping on 4 individual plates. Spread 1 to 2 tablespoons of sauce down the center of the breasts. Garnish with cilantro and serve immediately. Pass the remaining sauce in a bowl.

Makes 4 servings

CHICKEN AND GREEN CHILE OMELET

Omelets are always popular and can be served any time of the day. Fillings can include a variety of choice ingredients. This recipe will generously serve one, but make as many as you need to serve your family or guests.

FILLING

¼ cup finely chopped cooked chicken breast

¼ cup (1 ounce) shredded Monterey Jack cheese

2 green onions including some tender green tops, chopped

1 tablespoon canned diced green chiles

OMELET

3 large eggs

1 tablespoon water

⅛ teaspoon salt

Freshly ground pepper

1 tablespoon butter

To make the filling: In a small bowl, combine the chicken, cheese, onions, and chiles and set aside.

To make the omelet: In a medium bowl, whisk together the eggs, water, salt, and pepper to taste. Heat an 8-inch omelet pan or nonstick skillet over medium heat. Add the butter and swirl to coat the bottom of the pan. When the butter foams, pour in the egg mixture and let it set for 30 seconds. Tip the skillet and use a spatula to lift around the edge to allow the uncooked egg mixture to flow underneath. Continue to do this until the top is almost dry, 3 to 4 minutes.

Spoon the chicken mixture over one half of the omelet. Fold the other side over to cover it. Let stand for a few seconds to allow the chicken mixture to warm and the cheese to melt. Turn out onto a warmed plate and serve immediately.

Makes 1 serving

CHICKEN HASH

Here is one of my husband Reed's favorite supper dishes. It consists of fried potatoes, vegetables, chicken, and a poached egg on top (it's the poached egg he likes).

4 new red potatoes (about 1½ pounds), scrubbed and halved	1 teaspoon salt, divided
1 to 2 tablespoons vegetable oil	Freshly ground pepper
8 green onions including some tender green tops, chopped	¾ cup cubed cooked chicken
½ cup diced red bell pepper	4 large poached eggs (facing page)
1 tablespoon chopped fresh sage or 1 teaspoon ground sage	Chopped fresh parsley for garnish
	Tomato wedges for serving

Place the potatoes in a medium saucepan over high heat with salted water to cover and bring to a boil. Reduce the heat to medium-low and cook until almost tender, 15 to 20 minutes. Drain and, when cool, cut into ¾-inch cubes.

In a large skillet over medium heat, warm 1 tablespoon of the oil. Add the potatoes, onions, bell pepper, sage, salt, and pepper to taste and sauté until the potatoes are lightly browned and the vegetables are tender, about 10 minutes, stirring occasionally. Add more oil, if needed. Add the chicken and stir until the chicken is heated through, about 2 minutes.

Divide the hash evenly among 4 plates and top each serving with a poached egg. Sprinkle with chopped parsley and serve with tomato wedges.

Makes 4 servings

POACHED EGGS

In an egg poacher, follow the manufacturer's directions for perfect poached eggs. Eggs poached in a pan of water will look a bit more uneven around the edges than eggs poached in an egg poacher, and some of the white may be lost.

1 teaspoon cider vinegar (optional; vinegar helps hold the shape)

1 teaspoon salt (optional)

4 large eggs

In a deep skillet or saucepan over medium-high heat, bring 1½ inches of water to a gentle boil. Reduce the heat to low. Add the vinegar and salt. Break 1 egg into a small bowl or cup and slip it from the bowl into the water. Repeat with the remaining eggs, adding the eggs clockwise. Cover and simmer for 3 to 4 minutes, or to desired doneness. Do not allow the water to boil. Remove the eggs with a slotted spoon in the order they were added to the pan and blot the bottoms with a paper towel. Trim the edges with kitchen scissors for a neat, even look, if desired.

Makes 4 eggs

CHICKEN
FROM THE OVEN

Oven dishes are convenient to make because, once they are assembled, very little attention is required.

In this chapter, chicken from the oven will answer all of your needs and will simplify your meal planning. There is a recipe for every occasion, from company dishes for entertaining to quick and easy recipes for friends and family. You will find ethnic-inspired dishes, updated classics, some old favorites with a new twist, and many new, contemporary dishes. Try Chutney-Glazed Chicken Breasts; Oven-Fried Sesame Chicken; Chicken Thighs with Spicy Orange Sauce; Coq au Vin; Roasted Whole Chicken with Lemon-Thyme Sauce; Crab-Stuffed Chicken Breasts with Mushroom-Cheese Sauce; and many more.

EASY OVEN-BARBECUED CHICKEN

You don't have to wait until summer to enjoy the flavor of barbecued chicken. Here the chicken bakes in a quick barbecue sauce in the oven with the same good results. Bake some potatoes alongside for an easy oven meal.

1   chicken (3½ to 4 pounds), cut into serving
    pieces, excess fat and skin trimmed
¼   cup ketchup
¼   cup dry red wine
¼   cup soy sauce
1   tablespoon vegetable oil
1   teaspoon Worcestershire sauce

Place the chicken in a lightly sprayed or oiled 9-by-13-inch glass baking dish. In a medium bowl, whisk together the ketchup, wine, soy sauce, oil, and Worcestershire sauce. Pour over the chicken and marinate for 30 minutes at room temperature.

Preheat the oven to 350°F. Bake, uncovered, until the chicken is no longer pink in the center, about 1 hour. Spoon some of the sauce over the chicken once during baking.

Makes 4 servings

CHICKEN WITH SWEET-AND-SOUR SAUCE

Who needs Chinese takeout when you can make this easy dish at home? Serve with rice or Chinese noodles.

SAUCE

¼ cup packed brown sugar

¼ cup water

2 tablespoons cornstarch

¼ cup cider vinegar

¼ cup pineapple juice

2 tablespoons soy sauce

1 tablespoon vegetable oil

¼ teaspoon ground ginger

1 chicken (3½ to 4 pounds), cut into serving pieces, excess fat and skin trimmed

Preheat the oven to 350°F. To make the sauce, in a medium saucepan over medium heat, stir together the sugar, water, and cornstarch until the sugar is dissolved. Add the vinegar, juice, soy sauce, oil, and ginger and mix well. Stir until bubbly and slightly thickened, about 5 minutes.

Place the chicken in a lightly sprayed or oiled 9-by-13-inch glass baking dish. Spoon the sauce over it and bake, uncovered, until the chicken is no longer pink in the center, about 1 hour, turning over once. Serve on a platter with the sauce.

Makes 4 servings

BAKED SPICY CHICKEN

You can see why this recipe is popular with busy cooks. The chicken is simply coated with a spicy mayonnaise mixture and then rolled in crumbs and baked in the oven at a high temperature for a crispy finish.

½ cup mayonnaise
¼ cup well-shaken buttermilk
2 teaspoons chili powder
1 teaspoon paprika
½ teaspoon salt
⅛ teaspoon cayenne
2 cups fine dried bread crumbs
1 chicken (3½ to 4 pounds), cut into serving
    pieces, excess fat and skin trimmed

Preheat the oven to 425°F. In a medium, shallow bowl, mix together the mayonnaise, buttermilk, chili powder, paprika, salt, and cayenne. Spread the crumbs on a piece of waxed paper. Coat each chicken piece in the mayonnaise mixture, then roll it in the bread crumbs. Place the chicken in a lightly sprayed or oiled 9-by-13-inch baking dish. Bake, uncovered, for 25 minutes, then reduce the heat to 350°F and bake until the chicken is no longer pink in the center, about 30 minutes longer.

Makes 4 servings

BAKED CHICKEN IN YOGURT SAUCE

On nights when time is at a premium, here is a recipe that goes together in minutes. The chicken is topped with a tangy yogurt sauce and baked until tender and juicy.

1   cup nonfat plain yogurt
½   cup mayonnaise
¼   cup (1 ounce) freshly grated Parmesan cheese
1   tablespoon fresh lemon juice
1   tablespoon Dijon mustard
1   teaspoon Worcestershire sauce
¼   teaspoon dried thyme
¼   teaspoon salt
    Freshly ground pepper
2   drops Tabasco sauce
1   chicken (3½ to 4 pounds) cut into serving pieces, excess fat and skin trimmed
4   green onions including some tender green tops, sliced

Preheat the oven to 350°F. In a medium bowl, mix together all the ingredients except the chicken and onions. Arrange the chicken in a lightly sprayed or oiled 9-by-13-inch glass baking dish. Spread the sauce over it and bake for 30 minutes. Spoon some of the sauce over the chicken and add the onions on top. Bake until the chicken is no longer pink in the center, about 30 minutes longer.

Makes 4 servings

COLD NIGHT STEW

Lots of fresh vegetables make this healthful stew real comfort food. If you have leftovers, it is even better the next day. Serve with hot biscuits.

1	tablespoon vegetable oil
1	chicken (3½ to 4 pounds), cut into serving pieces, excess fat and skin trimmed
1½	cups Basic Chicken Stock (page 29) or reduced-sodium chicken broth
3	carrots, cut diagonally into 1-inch slices
1	turnip, peeled and quartered
1	small yellow onion, quartered
3 or 4	whole garlic cloves, peeled
1¼	teaspoons salt
½	teaspoon paprika
¼	teaspoon dried marjoram
¼	teaspoon dried thyme
	Freshly ground pepper to taste
6	small new red potatoes (about 12 ounces), unpeeled, scrubbed, and halved
8	ounces mushrooms, halved
1	cup peas, fresh or frozen
¼	cup all-purpose flour
½	cup water

Preheat the oven to 350°F. In a large Dutch oven over medium-high heat, warm the oil. In 2 batches, cook the chicken until lightly browned, 10 to 15 minutes, turning often. Transfer to a plate. Pour off the excess grease and return the chicken to the Dutch oven. Add the stock, carrots, turnip, onions, garlic, and seasonings. Cover and bake for 30 minutes. Add the potatoes and mushrooms. Bake, covered, for 30 minutes longer. Add the peas and bake, uncovered, until all the vegetables are tender and the chicken is no longer pink in the center, about 10 minutes longer.

To make the gravy, in a small bowl, mix the flour and water. Add the mixture to the juices in the Dutch oven and cook, stirring constantly, until slightly thickened, about 2 minutes. Serve the chicken and vegetables in large bowls.

Makes 6 servings

FAMILY-NIGHT CHICKEN STEW

This is a repeat from one of my earlier books because it is by far the easiest and best chicken stew. Now it comes with a story. During the devastating fires in Southern California several years ago, a lady whose house was in the line of fire was staying out of town with her daughter. The daughter prepared this stew for dinner, and the lady said it was truly comfort food during a trying time and helped her through the ordeal. The daughter later notified me that her mother's house had been saved.

1   chicken (3½ to 4 pounds) cut into serving pieces, excess fat and skin trimmed
1   yellow onion, quartered
3   carrots, cut into 1-inch pieces
3   celery stalks, cut into 1-inch pieces
1   can (14½ ounces) whole tomatoes including juice, cut up
1   red bell pepper, cut into 1-inch pieces
8   ounces whole medium white mushrooms
1   cup dry white wine
½   cup fine dried bread crumbs
¼   cup quick-cooking tapioca
1½ teaspoons salt

Preheat the oven to 325°F. In a lightly sprayed or oiled 4-quart casserole dish, combine all the ingredients. Bake, covered, for 2 hours. Remove the lid, stir, and bake, uncovered, to reduce some of the liquid, 20 minutes longer.

Makes 6 servings

OVEN-GLAZED CHICKEN ON RICE

Sometimes the easiest recipes are the best. Just put chicken with this orange-soy glaze in the oven and enjoy a glass of wine while it bakes. Serve with rice to absorb some of the delicious sauce.

ORANGE-SOY GLAZE

¼ cup fresh orange juice

3 tablespoons soy sauce

2 tablespoons vegetable oil

1 tablespoon grated orange zest

1 tablespoon honey

1 teaspoon paprika

½ teaspoon ground mustard

¼ teaspoon salt

1 chicken (3½ to 4 pounds) cut into serving pieces, excess fat and skin trimmed

1 cup long-grain white rice, cooked according to package directions (3 cups cooked)

Preheat the oven to 350°F. To make the glaze, in a medium bowl, whisk together all the glaze ingredients. Place the chicken in a lightly sprayed or oiled 9-by-13-inch glass baking dish. Pour the glaze over it. Bake, uncovered, until the chicken is no longer pink in the center and lightly browned on top, about 1 hour. Spoon the juices over the chicken and serve on the rice.

Makes 4 servings

CHICKEN ASTORIA

When any of my relatives visited Aunt Henrietta, who lived in Astoria, Oregon, she always served this chicken dish. It soon became known by this name. She died a few years ago at age 98, but we still enjoy her recipe. Serve with baked potatoes.

6 to 8 bacon strips, uncooked
1 chicken (3½ to 4 pounds) cut into serving pieces, excess fat and skin trimmed
¼ cup (½ stick) butter
½ cup chopped yellow onion
½ cup ketchup
2 tablespoons cider vinegar
2 tablespoons water
1 tablespoon honey
1 teaspoon Worcestershire sauce
½ teaspoon salt
　 Freshly ground pepper

Preheat the oven to 350°F. Place the bacon in the bottom of a 9-by-13-inch glass baking dish. Place the chicken on top in 1 layer.

In a medium saucepan over medium heat, melt the butter. Add the onions and sauté until tender, about 5 minutes. Add the ketchup, vinegar, water, honey, Worcestershire sauce, salt, and pepper to taste and simmer until the flavors are blended, 2 to 3 minutes. Pour the sauce over the chicken. Bake, uncovered, until the chicken is no longer pink in the center, about 1 hour.

Makes 4 to 6 servings

CHICKEN AND DUMPLINGS

Just like mother used to make, this classic dish has been a longtime favorite and it still rates high on the list of comfort food.

½ cup all-purpose flour
¾ teaspoon salt, divided
   Freshly ground pepper
1 chicken (3½ to 4 pounds) cut into serving pieces, excess fat and skin trimmed
1 tablespoon butter
2 tablespoons vegetable oil, divided
3 carrots, sliced diagonally into 1-inch pieces
2 celery stalks, sliced diagonally into 1-inch slices

1 cup chopped yellow onion
½ cup chopped red bell pepper
4 ounces mushrooms, sliced
1 garlic clove, minced
4 cups Basic Chicken Stock (page 29) or reduced-sodium chicken broth
1 bay leaf
½ teaspoon dried thyme
1 package (10 ounces) frozen peas, thawed
   Buttermilk Dumplings (facing page)

On a sheet of waxed paper, combine the flour, ¼ teaspoon of the salt, and pepper to taste. Roll the chicken in the mixture to coat. Set aside the remaining mixture (about ¼ cup).

In a large Dutch oven over medium-high heat, melt the butter with 1 tablespoon of the oil. Cook the chicken in 2 batches until lightly browned, 10 to 15 minutes, turning often. Add more oil, if needed. Transfer the chicken to a plate.

Preheat the oven to 350°F. Add the remaining 1 tablespoon oil to the Dutch oven over medium heat and sauté the vegetables until tender, about 5 minutes. Add the reserved flour mixture and stir until bubbly. Add the stock, bring to a boil, and whisk until smooth. Add the bay leaf, thyme, and remaining ½ teaspoon salt. Return the chicken to the Dutch oven.

Cover and bake until the chicken is no longer pink in the center, about 1 hour. Meanwhile, make the dumplings.

Remove the lid and discard the bay leaf. Stir in the peas. Drop the dumplings on top of the chicken in 12 heaping tablespoonfuls, keeping them spaced apart. Cover, and bake until a toothpick comes out clean when inserted into a dumpling, 10 to 12 minutes. Serve immediately in large bowls.

Makes 6 servings

BUTTERMILK DUMPLINGS
 2 cups all-purpose flour
 1 tablespoon baking powder
 ½ teaspoon salt
 ¼ teaspoon baking soda
 1 cup well-shaken buttermilk

In a bowl, mix the flour, baking powder, salt, and baking soda. With a fork, stir in the buttermilk until the dough is just blended. Add to the chicken as directed.

Makes about 12 dumplings

FRUITED CURRIED CHICKEN

Peaches and prunes add a new flavor to this easy chicken dish. Serve on a large platter garnished with parsley and offer the toppings in bowls.

1 chicken (3½ to 4 pounds), quartered, excess fat and skin trimmed
½ teaspoon salt
 Freshly ground pepper
1 can (15 ounces) peach halves, drained and juice reserved
½ cup Basic Chicken Stock (page 29) or reduced-sodium chicken broth
2 tablespoons melted butter

1 teaspoon curry powder
1 cup pitted dried prunes
 Parsley sprigs for garnish
2 tablespoons cornstarch
3 tablespoons cold water

Toppings: Unsalted peanuts, flaked coconut, chutney

Preheat the oven to 350°F. Season the chicken with salt and pepper to taste. Put it in a lightly sprayed or oiled 2½-quart casserole. In a small bowl, mix together the reserved peach juice, the stock, butter, and curry powder. Pour it over the chicken. Cover and bake for 45 minutes. Add the peaches and prunes to the casserole. Cover and cook until the chicken is no longer pink in the center and the fruit is hot, about 15 minutes longer. Transfer the chicken to a platter and arrange the fruit around it; garnish with parsley. Pour the juices into a small pan. In a small cup, blend the cornstarch and water. Pour the mixture into the juices and cook over medium heat until thickened, about 1 minute. Pour over the chicken and fruit. Serve the toppings in bowls.

Makes 4 servings

BAKED MUSTARD CHICKEN QUARTERS

If you like mustard, you'll love this recipe. The chicken is brushed with a bold sauce of two mustards and baked. This easy dish can be prepared in minutes and is good to make after a busy day. Bake potatoes alongside to complete the menu.

¼ cup Dijon mustard
¼ cup prepared yellow mustard
1 tablespoon vegetable oil
1 tablespoon red wine vinegar
1 teaspoon dried thyme
½ teaspoon salt
¼ teaspoon freshly ground pepper
1 chicken (3½ to 4 pounds), quartered, excess
   fat and skin trimmed

Preheat the oven to 350°F. In a small bowl, mix together all the ingredients except the chicken. Place the chicken, skin-side up, in a lightly sprayed or oiled 9-by-13-inch glass baking dish. Spread the sauce evenly on top of the chicken, covering completely. Let it stand for 10 minutes at room temperature. Bake, uncovered, until the chicken is no longer pink in the center, about 1 hour.

Makes 4 servings

COQ AU VIN

In French, *coq au vin* simply means "chicken cooked in wine." This classic dish is composed of chicken pieces, bacon, mushrooms, onions, and herbs baked together in red wine. This makes an elegant dish for a company dinner. Serve with noodles or mashed potatoes.

4 slices bacon (about 4 ounces), diced
1 package (about 3 pounds) premium chicken parts (2 legs, 2 thighs, and 2 half breasts with bone), excess fat and skin trimmed
½ teaspoon salt; plus more to taste
  Freshly ground pepper
3 tablespoons butter
1 cup chopped yellow onion
8 ounces medium mushrooms, quartered
1 garlic clove, minced
3 tablespoons all-purpose flour

1 cup Basic Chicken Stock (page 29) or reduced-sodium chicken broth
1 cup dry red wine
2 tablespoons tomato paste
½ teaspoon dried thyme
½ teaspoon dried marjoram
1 bay leaf
1 cup frozen or canned small pearl onions, drained
3 tablespoons chopped fresh parsley

Preheat the oven to 350° F. In a Dutch oven over medium-high heat, cook the bacon until crisp, about 5 minutes. With a slotted spoon, remove it to a large plate, leaving the bacon drippings in the pan. Add the chicken and cook in batches until lightly browned, 10 to 15 minutes, turning often. Season the chicken with salt and pepper to taste. As it browns, transfer the chicken to the plate holding the bacon. Reduce the heat to medium. Add the butter, onions, mushrooms, and garlic and sauté until tender, about 5 minutes. Add the flour and stir until bubbly. Add the stock, wine, tomato paste, thyme, marjoram, the ½ teaspoon salt, pepper to taste, and the bay leaf. Stir until thickened, about 2 minutes. Return the bacon and chicken and any accumulated juices to the Dutch oven.

Bake until the chicken is no longer pink in the center, about 50 minutes. Add the pearl onions and bake until the onions are warmed, 10 minutes longer. Discard the bay leaf. Sprinkle with the parsley before serving.

Makes 6 to 8 servings

MOROCCAN CHICKEN WITH RICE AND APRICOTS

One of the best ways to add variety to your menu is to serve a chicken dish with new flavors and ingredients. Here, apricots and exotic spices are added and the stew is topped with feta cheese. Serve with warm pita bread.

1½ tablespoons olive oil, divided

1 chicken (3½ to 4 pounds), cut into serving pieces, excess fat and skin trimmed

1 small yellow onion, chopped

3 garlic cloves, minced

1 cup uncooked brown rice

½ teaspoon salt

½ teaspoon ground coriander

½ teaspoon ground ginger

½ teaspoon paprika

¼ teaspoon ground cumin

¼ teaspoon fennel seeds

¼ teaspoon ground cinnamon

Freshly ground pepper

2 cups Basic Chicken Stock (page 29) or reduced-sodium chicken broth

¼ cup fresh orange juice

¾ cup dried apricots

¼ cup chopped fresh parsley

Preheat the oven to 350°F. In a Dutch oven over medium-high heat, warm 1 tablespoon of the oil. Add the chicken and cook until lightly browned on all sides, 10 to 15 minutes, turning often. Transfer the browned chicken to a plate. Reduce the heat to medium. Add the remaining ½ tablespoon oil. Add the onions and garlic and sauté until tender, about 5 minutes. Stir in the rice and seasonings and mix well. Return the chicken to the pan. Add the stock and orange juice. Bake, covered, for 30 minutes. Add the apricots and bake, covered, until the chicken is no longer pink in the center, the rice is tender, and the liquid is absorbed, about 30 minutes longer. Place on a platter with the chicken and apricots on top of the rice, and sprinkle with the parsley.

Makes 4 to 6 servings

CHICKEN CACCIATORE

Cacciatore is Italian for "hunter." It refers to food cooked "hunter style" with mushrooms, onions, tomatoes, herbs, and often wine. This is a popular dish prepared with chicken. Serve on soft polenta or noodles.

¼ cup all-purpose flour
1 teaspoon salt
 Freshly ground pepper
1 package (about 3 pounds) premium chicken parts (2 legs, 2 thighs, and 2 half breasts with bone), excess fat and skin trimmed
2 tablespoons olive oil, plus more if needed
1 cup chopped yellow onion
½ red bell pepper, chopped
8 ounces fresh mushrooms, sliced
1 garlic clove, minced

1 can (14½ ounces) whole tomatoes including juice, coarsely chopped in a food processor
1 can (8 ounces) tomato sauce
½ cup dry red wine
3 tablespoons chopped fresh parsley
½ teaspoon dried basil
¼ teaspoon dried marjoram
¼ teaspoon dried thyme
¼ teaspoon dried oregano
 Freshly grated Parmesan cheese for topping
 Basic Polenta (facing page)

Preheat the oven to 350°F. On a large piece of waxed paper, mix together the flour, salt, and pepper to taste. Roll the chicken pieces in the mixture to coat evenly. Reserve any remaining flour mixture.

In a large nonstick skillet over medium heat, warm the oil. Add the chicken and cook until lightly browned on all sides, 10 to 15 minutes, turning often. Transfer it to a lightly sprayed or oiled 3-quart casserole.

In the same skillet, add the onions, bell pepper, mushrooms, and garlic and sauté until tender, about 5 minutes, adding more oil if needed. Add to the chicken in the casserole.

In the same skillet over medium heat, add the tomatoes and juices, tomato sauce, wine, parsley, herbs, and any remaining flour mixture. Stir for a few minutes until blended. Pour over the chicken and vegetables.

Cover and bake until the chicken is tender and no longer pink in the center, about 1 hour. Uncover and add salt and pepper, if needed. Sprinkle with the cheese and bake, uncovered, until golden and the cheese is melted, about 10 minutes longer. Serve on the polenta.

Makes 6 servings

BASIC POLENTA

Polenta can be served soft in a bowl or chilled until set, then sliced, and fried or grilled.

- 1 cup yellow cornmeal
- 3½ cups cold water, divided
- ¼ teaspoon salt
- 1 tablespoon butter
- ¼ cup (1 ounce) freshly grated Parmesan cheese

In a bowl, mix the cornmeal with 1 cup of the water. In a deep saucepan over high heat, combine the remaining 2½ cups water and salt and bring to a boil. Slowly pour the cornmeal mixture into the boiling water, stirring constantly. Reduce the heat to low and simmer, uncovered, stirring constantly until thick and smooth, 3 to 4 minutes. Remove from the heat. Stir in the butter and cheese.

Makes 4 to 6 servings

TEX-MEX CHICKEN AND CHILES

Set the mood for this delicious dish of chicken baked in a chile-tomato sauce by serving guacamole and chips or quesadillas for starters. Add a side dish of rice to the menu.

3 tablespoons vegetable oil, divided

1 chicken (3½ to 4 pounds) cut into serving pieces, excess fat and skin trimmed

1 can (7 ounces) whole green chiles, drained, split, seeded, and cut into large pieces

½ cup chopped yellow onion

1 garlic clove, minced

1½ tablespoons all-purpose flour

1 can (15 ounces) Mexican-style tomatoes including juice, chopped

1 can (8 ounces) tomato sauce

2 tablespoons chopped fresh cilantro

1 teaspoon dried oregano

1 teaspoon chili powder

½ teaspoon salt

¼ teaspoon ground cumin

Freshly ground pepper

1 cup pitted black olives

Preheat the oven to 350°F. In a large skillet over medium-high heat, warm 2 tablespoons of the oil. Add the chicken and cook until lightly browned on all sides, about 15 minutes, turning often. Transfer it to a lightly sprayed or oiled 9-by-13-inch glass baking dish. Lay the chile pieces on top of the chicken. In the same skillet over medium heat, add the remaining 1 tablespoon oil and sauté the onions and garlic until tender, about 5 minutes. Add the flour and stir until bubbly. Add the tomatoes, tomato sauce, cilantro, seasonings, and pepper to taste and stir until thickened. Simmer until the flavors are blended, 2 to 3 minutes.

Pour the sauce over the chicken. Cover and bake for 45 minutes. Uncover, add the olives, and spoon some of the sauce over the chicken. Bake, uncovered, until the chicken is no longer pink in the center, about 15 minutes longer.

Makes 4 servings

CRISP OVEN-FRIED CHICKEN

Fried chicken is always popular, especially when it can be done in the oven. Cornflakes and butter are the key to this oven-fried chicken. No browning is necessary, saving time and mess.

3 to 4 cups cornflakes or other cereal flakes, crushed
¼ cup (½ stick) butter
1 large egg
2 teaspoons salt
1 teaspoon water
1 teaspoon freshly ground pepper
1 chicken (3½ to 4 pounds), cut into serving pieces, excess fat and skin trimmed

Preheat the oven to 375°F. Place the cornflakes in a large plastic bag and crush with a rolling pin until fine, then transfer to a piece of waxed paper. Melt the butter in a 9-by-13-inch glass baking dish in the oven. Remove the dish from the oven. In a shallow bowl, beat together the egg, salt, water, and pepper. Roll the chicken in the butter, then the egg mixture, and then coat with the cornflakes on all sides. Place it in the baking dish and bake, uncovered, until the chicken is no longer pink in the center and is crispy on the outside, about 1 hour.

Makes 4 servings

OVEN-FRIED SESAME CHICKEN

Sesame seeds give a nutty flavor and crunch to this "fried" chicken. Sesame seeds come in various shades of brown and red, but the most common variety is ivory. They are very versatile and can be used in baked goods, salads, and other savory dishes. They are available in bulk, packages, or jars; bulk is the best buy. Store in a plastic bag in the refrigerator or freeze.

¼ cup (½ stick) butter
1 large egg
¼ cup whole milk
½ cup all-purpose flour
¼ cup sesame seeds
1 teaspoon salt
   Freshly ground pepper
1 chicken (3 to 4 pounds) cut into serving pieces,
   excess fat and skin trimmed

Preheat the oven to 375°F. Melt the butter in a 9-by-13-inch glass baking dish in the oven. In a shallow bowl, beat together the egg and milk. On a piece of waxed paper, mix together the flour, sesame seeds, salt, and pepper to taste. Dip the chicken pieces in the egg-milk mixture, then roll in the flour mixture. Place it in the baking dish and turn to coat in butter. Bake, uncovered, until the chicken is no longer pink in the center and is crispy on the outside, about 1 hour.

Makes 4 servings

FLB OVEN-FRIED CHICKEN ON THE RIVER

When my Friday Lunch Bunch comes to our cabin every summer for a potluck, I always provide this chicken. You don't have to stand over a hot stove frying chicken with this method, and it has the same good, old-fashioned flavor as stove-top fried chicken. It is an easy way to prepare chicken for a crowd and can be served hot or cold.

½ cup all-purpose flour

½ cup fine dried bread crumbs

¼ cup (1 ounce) freshly grated Parmesan cheese

1 teaspoon dried thyme

1 teaspoon dried basil

1 teaspoon salt

Freshly ground pepper

1 cup well-shaken buttermilk

½ cup (1 stick) butter or margarine

2 packages (about 6 pounds) premium chicken parts (4 thighs, 4 drumsticks, and 4 half breasts with bone), excess fat and skin trimmed

Preheat the oven to 400°F. On a large piece of waxed paper, combine the flour, crumbs, cheese, thyme, basil, salt, and pepper to taste. Pour the buttermilk into a shallow dish. Melt the butter in a jelly-roll pan in the oven.

Dip a few pieces of chicken in the buttermilk, shake off the excess, then roll them in the flour and crumb mixture. Roll the chicken in the butter in the jelly-roll pan and leave it in the pan. Repeat with the remaining chicken. Bake, uncovered, until the chicken is crispy and no longer pink in the center, about 1 hour.

Makes 6 to 8 servings

DEVILED FRIED CHICKEN

This spicy chicken is browned on top of the stove, then baked in the oven for a crispy finish. It is good hot or cold and is sure to be the star at a picnic, served with your favorite potato salad. Chill the chicken thoroughly and transport it in a cooler chest.

1   cup well-shaken buttermilk
2   tablespoons Dijon mustard
1   tablespoon prepared yellow mustard
1   teaspoon ground mustard
2   teaspoons cayenne, divided
2   teaspoons salt, divided

1   teaspoon paprika
1   teaspoon ground cumin
1   chicken (3½ to 4 pounds), cut into serving pieces, excess fat and skin trimmed
½   cup all-purpose flour
2 to 3   tablespoons vegetable oil

In a large bowl, mix together the buttermilk, all the mustards, 1 teaspoon of the cayenne, 1 teaspoon of the salt, the paprika, and cumin. Add the chicken pieces and turn to coat. Cover and refrigerate for several hours, turning once.

On a piece of waxed paper, mix together the flour, the remaining 1 teaspoon cayenne, and the remaining 1 teaspoon salt. Remove the chicken from the buttermilk mixture and shake off the excess. Coat the chicken evenly with the flour mixture.

Preheat the oven to 350°F. In a large skillet over medium heat, warm 2 tablespoons of the oil. Add the chicken and cook until lightly browned on all sides, 10 to 15 minutes, turning often. Add more oil, if needed. Transfer to a lightly sprayed or oiled 9-by-13-inch glass baking dish. Bake, uncovered, until the chicken is no longer pink in the center, about 1 hour.

Makes 4 servings

OVEN-FRIED CHIPOTLE CHICKEN

Chipotle chiles add variety to this fried chicken. They have a smoky, spicy flavor that changes the dish into an experience. Serve with a vegetable and a salad of sliced oranges, avocado, and green onions with a vinaigrette dressing.

1   cup well-shaken buttermilk

1   tablespoon chopped canned chipotle chiles in adobo sauce (see Note), plus 1 teaspoon sauce

1   garlic clove, minced

1   package (about 3 pounds) premium chicken parts (2 legs, 2 thighs, and 2 half breasts with bone), excess fat and skin trimmed

1¼ cups fine dried bread crumbs

½   cup (2 ounces) shredded Monterey Jack cheese

1   teaspoon coarse salt

½   teaspoon ground cumin

½   teaspoon dried oregano
    Vegetable cooking spray

In a large shallow bowl, mix together the buttermilk, chipotles, adobo sauce, and garlic. Add the chicken and turn to coat. Cover and marinate in the refrigerator for about 2 hours, turning once.

Preheat the oven to 350°F. On a piece of waxed paper, mix together the crumbs with the cheese and seasonings. Remove the chicken from the buttermilk mixture and shake off the excess. Roll the chicken in the crumb mixture to coat. Arrange it in a lightly sprayed or oiled 9-by-13-inch glass baking dish. Spray the chicken lightly with cooking spray. Bake until the chicken is crispy on the outside and no longer pink in the center, about 1 hour.

Makes 4 to 6 servings

NOTE: Leftover chipotle chiles in adobo sauce can be frozen in a covered jar for up to 6 months.

CHICKEN WITH 40 CLOVES OF GARLIC

Don't let the forty cloves of garlic intimidate you. When garlic is cooked, it becomes mild in flavor and buttery in texture. This recipe may have been created by the late James Beard in the early 1980s, but since then, there have been many variations.

3 tablespoons olive oil

1 package (about 3 pounds) premium chicken parts (2 legs, 2 thighs, and 2 half breasts with bone), excess fat and skin trimmed
Salt and freshly ground pepper

1 large yellow onion, chopped

3 sprigs fresh rosemary or 1 teaspoon dried rosemary

2 or 3 sprigs fresh thyme or ½ teaspoon dried thyme

4 sprigs fresh parsley

40 garlic cloves (about 2 large heads), separated and peeled

½ cup Basic Chicken Stock (page 29) or reduced-sodium chicken broth

¼ cup dry white wine
Toasted French bread slices for serving

Preheat the oven to 350ºF. In a Dutch oven over medium-high heat, warm the oil. Sprinkle the chicken with salt and pepper to taste. Add the chicken to the pot and cook until lightly browned on all sides, 10 to 15 minutes, turning often. Transfer it to a platter. Reduce the heat to medium, add the onions and sauté until tender, about 5 minutes. Return the chicken to the pot and tuck the herb sprigs and garlic in and around the chicken pieces. Pour the stock and wine over all.

Bake, covered, for 30 minutes. Baste the chicken with the accumulated juices and continue to bake, covered, until the chicken is cooked through, about 30 minutes longer. Transfer the chicken and 10 or 12 garlic cloves to a platter. Discard the herb sprigs. Transfer the pan juices and half of the garlic cloves to a food processor and process until smooth. Pour some of the sauce over the chicken and pass the remaining sauce in a bowl or pitcher. Mash the remaining garlic cloves and eat with the chicken or spread on toast.

Makes 6 servings

CRUNCHY BAKED CHICKEN BREASTS

When it comes to a quick dinner, many cooks turn to boned and skinned chicken breasts because they cook fast and are easy to prepare. Here, they are dipped in a rich sour cream sauce, then coated with crumbs and baked in the oven.

¼ cup (½ stick) butter
½ cup sour cream
1 teaspoon paprika
1 teaspoon salt
½ teaspoon dried thyme
⅛ teaspoon ground white pepper
1 cup dried coarse bread crumbs
   (preferably sourdough)

4 boned and skinned chicken breast halves
   (about 2 pounds)
1 cup long-grain white rice, cooked according to
   package directions (3 cups cooked)
   Parsley sprigs for garnish

Preheat the oven to 350°F. Melt the butter in a 8-by-8-inch glass baking dish in the oven. In a medium, shallow bowl, mix together the sour cream, paprika, salt, thyme, and pepper. Place the crumbs on a piece of waxed paper. Dip the chicken breasts in the sour cream mixture, then coat them with the crumbs. Place them in the baking dish and turn to coat in the butter. Bake until the chicken is cooked through, about 30 minutes. To serve, place the rice on a large platter and arrange the chicken on top, garnishing with the parsley.

Makes 4 servings

BAKED ALMOND-COATED CHICKEN BREASTS

Bake these crunchy chicken breasts along with sweet potatoes for an all-oven entrée. The almond coating keeps the breasts moist as they bake.

¼ cup chopped blanched almonds

¼ cup all-purpose flour

3 tablespoons freshly grated Parmesan cheese

½ teaspoon dried rosemary

½ teaspoon salt

Freshly ground pepper

⅓ cup well-shaken buttermilk

6 boned and skinned chicken breast halves (about 3 pounds)

¼ cup (½ stick) butter or margarine, melted

Preheat the oven to 350°F. On a piece of waxed paper, mix together the almonds, flour, Parmesan, rosemary, salt, and pepper to taste. Pour the buttermilk in a shallow dish. Dip the chicken in the buttermilk, shake off the excess, and roll it in the nut-flour mixture to coat.

Place the chicken breasts in a lightly sprayed or oiled 9-by-9-inch glass baking dish and drizzle with the butter. Bake, uncovered, until the chicken is cooked through, about 30 minutes.

Makes 4 to 6 servings

SWEET HONEY-MUSTARD CHICKEN BAKE

Here is a quick recipe you will love to make when time is short. It is simple but good.

6 boned and skinned chicken breast halves
 (about 3 pounds)
 Coarse salt and freshly ground pepper
 Vegetable oil cooking spray
½ cup honey
¼ cup prepared yellow mustard
 Dash curry powder (optional)

Preheat the oven to 350°F. In a lightly sprayed or oiled glass baking dish, arrange the chicken breasts. Sprinkle them with salt and pepper to taste and spray with vegetable oil. In a small bowl, mix together the honey, mustard, and curry powder, if using, and brush on top of the chicken. Bake until the chicken is cooked through, about 30 minutes.

Makes 6 servings

BAKED HERBED CHICKEN BREASTS

In this no-fuss dish, chicken breasts are thoroughly coated in a flavorful mixture of yogurt, mustard, and herbs and rolled in a crumb coating, then baked. Browning is not necessary.

½   cup nonfat plain yogurt

1   tablespoon Dijon mustard

½   teaspoon salt

    Freshly ground pepper

½   cup dried coarse bread crumbs

¼   cup (1 ounce) freshly grated Parmesan cheese

¼   cup chopped fresh parsley

¼   teaspoon dried basil

¼   teaspoon dried rosemary

¼   teaspoon dried thyme

¼   teaspoon paprika

6   boned and skinned chicken breast halves (about 3 pounds)

Preheat the oven to 400°F. In a pie plate, mix together the yogurt, mustard, salt, and pepper to taste. On a piece of waxed paper or a plate, mix together the remaining ingredients except the chicken. Coat the chicken pieces in the yogurt mixture and then roll them in the crumb mixture. Pat the crumbs with your fingers to make them adhere.

Place in a lightly sprayed or oiled 7-by-11-inch glass baking dish and bake until the chicken is lightly browned and cooked through, about 30 minutes.

Makes 4 to 6 servings

CHICKEN BREASTS WITH HAM AND SWISS CHEESE

For the short-order cook, these chicken breasts are topped with ham and cheese and baked for a superb combination.

1   tablespoon vegetable oil

4   boned and skinned chicken breast halves (about 2 pounds)

½   teaspoon dried thyme
    Salt and freshly ground pepper

½   cup chopped yellow onion

2   garlic cloves, minced

1   cup Basic Chicken Stock (page 29) or reduced-sodium chicken broth

¼   cup dry white wine

1   ham slice (about 4 ounces), cut into ½-inch strips

4   slices Swiss cheese, cut into ½-inch strips

Preheat the oven to 375°F. In a large skillet over medium-high heat, warm the oil. Add the chicken and cook until lightly browned, about 5 minutes on each side, turning once. Season with the thyme, and salt and pepper to taste. Transfer the chicken to a lightly sprayed or oiled 8-by-8-inch glass baking dish. Reduce the heat to medium. Add the onions and garlic to the skillet and sauté until tender, about 5 minutes. Add the stock and wine and cook for several minutes. Pour over the chicken. Layer with the ham and cheese strips. Bake, uncovered, until the chicken is cooked through and the cheese is melted, about 30 minutes.

Makes 4 servings

GLAZED ORANGE MARMALADE CHICKEN BREASTS

For a tempting aroma and outstanding flavor, the chicken bakes in the oven with a simple glaze of orange marmalade and soy sauce. Very easy!

4   boned and skinned chicken breast halves
    (about 2 pounds)
    Vegetable oil for brushing on chicken
½   cup sweet orange marmalade
2   tablespoons soy sauce
1   teaspoon ground mustard
1   teaspoon salt
    Freshly ground pepper

Preheat the oven to 400°F. Place the chicken in a lightly sprayed or oiled 8-by-8-inch glass baking dish. Brush with oil. In a small bowl, mix together the marmalade, soy sauce, mustard, salt, and pepper to taste and spread it on the chicken. Bake, uncovered, until the chicken is cooked through, about 30 minutes.

Makes 4 servings

CHICKEN BREASTS WITH CHEESE AND MUSHROOM FILLING

A tasty filling tucked under the skin of these chicken breasts adds flavor and keeps them moist while they bake. This is one of those company dishes that can be made ahead.

4   bone-in, skin-on chicken breast halves (about 4 pounds)
Salt and freshly ground pepper
⅓   cup cottage cheese
2   mushrooms, finely chopped
¼   cup (1 ounce) freshly grated Parmesan cheese

2   teaspoons chopped fresh parsley
½   teaspoon dried basil
1   tablespoon olive oil
Paprika for sprinkling on top
Basil leaves for garnish

Preheat the oven to 375°F. Loosen the skin from the chicken breasts with your fingers, leaving one side attached. Season with salt and pepper to taste under the skin. In a medium bowl, mix together the cottage cheese, mushrooms, Parmesan, parsley, and dried basil. Spoon 1 to 2 tablespoons of the cottage cheese mixture under the skin of each chicken breast and stretch the skin over the filling. Secure with a toothpick. Brush the skin with oil and sprinkle with paprika. Place in a lightly sprayed or oiled 7-by-11-inch glass baking dish. Bake until the skin is lightly browned and the chicken is cooked through, about 35 minutes. Transfer the chicken to a warmed platter and remove the toothpicks. Garnish with basil leaves.

Makes 4 servings

CHICKEN BREASTS AND ONIONS IN SOUR CREAM SAUCE

These chicken breasts, with a creamy sauce lightly flavored with sage, make an elegant dish with a sophisticated touch. It makes a nice company dinner to serve with green beans and toasted slivered almonds. Add a fresh fruit salad to complete the meal.

4 boned and skinned chicken breast halves (about 2 pounds)
1 teaspoon ground sage
  Salt and freshly ground pepper
1 tablespoon vegetable oil
½ yellow onion, sliced and separated into rings

½ cup sour cream
1 tablespoon all-purpose flour
1 teaspoon Dijon mustard
½ cup dry white wine
¼ cup chopped fresh parsley

Preheat the oven to 350°F. Sprinkle the chicken breasts generously with the sage, and salt and pepper to taste. In a large skillet over medium heat, warm the oil. Add the chicken breasts and brown, about 5 minutes on each side, turning once. Transfer the breasts to a lightly sprayed or oiled 8-by-8-inch glass baking dish. Lay the onion rings on top.

In a small bowl, blend together the sour cream, flour, and mustard. Add the wine to the skillet and boil for 1 minute. Remove from the heat and whisk in the sour cream mixture and parsley and blend well. Pour over the breasts. Bake, uncovered, until the chicken is cooked through and the sauce is bubbly, 25 to 30 minutes.

Makes 4 servings

APRICOT-PEANUT-GINGER CHICKEN BREASTS

Peanut butter, apricot, and spices in an Asian-inspired sauce are spread over chicken and sprinkled with crumbs for an easy, exotic-flavored oven dish. Serve rice or Chinese noodles as an accompaniment.

½ cup chunky peanut butter, at room temperature
½ cup apricot preserves
½ cup dried coarse bread crumbs
1 teaspoon ground ginger
1 teaspoon curry powder

½ teaspoon salt
Dash ground cinnamon
Freshly ground pepper
6 boned and skinned chicken breast halves (about 3 pounds)

Preheat the oven to 350°F. In a medium bowl, mix together the peanut butter and preserves until blended. In another medium bowl, mix together the crumbs, ginger, curry powder, salt, cinnamon, and pepper to taste. Place the chicken in a lightly sprayed or oiled 7-by-11-inch glass baking dish. Spread with the peanut butter mixture, covering completely, then sprinkle with the crumb mixture. Press with your fingersto make the crumbs adhere to the chicken. Bake, uncovered, until the chicken is cooked through, about 30 minutes.

Makes 4 to 6 servings

CHUTNEY-GLAZED CHICKEN BREASTS

A fruity chutney glaze enhances these baked chicken breasts, which go well with curried rice. Chutney is a spicy condiment that includes fruit, vinegar, sugar, and spices and can be purchased at most supermarkets.

6   boned and skinned chicken breast halves
     (about 3 pounds)
     Olive oil for brushing
     Salt and freshly ground pepper
½   cup mango chutney (preferably Major Grey's)

Preheat the oven to 375°F. In a lightly sprayed or oiled 7-by-11-inch glass baking dish, place the chicken breasts. Brush them with oil and season with salt and pepper to taste. Bake, uncovered, for 20 minutes. Spread about 1 tablespoon chutney on top of each breast, covering completely. Bake until the chicken is cooked through and the glaze is set, about 10 minutes longer.

Makes 4 to 6 servings

ASIAN CHICKEN BREASTS AND RICE WITH CASHEWS

In this delightful dish, chicken breasts bake in a pungent sauce served on a bed of rice and topped with chopped nuts.

½ cup soy sauce

¼ cup honey

2 teaspoons ground mustard

¼ teaspoon ground ginger

6 boned and skinned chicken breast halves (about 3 pounds)

1 cup long-grain white rice, cooked according to package directions (3 cups cooked)

½ cup coarsely chopped unsalted cashews

Preheat the oven to 350°F. In a medium bowl, whisk together the soy sauce, honey, mustard, and ginger. Arrange the chicken in a lightly sprayed or oiled 7-by-11-inch glass baking dish and pour the sauce over. Bake, uncovered, until the chicken is cooked through, about 30 minutes. Place the rice on a large platter and arrange the chicken on top. Pour the sauce over it and sprinkle with the cashews.

Makes 4 to 6 servings

CHICKEN BREASTS, GREEK STYLE

This is a very simple way to prepare chicken breasts with a lot of style and flavor. Serve with sliced cucumbers and Yogurt-Dill Sauce.

6 boned and skinned chicken breast halves (about 3 pounds)
   Olive oil for brushing
1 teaspoon dried oregano
   Salt and freshly ground pepper

1 red bell pepper, chopped
1 plum tomato, chopped
1 cup crumbled feta cheese
   Juice of 1 lemon
   Yogurt-Dill Sauce (recipe follows)

Preheat the oven to 350°F. Arrange the chicken breasts in a lightly sprayed or oiled 7-by-11-inch glass baking dish. Brush them with olive oil. Season each breast with the oregano, and salt and pepper to taste. Divide the bell pepper, tomato, and feta evenly on top of each chicken breast. Drizzle the lemon juice over all. Bake, uncovered, until the chicken is cooked through, about 30 minutes. Pass the Yogurt-Dill Sauce.

Makes 4 to 6 servings

YOGURT-DILL SAUCE

1 cup nonfat plain yogurt
1 teaspoon fresh lemon juice
1 tablespoon chopped fresh dill or 1 teaspoon dried dill
½ teaspoon salt

In a small bowl, mix together all the ingredients. Keep refrigerated and bring to room temperature to serve.

Makes about 1 cup

CHICKEN BREASTS, MEXICAN STYLE

Make mealtime special by serving chicken breasts and corn in a spicy tomato sauce. Garnish with olives and avocado slices for more flavor and contrast. Serve over hot rice.

1½ tablespoons vegetable oil, divided

6 boned and skinned chicken breast halves (about 3 pounds)

1 cup chopped yellow onion

½ red bell pepper, chopped

1 garlic clove, minced

1 can (14½ ounces) Mexican-style tomatoes including juice

1 cup corn kernels, fresh or frozen

1 can (4 ounces) diced green chiles, drained

½ teaspoon chili powder

½ teaspoon ground cumin

½ teaspoon paprika

½ teaspoon salt

Freshly ground pepper

1 cup (4 ounces) shredded Monterey Jack cheese

½ cup pitted ripe olives

1 avocado, peeled, pitted, and sliced

Preheat the oven to 350°F. In a medium skillet over medium-high heat, warm 1 tablespoon of the oil. Cook the chicken breasts until lightly browned, about 5 minutes on each side. Transfer them to a lightly sprayed or oiled 7-by-11-inch glass baking dish. In the same skillet over medium heat, warm the remaining ½ tablespoon oil, if needed. Add the onions, bell pepper, and garlic and sauté until the vegetables are tender, about 5 minutes. Add the tomatoes, corn, chiles, and seasonings and mix well. Pour the mixture over the chicken and bake, uncovered, until the chicken is cooked through and the sauce is bubbly, about 30 minutes. Sprinkle with the cheese and tuck in the olives. Bake until the cheese melts, about 5 minutes longer. Arrange the avocado slices on top and serve.

Makes 4 to 6 servings

BAKED CURRIED CHICKEN BREASTS

These chicken breasts bake in a flavorful curry sauce to serve over a bed of rice. Curry powder is a blend of about twenty spices, herbs, and seeds, used extensively in Indian cooking. It is very pungent and should be used according to your taste. For an attractive plate, sauté some bright green sugar snap peas to go alongside. Shallots have a mild onion flavor and look like a large clove of garlic. They are available year-round.

CURRY SAUCE

2   shallots, cut up

2   garlic cloves, cut up

1   tablespoon peeled, chopped fresh ginger or
    1 teaspoon ground ginger

2   sprigs fresh parsley, torn, plus additional
    sprigs for garnish

¾   cup nonfat plain yogurt

1   tablespoon fresh lemon juice

1   teaspoon curry powder or more to taste

½   teaspoon salt
    Freshly ground pepper

4   boned and skinned chicken breast halves
    (about 2 pounds)

1   cup long-grain white rice, cooked according
    to package directions (3 cups cooked)

¼   cup chopped unsalted peanuts

Preheat the oven to 350°F. To make the curry sauce, in a food processor, combine the shallots, garlic, ginger, and parsley and process until finely chopped. Add the yogurt, lemon juice, curry powder, salt, and pepper to taste and blend. Put the chicken in a lightly sprayed or oiled 7-by-11-inch glass baking dish. Pour the curry sauce over it. Bake until the chicken is cooked through, about 30 minutes. Serve the chicken and sauce on top of the rice and sprinkle with the peanuts. Garnish with parsley sprigs.

Makes 4 servings

SPICY CHICKEN BREASTS, CUBAN STYLE

Experience some new flavors in these lively chicken breasts accented with a blend of Cuban spices. Serve with cooling drinks and a rich chocolate dessert.

4   boned and skinned chicken breast halves
    (about 2 pounds)
    Salt and freshly ground pepper
2   tablespoons olive oil, divided
1   cup diced yellow onion
1   garlic clove, minced
1   can (14½ ounces) crushed tomatoes
1   teaspoon ground cumin

1   teaspoon dried basil
½   teaspoon dried oregano
¼   teaspoon ground cinnamon
⅛   teaspoon ground cloves
10 pimiento-stuffed olives, sliced
¼   cup dry red wine
1   tablespoon drained capers
1   tablespoon brown sugar

Preheat the oven to 350°F. Cut the chicken breasts into large pieces. Season with salt and pepper to taste. In a large skillet over medium-high heat, warm 1 tablespoon of the oil. Add the chicken and sauté until lightly browned, about 5 minutes on each side. Transfer to a lightly sprayed or oiled 2-quart casserole. Add the remaining 1 tablespoon oil to the skillet. Reduce the heat to medium and sauté the onions and garlic until tender, about 5 minutes. Add the tomatoes and seasonings and simmer for 1 minute. Stir in the olives, wine, capers, and sugar and mix well. Pour the sauce over the chicken. Bake, covered, until the chicken is cooked through and the flavors are blended, about 30 minutes.

Makes 4 servings

STUFFED CHICKEN BREASTS WITH SAUSAGE, SPINACH, AND MUSHROOMS

The savory stuffing highlights this great company dish and adds a lot of flavor to the chicken. This takes time, so prepare the chicken ahead and bake later. A final glaze adds to the appeal. Serve with orzo and chives as a side dish.

8 ounces bulk pork sausage

6 ounces mushrooms, stems trimmed and caps coarsely chopped

8 green onions including some tender green tops, sliced

2 garlic cloves, minced
Vegetable oil, if needed

1 bag (5 ounces) spinach, stemmed, cooked, drained, squeezed dry with paper towels, and chopped, or 1 package (10 ounces) chopped frozen spinach, thawed and squeezed dry

½ cup dried coarse bread crumbs

½ teaspoon salt

⅛ teaspoon freshly ground pepper

½ cup dry white wine, divided

½ cup (2 ounces) shredded Swiss cheese

8 boned and skinned chicken breast halves (3½ to 4 pounds)

1 to 2 tablespoons butter

1½ cups Basic Chicken Stock (page 29) or reduced-sodium chicken broth

3 tablespoons water

1½ tablespoons cornstarch

In a large skillet over medium heat, add the sausage, mushrooms, onions, and garlic, and sauté, breaking up the sausage with a spoon until it is no longer pink and the vegetables are tender, 6 to 7 minutes. Add oil, if needed. Stir in the spinach and bread crumbs. Season with the salt and pepper. Add ¼ cup of the wine and the cheese and mix well.

Preheat the oven to 350°F. Place the chicken breasts between 2 pieces of plastic wrap and pound with the flat side of a meat mallet, to ⅜ inch thick. Divide the sausage-spinach mixture among the 8 breasts. Roll up from the small end and secure with a toothpick.

In the same large skillet over medium heat, melt 1 tablespoon of the butter. Add the chicken and cook until lightly browned, 5 to 6 minutes on each side, turning once. Add more butter, if needed. Transfer the chicken, seam-side down, to a lightly sprayed or oiled 9-by-13-inch glass baking dish. Add the stock and remaining ¼ cup wine to the skillet. In a small bowl, blend the cornstarch and water. Add to the stock and stir until thickened, about 1 minute. Pour over the chicken. Bake, uncovered, until the chicken is cooked through, about 35 minutes. Transfer the chicken to a warmed platter and remove the toothpicks.

Makes 8 servings

CHEESE AND PESTO–FILLED CHICKEN BREASTS WITH MUSHROOM SAUCE

This sounds like a fancy dish, but it is easy to make and is a great company dish. You will need thick fillets to make a pocket for this flavorful cheese-pesto filling. Pesto has many uses in soups, sandwiches, and as an accent for seafood and meats.

4   thick boned and skinned chicken breast
    halves (about 2 pounds)
⅓   cup ricotta or cottage cheese
¼   cup fine dried bread crumbs
3   tablespoons Basil Pesto (page 99)
    or purchased pesto

1   large egg, lightly beaten
¼   teaspoon salt
    Freshly ground pepper
    Olive oil for brushing
    Mushroom Sauce (facing page)

Preheat the oven to 375°F. With a sharp knife, horizontally cut a pocket in each breast. In a medium bowl, mix together the cheese, crumbs, pesto, egg, salt, and pepper to taste. Spoon about 2 table-spoons of the mixture in each pocket and secure with a toothpick. Put the chicken in a lightly sprayed or oiled 7-by-11-inch glass baking dish and brush with oil. Bake, uncovered, for 10 minutes. Reduce the heat to 350°F. Pour the mushroom sauce over the top and bake until bubbly and the chicken is cooked through, about 25 minutes longer. Transfer the chicken to a warmed platter and remove the toothpicks.

Makes 4 to 6 servings

MUSHROOM SAUCE

This can be made ahead and warmed before using.

2 tablespoons butter

¼ cup finely chopped yellow onion

6 ounces mushrooms, sliced

2 tablespoons all-purpose flour

½ cup Basic Chicken Stock (page 29) or reduced-sodium chicken broth

½ cup half-and-half or whole milk

2 tablespoons dry white wine

¼ teaspoon salt

Dash ground white pepper

In a medium saucepan over medium heat, melt the butter. Add the onions and mushrooms and sauté until tender, about 5 minutes. Add the flour and stir until bubbly. Add the stock and half-and-half and stir until thickened, about 2 minutes. Add the wine, salt, and pepper and mix well.

Makes about 1½ cups

CRAB-STUFFED CHICKEN BREASTS WITH MUSHROOM-CHEESE SAUCE

My husband, Reed, entered this recipe in an Oregon Fryer Commission contest and won first prize—$100 and a year's supply of chicken! This makes an elegant company dish to serve with rice.

4 boned and skinned chicken breast halves
   (about 2 pounds)
   Crab Filling (facing page)
   Mushroom-Cheese Sauce (facing page)
1 cup long-grain white rice, cooked according
   to package directions (3 cups cooked)

Preheat the oven to 375°F. Place the chicken breasts between 2 sheets of plastic wrap and pound with the flat side of a meat mallet to ⅜ inch thick. Lay the chicken breasts on a flat surface. Divide the filling equally between them. Roll up from the small end and secure with a toothpick. Place seam-side down in a lightly sprayed or oiled 7-by-11-inch glass baking dish. Add any remaining filling on top. Cover and bake for 25 minutes. Uncover and spoon the Mushroom-Cheese Sauce over the chicken. Bake, uncovered, until the chicken is cooked through and the sauce is bubbly, about 15 minutes longer. To serve, transfer the chicken rolls to a warmed platter and remove the toothpicks. Spoon the sauce over the chicken.

Makes 4 servings

CRAB FILLING

8 ounces Dungeness crabmeat, flaked and picked over for shell pieces
⅓ cup Mushroom-Cheese Sauce (recipe follows)
¼ cup dried coarse bread crumbs, preferably sourdough
2 tablespoons chopped fresh parsley
¼ teaspoon salt

In a medium bowl, mix together the crab, sauce, bread crumbs, parsley, and salt. Refrigerate until needed.

Makes about 2 cups

MUSHROOM-CHEESE SAUCE

5 tablespoons butter
8 ounces mushrooms, sliced (quartered and sliced if large)
6 green onions including some tender green tops, sliced
¼ cup all-purpose flour
1 cup Basic Chicken Stock (page 29) or reduced-sodium chicken broth
½ cup whole milk
1 cup (4 ounces) shredded Swiss cheese
2 tablespoons dry white wine
½ teaspoon dried thyme
½ teaspoon salt
Freshly ground pepper

In a large saucepan over medium heat, melt the butter. Add the mushrooms and onions and sauté until tender, about 5 minutes. Add the flour and stir until bubbly. Add the stock and milk and stir until thickened, about 2 minutes. Add the cheese, wine, thyme, salt, and pepper to taste. Stir until the cheese is melted. Set aside.

Makes about 2 cups

STUFFED CHICKEN BREASTS WITH PECANS

These stuffed chicken breasts, with a mushroom–cream cheese filling and a crunchy nut coating, are a standout. For easy entertaining, they can be made ahead and baked later. Serve with buttered broccoli for a bright color and flavor.

4 .boned and skinned chicken breast halves (about 2 pounds)
  Salt and freshly ground pepper
3 tablespoons butter, divided
4 ounces medium mushrooms, sliced
4 green onions including some tender green tops, sliced
3 ounces cream cheese, at room temperature

1½ teaspoons Dijon mustard
 2 tablespoons finely chopped fresh parsley
 ½ teaspoon dried thyme
 ¼ cup well-shaken buttermilk
 ½ cup finely chopped pecans
 ½ cup fine dried bread crumbs

Preheat the oven to 375°F. Place the chicken breasts between 2 sheets of plastic wrap and pound with the flat side of a meat mallet to ⅜ inch thick. Season generously with salt and pepper. In a medium skillet over high heat, melt 1 tablespoon of the butter. Add the mushrooms and onions and sauté until tender, about 5 minutes. Set aside.

In a small bowl, mix the cream cheese, Dijon, parsley, and thyme. Spread the mixture on 1 side of each chicken breast. Divide the mushroom mixture evenly on top. Roll the chicken up from the small end and secure with a toothpick.

Put the buttermilk in a pie plate. Mix together the pecans and crumbs on a piece of waxed paper. Roll the chicken breasts in the buttermilk and then in the nut-crumb mixture, covering completely. Place them seam-side down in a lightly sprayed or oiled 7-by-11-inch glass baking dish. Melt the remaining 2 tablespoons butter and drizzle it over the chicken breasts. Bake, uncovered, until the chicken is cooked through, about 35 minutes. Transfer the chicken rolls to a warmed platter and remove the toothpicks.

Makes 4 servings

CHICKEN SALTIMBOCCA

This is a variation of the famous Italian dish, veal saltimbocca, using chicken instead of the veal. Chicken is always available and is less expensive than veal, and it works well as an alternative.

4 boned and skinned chicken breast halves (about 2 pounds)
¼ cup all-purpose flour
½ teaspoon salt
Freshly ground pepper
4 thin slices mozzarella cheese
4 thin slices prosciutto

4 large fresh sage leaves, chopped, or 1 teaspoon dried sage
4 tablespoons (½ stick) butter, divided
½ cup dry white wine
½ cup Basic Chicken Stock (page 29) or reduced-sodium chicken broth
Sage leaves for garnish

Preheat the oven to 375°F. Place the chicken between 2 pieces of plastic wrap and pound with the flat side of a meat mallet to ⅜ inch thick. On a large piece of waxed paper, mix together the flour, salt, and pepper to taste and set aside. On each chicken breast, layer a slice of cheese, a slice of prosciutto, and a sprinkle of sage. Roll up from the small end and secure with a toothpick. Roll each breast in the flour mixture to coat evenly. (They can be made ahead up to this point.)

In a large skillet over medium-high heat, melt 3 tablespoons of the butter. Add the chicken and cook until lightly browned, about 5 minutes on each side. Transfer, seam-side down, to a lightly sprayed or oiled 7-by-11-inch glass baking dish and bake, uncovered, for 15 minutes.

Meanwhile, add the wine and stock to the same skillet over medium heat, stirring to loosen the browned bits. Boil for 2 minutes to reduce slightly. Whisk in the remaining 1 tablespoon butter, small pieces at a time, until the sauce is smooth. Pour the sauce over the chicken rolls, return to the oven, and bake, covered, until the chicken is cooked through, about 20 minutes longer.

Transfer the chicken rolls to a warmed platter and remove the toothpicks. Spoon the sauce over and garnish with sage leaves. Serve immediately.

Makes 4 servings

CHICKEN ROLLS, ITALIAN STYLE

Plan ahead for a dinner party with these enticing chicken breasts filled with prosciutto, mozzarella cheese, and pine nuts and baked in a well-seasoned tomato sauce. Serve with a mixed green salad and Italian dressing. This recipe can easily be doubled.

4 boned and skinned chicken breast halves (about 2 pounds)
Italian Filling (facing page)
1 tablespoon olive oil
Tomato Sauce (facing page)
½ cup (2 ounces) freshly grated Parmesan cheese

Preheat the oven to 375°F. Place the chicken breasts between 2 pieces of plastic wrap and pound with the flat side of a meat mallet to ⅜ inch thick. Divide the filling evenly between the chicken breasts. Roll up from the small end and secure with a toothpick.

In a large skillet over medium heat, warm the oil. Add the chicken rolls and cook until lightly browned, about 5 minutes on each side. Transfer to a lightly sprayed or oiled 2-quart casserole. Pour the sauce over the chicken and bake, covered, until the sauce is bubbly, about 30 minutes. Uncover, sprinkle with the Parmesan, and bake, uncovered, until the cheese melts, about 5 minutes longer. Transfer the chicken rolls to a warmed platter and remove the toothpicks.

Makes 4 to 6 servings

ITALIAN FILLING

½ cup (2 ounces) shredded mozzarella cheese
¼ cup chopped fresh flat-leaf parsley
2 ounces chopped prosciutto
¼ cup toasted pine nuts, chopped
2 tablespoons minced green onions including
    some tender green tops
1 tablespoon olive oil

To make the filling, mix together all the ingredients in a small bowl.

Makes about ¾ cup

TOMATO SAUCE

1 tablespoon olive oil
1 cup chopped yellow onion
1 large garlic clove, minced
1 can (15½ ounces) Italian-style tomatoes
¼ cup chopped fresh flat-leaf parsley
3 tablespoons dry red wine
1 teaspoon dried oregano
¼ teaspoon salt
    Freshly ground pepper

To make the sauce, in the same skillet used for browning the chicken rolls, over medium heat, add the oil. Add the onions and garlic and sauté until tender, about 5 minutes. Add the tomatoes, parsley, wine, oregano, salt, and pepper to taste. Simmer for 5 minutes. Transfer to a food processor and process until blended, but still slightly chunky.

Makes about 3 cups

CHICKEN CORDON BLEU

Cordon bleu is a classic dish of coated chicken breasts filled with prosciutto and cheese and usually fried. In this version, it is baked but still has the same inviting appeal and delicious flavor.

5 tablespoons butter
4 boned and skinned chicken breast halves (about 2 pounds)
1 teaspoon salt, divided
Freshly ground pepper
8 thin slices prosciutto

4 thin slices Gruyère or Swiss cheese
⅓ cup all-purpose flour
½ teaspoon dried thyme
2 large eggs, lightly beaten
2 teaspoons water
1 cup dried coarse bread crumbs

Preheat the oven to 350°F. Melt the butter in an 8-by-8-inch glass baking dish in the oven and set aside. Remove the dish from the oven. Place the chicken breasts between 2 pieces of plastic wrap and pound with the flat side of a meat mallet to ⅜ inch thick. Lay the chicken breasts on a flat surface and season with ½ teaspoon of the salt and pepper to taste. Layer each with 2 slices of prosciutto and 1 slice of cheese, leaving a ½-inch margin on all sides. Fold the breasts in half and secure with a toothpick. Combine the flour, thyme, remaining ½ teaspoon salt, and pepper to taste on a piece of waxed paper. In a shallow bowl, mix together the eggs and water. Place the crumbs on a piece of waxed paper. Coat each chicken breast with the flour mixture, shaking off the excess, then the egg mixture, and finally with the crumbs, patting them with your fingers to make the crumbs adhere. Place the chicken in the baking dish and turn to coat with butter. Bake until golden brown and cooked through, about 35 minutes, turning once. Transfer the chicken to a warmed platter and remove the toothpicks.

Makes 4 servings

SCOTT'S CHICKEN AND LAMB MEATLOAF

Chicken and lamb are low in fat and cholesterol and will appeal to those concerned with diet issues. Because chicken and lamb are both mild in flavor, some bold seasonings are added. My son Scott's favorite seasoning is soy sauce, and it works well here. This makes a large meatloaf with leftovers for delicious sandwiches the next day.

1½ pounds ground chicken
1½ pounds ground lamb
 1 cup diced celery
 ½ cup quick-cooking oats, finely chopped in a food processor
 ½ cup diced yellow onion
 1 medium tomato, chopped

1 large egg
1 tablespoon Worcestershire sauce
2 garlic cloves, minced
5 tablespoons soy sauce, divided (Scott uses more)

Preheat the oven to 350°F. In a medium bowl, mix together all the ingredients except 2 tablespoons of the soy sauce. Place in a lightly sprayed or oiled 7-by-11-inch glass baking dish. Spread the remaining 2 tablespoons soy sauce on top. Bake until firm and lightly browned, about 1 hour. Let stand for 10 minutes before serving. Cut into squares to serve.

Makes 6 to 8 servings

BAKED CHICKEN DIJON WITH SWISS CHEESE

Don't tell your guests how easy it is to make this simple, yet impressive, dish! Include a mushroom pilaf and a tossed green salad.

DIJON SAUCE

⅓ cup nonfat plain yogurt
2 tablespoons Dijon mustard
1 garlic clove, minced
¼ teaspoon dried thyme
¼ teaspoon salt
   Freshly ground pepper

8 boned and skinned chicken breast halves
   (about 4 pounds)
2 cups (8 ounces) shredded Swiss cheese

Preheat the oven to 350°F. To make the sauce, in a small bowl, mix together all the sauce ingredients. Place the chicken in a lightly sprayed or oiled 9-by-13-inch glass baking dish and spread the sauce on top.

Bake, uncovered, until the chicken is cooked through, about 35 minutes. Sprinkle with the cheese and bake until the cheese melts, about 5 minutes longer.

Makes 8 servings

CHICKEN IN TOMATO SAUCE ON POLENTA

In this rustic Italian dish, drumsticks and thighs bake in a well-seasoned sauce on top of a polenta base for a great meal. Serve with a tossed green salad and sourdough bread.

3½ cups Basic Chicken Stock (page 29) or reduced-sodium chicken broth
1 cup yellow cornmeal
1 to 2 tablespoons olive oil
4 chicken drumsticks (about 1 pound)
4 bone-in chicken thighs (about 1½ pounds)
¾ teaspoon salt, divided
Freshly ground pepper
1 cup chopped yellow onion
½ cup chopped red or green bell pepper

4 ounces mushrooms, sliced
1 garlic clove, minced
1 can (14½ ounces) Italian-style tomatoes, lightly puréed in a food processor
2 tablespoons tomato paste (see Note)
2 tablespoons dry red wine
½ teaspoon dried basil
¼ teaspoon dried oregano
½ cup (2 ounces) freshly grated Parmesan cheese

Preheat the oven to 375°F. In a lightly sprayed or oiled 9-by-13-inch glass baking dish, stir together the stock and cornmeal until mixed. Bake until firm, about 35 minutes.

In a large skillet over medium heat, warm 1 tablespoon of the oil. Add the chicken and cook until lightly browned on all sides, 10 to 15 minutes. Season with ¼ teaspoon of the salt and pepper to taste. Transfer to a plate. Add the onions, bell pepper, mushrooms, garlic, and more oil, if needed and sauté until tender, about 5 minutes. Add the tomatoes, tomato paste, wine, basil, oregano, and remaining ½ teaspoon salt, and simmer for 5 minutes. Lay the chicken on top of the baked polenta. Pour the sauce over it and sprinkle with the Parmesan. Bake, uncovered, until the chicken is no longer pink in the center, about 40 minutes. Let stand for 5 to 10 minutes before serving.

Makes 4 servings

NOTE: Tomato paste can be purchased in a tube and used as called for in the recipe. Keep refrigerated. Leftover tomato paste can be frozen.

BISTRO VEGETABLE STEW WITH DRUMSTICKS

Here is a big pot of fresh vegetables combined with chicken drumsticks for a cozy winter meal. Drumsticks appeal to those who prefer dark meat. Serve with a tossed green salad, warm croissants, and red wine.

½ cup all-purpose flour
1 teaspoon salt, divided
   Freshly ground pepper
3 tablespoons olive oil, divided
8 chicken drumsticks (about 2 pounds)
1 cup chopped yellow onion
4 ounces medium mushrooms, quartered
3 carrots, cut diagonally into 1-inch slices
2 celery stalks, cut into 1-inch slices
2 garlic cloves, minced

2 cups Basic Chicken Stock (page 29) or reduced-sodium chicken broth
4 small new potatoes (about 1 pound), unpeeled, scrubbed, and halved
1 can (14½ ounces) whole tomatoes including juice, chopped
1 teaspoon dried basil
½ teaspoon dried rosemary
¼ cup cold water

Preheat the oven to 350°F. On a piece of waxed paper, combine the flour, ½ teaspoon of the salt, and pepper to taste. Add the chicken and turn to coat. Reserve the remaining flour mixture. In a Dutch oven over medium-high heat, warm 2 tablespoons of the oil. Add the drumsticks and cook until lightly browned on all sides, 10 to 15 minutes, turning often. Transfer them to a plate. Add the remaining 1 tablespoon oil and sauté the onions, mushrooms, carrots, celery, and garlic until tender, about 5 minutes. Return the chicken to the pan. Add the stock, potatoes, tomatoes, seasonings, and remaining ½ teaspoon salt. Bake, covered, until the chicken is cooked through and the vegetables are tender, about 1 hour. To thicken the sauce, in a small bowl, mix together 2½ tablespoons of the remaining flour with ¼ cup cold water. Add to the sauce and stir until thickened, about 1 minute.

Makes 4 servings

BAKED CHICKEN THIGHS AND RICE
WITH HONEY-MUSTARD SAUCE

For fast flavor, these thighs are baked on a bed of rice, then highlighted with a sweet mustard sauce for an easy weekend meal. Serve with steamed spinach.

1 cup uncooked long-grain white rice

8 boned and skinned chicken thighs (about 3 pounds)

Salt and freshly ground pepper

2¼ cups Basic Chicken Stock (page 29) or reduced-sodium chicken broth, hot

¾ cup nonfat plain yogurt

¼ cup honey

2 tablespoons Dijon mustard

2 tablespoons soy sauce

½ teaspoon ground ginger

Preheat the oven to 350°F. Spread the rice in a lightly sprayed or oiled 2-quart casserole. Arrange the thighs on top and sprinkle them with salt and pepper. Pour the stock over. Bake, covered, for 40 minutes.

In a medium bowl, whisk together the yogurt, honey, Dijon, soy sauce, and ginger. Spread the yogurt mixture over the chicken and rice. Bake, uncovered, until the rice is tender and the chicken is cooked through, about 10 minutes longer.

Makes 4 servings

ROASTED CHICKEN THIGHS AND VEGETABLES

Roasting the chicken and vegetables together at a high temperature is another way to flavor chicken. It also brings out the intense, natural flavors of the vegetables.

8   boned and skinned chicken thighs (about 3 pounds)

6   small new potatoes (about 1½ pounds), unpeeled, scrubbed, and halved

2   red bell peppers, cut into 1-inch strips

½   yellow onion, cut into ½-inch wedges

2   tablespoons olive oil

4 to 6   garlic cloves, halved

½   teaspoon dried thyme

Salt and freshly ground pepper

¼   cup dry white wine

Preheat the oven to 400°F. In a large bowl, toss all the ingredients together except the wine and arrange in a 9-by-13-inch glass baking dish.

Roast the chicken and vegetables for about 30 minutes. Turn the chicken over and pour the wine on top. Bake until the chicken is no longer pink in the center and the vegetables are tender-crisp, about 10 minutes longer.

Makes 4 to 6 servings

CHICKEN THIGHS WITH SPICY ORANGE SAUCE

For those who don't want to spend a lot of time in the kitchen, here is a recipe for you. A sweet-tart sauce with spices and soy sauce is simply poured over the thighs and baked. Rice makes a good accompaniment served with additional soy sauce.

ORANGE-SOY SAUCE

¾ cup fresh orange juice
3 tablespoons brown sugar
2 tablespoons soy sauce
1 tablespoon fresh lemon juice
1 teaspoon grated orange zest
1 teaspoon salt
½ teaspoon paprika
½ teaspoon ground ginger
   Dash nutmeg
   Freshly ground pepper

6 boned and skinned chicken thighs (about 2 pounds)
1 tablespoon cornstarch
2 tablespoons water
1 orange, sliced, for garnish
   Parsley sprigs for garnish

To make the sauce, in a saucepan over medium heat, stir the sauce ingredients together until the sugar dissolves and the flavors are blended, about 1 minute.

Preheat the oven to 350°F. Place the chicken in a lightly sprayed or oiled 7-by-11-inch glass baking dish. Pour the sauce over the chicken. Cover and bake for 15 minutes. Uncover, baste with the sauce, and continue to bake, uncovered, until the chicken is cooked through, about 15 minutes longer. Pour the sauce into a small pan over medium heat. Blend the cornstarch and water and stir into the sauce. Stir until thickened, about 1 minute. Transfer the chicken to a plate and pour the sauce over it. Garnish with orange slices and parsley.

Makes 4 servings

CHICKEN THIGHS WITH MANGO AND KIWI

Here, skinned chicken thighs bake with an Asian-inspired sauce and are then garnished with exotic fruit for an appealing presentation. Mangos originated in India, where they were once considered sacred. Now they are grown in warm climates around the world, including California and Florida, and are available year-round. The kiwi fruit is named after the kiwi bird. It looks like an egg with a covering of downy hair. Inside, it is a beautiful green with tiny seeds and a lovely fruity flavor.

8   bone-in chicken thighs (about 3 pounds), skin removed
½   cup fresh orange juice
¼   cup soy sauce
¼   cup water
2   teaspoons cornstarch
¼   teaspoon sugar

¼   cup chopped green onions including some tender green tops
¼   cup chopped unsalted cashews
1   kiwi, peeled and sliced, for garnish
1   mango, peeled, pitted, and sliced, for garnish

Preheat the oven to 350°F. Arrange the chicken in a lightly sprayed or oiled 7-by-11-inch glass baking dish.

In a small pan over medium heat, stir together the orange juice, soy sauce, water, cornstarch, and sugar and stir until the mixture bubbles and thickens, about 5 minutes. Pour over the chicken. Sprinkle the onions and cashews on top.

Bake, uncovered, until the chicken is no longer pink in the center, about 40 minutes. Baste with the sauce once while baking. Transfer to a platter and arrange the fruit around the chicken.

Makes 4 to 6 servings

APRICOT-CRANBERRY THIGHS

If you're looking for an alternative for a big turkey dinner for the holidays, try these meaty, moist chicken thighs with a sweet-tart topping. Bake sweet potatoes alongside and serve with additional cranberry sauce.

1 tablespoon butter
8 boned and skinned chicken thighs (about 3 pounds)
   Salt and freshly ground pepper
½ cup apricot preserves
½ cup homemade or purchased cranberry sauce
1 tablespoon cider vinegar
1 teaspoon ground mustard

Preheat the oven to 350°F. Melt the butter in a 7-by-11-inch glass baking dish in the oven. Add the chicken thighs and turn to coat. Season with salt and pepper to taste on all sides. Bake, covered, for 20 minutes.

In a medium bowl, mix together the apricot preserves, cranberry sauce, vinegar, and mustard. Spread over the chicken. Bake, uncovered, until the chicken is cooked through, about 10 minutes longer. Transfer to a plate and spoon some of the accumulated sauce in the dish over the chicken.

Makes 4 servings

BAKED CHICKEN REUBEN

This recipe was inspired by the famous Reuben sandwich, reportedly named for its creator, Arthur Reuben, owner of a once-famous New York delicatessen no longer in operation. If you like a Reuben sandwich, you will like this chicken with layers of sauerkraut, corned beef, and cheese. All of the good flavors are blended together as it bakes in the oven.

1 jar (16 ounces) sauerkraut, drained
1 teaspoon caraway seeds
½ teaspoon paprika
¼ teaspoon salt
  Freshly ground pepper

8 boned and skinned chicken thighs (about 3 pounds)
4 ounces thinly sliced corned beef
1 cup Thousand Island Dressing (page 89)
1½ cups (6 ounces) shredded Swiss cheese

In a medium bowl, mix together the sauerkraut, caraway seeds, paprika, salt, and pepper to taste. Place the thighs in a lightly sprayed or oiled 7-by-11-inch glass baking dish. Layer the corned beef on top of the chicken and cover with the sauerkraut mixture. Spread a light coating of dressing over all. Cover and bake for 30 minutes. Uncover and sprinkle the cheese on top. Bake until the chicken is no longer pink in the center and the cheese is melted, about 5 minutes longer.

Makes 4 to 6 servings

CHICKEN WITH SWEET POTATOES AND OKRA

This is a simplified version of a typical West African dish with a delicious peanut-flavored sauce, served over rice. Dark meat is typically called for in this recipe.

2 tablespoons peanut oil

3½ pounds bone-in chicken thighs and drumsticks (4 of each), excess fat and skin trimmed

1 cup chopped yellow onion

3 garlic cloves, chopped

1 can (14½ ounces) whole tomatoes, juice poured off and used for another purpose

1 cup Basic Chicken Stock (page 29) or reduced-sodium chicken broth

½ cup smooth peanut butter

¼ cup tomato purée

1 teaspoon salt

¼ teaspoon cayenne

1 large, dark orange sweet potato (¾ to 1 pound), peeled and cut into ½-inch chunks

1 package (10 ounces) frozen okra, thawed, rinsed, and dried

1 cup long-grain white rice, cooked according to package directions (3 cups cooked)

Preheat the oven to 350°F. In a large Dutch oven over medium heat, warm the oil. Add the chicken and cook it in batches until lightly browned on all sides, 10 to 15 minutes, turning often. Transfer it to a plate. To the same skillet, add the onions and garlic and sauté until tender, about 5 minutes.

In a food processor, add the tomatoes, stock, peanut butter, tomato purée, salt, and cayenne and process until smooth. Return the chicken to the pan. Pour the sauce over all. Bake, covered, for 20 minutes. Add the potatoes and okra and cook until the chicken is no longer pink in the center and the vegetables are tender, about 20 minutes longer. Serve over rice.

Makes 6 to 8 servings

CHICKEN AND FENNEL STEW, MEDITERRANEAN STYLE

This classic combination of thighs and drumsticks with fennel benefits from the flavor of olives and seasonings that give this dish a Mediterranean accent. Fennel is a vegetable with a bulblike base and celerylike stalks with a feathery green foliage that can be used as a garnish. Here, the fennel imparts a subtle licorice flavor that complements the chicken.

1 to 2 tablespoons olive oil, divided

4 chicken drumsticks (about 1 pound)

4 bone-in chicken thighs (about 1½ pounds)
Salt and freshly ground pepper

1 large fennel bulb, stalks and foliage removed (reserve some foliage for garnish), bulb thinly sliced lengthwise

1 cup chopped yellow onion

1 red bell pepper, sliced into strips

8 ounces mushrooms, halved

2 garlic cloves, minced

1 can (14½ ounces) whole tomatoes including juice, cut up

½ cup Basic Chicken Stock (page 29) or reduced-sodium chicken broth

2 tablespoons fresh lemon juice

1 teaspoon dried oregano

2 tablespoons all-purpose flour

¼ cup water

¼ cup pitted kalamata olives, drained

Preheat the oven to 350°F. In a Dutch oven over medium-high heat, warm 1 tablespoon of the oil. Add the drumsticks and thighs and cook until lightly browned on all sides, 10 to 15 minutes, turning often. Season with salt and pepper to taste while cooking. Transfer the chicken to a plate.

Reduce the heat to medium and sauté the fennel, onions, bell pepper, mushrooms, and garlic until tender, about 5 minutes. Add more oil if needed. Add the tomatoes, stock, lemon juice, and oregano and mix well. Return the chicken to the Dutch oven. Bake, covered, until the chicken is no longer pink in the center and the vegetables are tender, about 30 minutes. In a small bowl, blend the flour and water and stir into the stew until slightly thickened, about 1 minute. Add more salt, if needed. Add the olives and cook, uncovered, 5 minutes longer. Garnish each serving with a sprig of fennel foliage.

Makes 4 servings

BAKED CRUNCHY COATED DRUMSTICKS AND THIGHS

This appeals to many cooks because the thighs and drumsticks are rolled in a flavorful coating and then baked without browning. They are also good cold and are easily transported for a summer outing. A pasta salad is a good accompaniment.

½ cup nonfat plain yogurt

1 tablespoon Dijon mustard

¾ teaspoon salt

Freshly ground pepper

1½ cups fine dried bread crumbs

¼ cup (1 ounce) freshly grated Parmesan cheese

¼ cup chopped fresh parsley

2 tablespoons sesame seeds

½ teaspoon dried basil

½ teaspoon dried rosemary

½ teaspoon dried thyme

¼ teaspoon paprika

3 pounds bone-in chicken thighs and drumsticks, excess fat and skin trimmed

Preheat the oven to 375ºF. In a pie plate, mix the yogurt, mustard, salt, and pepper to taste. On a piece of waxed paper or a plate, combine the remaining ingredients except the chicken. Dip the chicken in the yogurt mixture, then in the crumb mixture. Place it in a lightly sprayed or oiled 9-by-13-inch glass baking dish. Bake until the chicken is no longer pink in the center and the coating is lightly browned and crispy, about 45 minutes. Serve hot or cold.

Makes 4 to 6 servings

HERBED PARMESAN DRUMSTICKS

Crispy drumsticks are equally delicious served hot or cold and are a popular finger food at parties or picnics. Kids love them.

½ cup (1 stick) butter

¾ cup fine dried bread crumbs (sourdough preferred)

½ cup all-purpose flour

½ cup (2 ounces) freshly grated Parmesan cheese

1 teaspoon dried marjoram

1 teaspoon dried basil

1 teaspoon dried oregano

¾ teaspoon salt

Freshly ground pepper

¾ cup well-shaken buttermilk

12 drumsticks (about 3½ pounds)

Preheat the oven to 375°F. Melt the butter in the oven in a jelly-roll pan and remove the pan when melted. On a large piece of waxed paper, combine the crumbs, flour, cheese, herbs, salt, and pepper to taste. Put the buttermilk in a shallow bowl. Dip the chicken in the buttermilk, then roll it in the crumb mixture to coat. Put the chicken in the pan, turning to coat all sides with the butter. Bake until the chicken is cooked through and crispy, about 45 minutes, turning once.

Makes 4 to 6 servings

CHICKEN THIGHS AND MUSHROOMS IN TOMATO SAUCE

My two teenage grandsons stopped by at about two o'clock when I was preparing this dish. As they looked longingly at the food, I said, "Are you guys hungry?" Yes, they were, so I finished it up, cooked some noodles, and fed them our dinner. Then we went out. That's what grandmas are for!

1 tablespoon vegetable oil, divided

4 bone-in chicken thighs (about 1½ pounds), excess fat and skin trimmed

½ teaspoon salt, divided
Freshly ground pepper

½ cup chopped yellow onion

8 ounces mushrooms, sliced

½ cup chopped red bell pepper

1 garlic clove, minced

1 can (14½ ounces) whole tomatoes, slightly puréed in a food processor

¼ cup red wine

1 teaspoon dried Italian seasoning

½ cup (2 ounces) shredded mozzarella cheese

1 tablespoon freshly grated Parmesan cheese

Preheat the oven to 350°F. In a medium skillet over medium heat, warm ½ tablespoon of the oil. Add the thighs and cook until lightly browned, about 5 minutes on each side. Season with ¼ teaspoon salt and pepper to taste. Transfer them to a 2-quart casserole. Add the remaining ½ tablespoon oil. Add the onions, mushrooms, bell pepper, and garlic and sauté until tender, 6 to 7 minutes. Add the tomatoes, wine, Italian seasoning, and remaining ¼ teaspoon salt, and mix well. Pour over the thighs. Bake, covered, until the chicken is no longer pink in the center, about 40 minutes. Sprinkle with the cheeses and bake, uncovered, until the cheeses melt, about 5 minutes longer.

Makes 4 servings

ROASTED WHOLE CHICKEN DIJON AND VEGETABLES

"Chicken every Sunday" was a special custom with some families in years past. Today, chicken is so plentiful, it is served several times a week in a variety of ways. Here chicken and vegetables are roasted together in one pan for a simple, yet delicious, meal.

1   chicken (3½ to 4 pounds), giblets removed, excess fat and skin trimmed
    Salt and freshly ground pepper
3   tablespoons butter
½   cup dry white wine
1   tablespoon Dijon mustard

1   tablespoon chopped fresh tarragon or 1 teaspoon dried tarragon
1   garlic clove, minced
3   new potatoes (about 12 ounces), unpeeled, scrubbed, and halved
2 or 3   carrots, cut diagonally into ¾-inch slices

Preheat the oven to 350°F. In a shallow roasting pan with a rack, place the chicken breast-side up and tuck the wings under the back. Sprinkle the chicken cavity with salt and pepper to taste. In a small saucepan over medium-low heat, melt the butter. Whisk in the wine, Dijon, tarragon, and garlic. Pour over the chicken.

Bake, uncovered, for 20 minutes. Add the potatoes and carrots to the pan and spoon the pan juices over the chicken and vegetables. Bake, uncovered, until the chicken is lightly browned and no longer pink in the center or a meat thermometer inserted in the thigh registers 180°F and the vegetables are tender, about 70 minutes longer. Transfer to a platter and arrange the vegetables around the chicken. Spoon the pan juices over everything. Let stand for 10 to 15 minutes before carving.

Makes 4 servings

HERB-ROASTED WHOLE CHICKEN

A simple herb butter baste ensures a moist, tender whole chicken while roasting. Bake acorn squash along with the chicken and serve with cranberry sauce for a delicious fall dinner.

1 chicken (3½ to 4 pounds), giblets removed, excess fat and skin trimmed
Salt and freshly ground pepper
½ yellow onion, quartered
1 celery stalk, cut up
1 garlic clove, minced

3 tablespoons butter
½ teaspoon dried basil
½ teaspoon dried sage
½ teaspoon dried thyme
Sage leaves for garnish

Preheat the oven to 350°F. In a shallow roasting pan with a rack, place the chicken breast-side up and tuck the wings under the back. Sprinkle the cavity with salt and pepper to taste. Place the onions, celery, and garlic in the cavity.

In a small pan, melt the butter with the seasonings. Brush it all over the chicken. Roast the chicken until lightly browned and no longer pink in the center or a meat thermometer inserted in the thigh registers 180°F, about 1½ hours. Let stand for 10 to 15 minutes before carving. Garnish with sage leaves.

Makes 4 servings

WHOLE CHICKEN WITH
SAGE DRESSING AND RICH GRAVY

You don't have to wait for the holidays to have this wonderful treat any time of the year. Stuff the chicken with the flavorful dressing and bake the remaining dressing in a casserole for a side dish. Serve with gravy and fluffy mashed potatoes.

1   chicken (3½ to 4 pounds), giblets removed, excess fat and skin trimmed
    Sage Dressing (facing page)
3   tablespoons butter, melted
    Salt and freshly ground pepper

¼   cup Basic Chicken Stock (page 29) or reduced-sodium chicken broth
½   cup dry white wine or water
    Rich Pan Gravy (facing page)

Preheat the oven to 350°F. Rinse the chicken inside and out under cold water and pat dry with paper towels. Loosely stuff the chicken cavity with dressing. Put the remaining dressing in a lightly sprayed or oiled 2-quart casserole dish and bake, covered, along with the chicken, until heated through, 35 to 40 minutes. In a shallow roasting pan with a rack, place the chicken breast-side up and tuck the wings under the back. Brush all over with the butter and sprinkle with salt and pepper to taste. Roast the chicken for 30 minutes. Pour the stock and wine over the chicken. Bake until no longer pink in the center or a meat thermometer inserted in the thigh registers 180°F, about 45 minutes longer. Remove the chicken from the pan to a platter. Let stand for 10 to 15 minutes before carving. Remove dressing from the cavity and place in a bowl. Pour off the pan juices to make the gravy.

Makes 4 to 6 servings

SAGE DRESSING

A classic bread stuffing or dressing.

8 to 10 cups day-old bread (sourdough preferred), cut into ½-inch cubes
½ cup (1 stick) butter
1 large yellow onion, chopped
2 celery stalks, chopped
2 garlic cloves, minced
1 cup Basic Chicken Stock (page 29) or reduced-sodium chicken broth
¼ cup minced fresh parsley
1 tablespoon minced fresh sage or 1 teaspoon ground sage
½ teaspoon dried thyme
½ teaspoon salt
Freshly ground pepper

In a large bowl, place the bread. In a medium skillet over medium heat, melt the butter. Add the onions, celery, and garlic and sauté until tender, 5 minutes. Stir in the stock, parsley, sage, thyme, salt, and pepper to taste. Pour over the bread and mix well.

Makes about 1½ quarts

RICH PAN GRAVY

Pan juices from a roasted chicken plus chicken stock will make about 2 cups total.

¼ cup all-purpose flour
½ cup water or cold chicken stock
Salt and freshly ground pepper

Place the roasting pan used for the chicken over medium heat. Add the juices and stock to the pan. In a small bowl or cup, whisk together the flour and water until blended. Add to the juices and whisk constantly until the sauce thickens, 1 to 2 minutes. Season with salt and pepper to taste.

Makes about 2 cups

NOTE: For a richer gravy, add 1 tablespoon butter and stir until melted.

ROASTED WHOLE CHICKEN WITH LEMON-THYME SAUCE

Thyme and lemon are perfect partners for roasted chicken. Fresh thyme is available in most supermarkets, as is dried thyme. Bake the new potatoes in the pan along with the chicken.

1 whole chicken (about 4 pounds), giblets removed, excess fat and skin trimmed
Juice of 1 lemon (reserve juiced lemon halves for cavity)
3 tablespoons butter
¼ cup chopped green onions including some tender green tops
Grated zest from ½ lemon

½ cup dry white wine
1 teaspoon paprika
1 teaspoon salt
Freshly ground pepper
¼ cup fresh thyme leaves or 1 tablespoon dried thyme, plus several sprigs for garnish
4 or 5 white new potatoes (about 2 pounds), scrubbed and quartered

Preheat the oven to 350°F. In a shallow roasting pan with a rack, place the chicken breast-side up. Add lemon halves to the cavity. Tuck the wings under the back and tie the legs together with twine. In a medium pan over medium heat, melt the butter. Add the onions and saute for 3 minutes. Add the zest, juice, wine, paprika, salt, pepper to taste, and thyme and cook 2 minutes longer. Pour half of the sauce over the chicken. Bake, uncovered, for 30 minutes. Add the potatoes to the pan. Place several thyme sprigs on top of the chicken. Pour the remaining sauce over the chicken and potatoes. Bake until the chicken is no longer pink in the center or a meat thermometer registers 180°F and the potatoes are tender, about 45 minutes longer. Transfer the chicken and potatoes to a platter and spoon some of the sauce over all. Let stand for 10 minutes before carving.

Makes 4 servings

ROASTED WHOLE CHICKEN WITH ORANGE-TERIYAKI SAUCE

The flavors of orange and soy are a good match to enhance the chicken as it bakes. Include Chinese noodles or rice as accompaniments.

MARINADE

½ cup sweet orange marmalade
¼ cup soy sauce
¼ cup fresh orange juice
1 tablespoon grated orange zest
1 tablespoon peeled grated fresh ginger
1 garlic clove, minced

1 chicken (3½ to 4 pounds), giblets removed, excess fat and skin trimmed
2 tablespoons cornstarch
3 tablespoons water

In a deep bowl large enough to hold the chicken, whisk together the marinade ingredients. Add the chicken and turn to coat. Cover and refrigerate for 3 to 4 hours, turning several times.

Preheat the oven to 350°F. Remove the chicken from the marinade. In a shallow roasting pan with a rack, place the chicken breast-side up and tuck the wings under the back. Pour the marinade over the chicken and roast until the chicken is no longer pink in the center or until a meat thermometer inserted in the thigh registers 180°F, about 1½ hours, basting once with the juices in the pan. Transfer to a platter and let stand for 10 to 15 minutes before carving.

To make the sauce, pour the pan juices into a small pan over medium heat. In a small bowl, mix together the cornstarch and water. Stir into the pan juices until thickened, about 2 minutes. Serve with the chicken.

Makes 4 to 6 servings

CHICKEN AND MUSHROOM CRÊPES

For a brunch or luncheon on a special occasion, serve these chicken-filled crêpes, baked in a cream cheese sauce. Baking eliminates the last-minute preparation of making the crêpes one by one. Allow one hour for the crêpe batter to set before using.

3 tablespoons butter	½ teaspoon salt
¼ cup chopped yellow onion	Freshly ground pepper
4 ounces mushrooms, sliced	2 tablespoons dry white wine
3 tablespoons all-purpose flour	¼ cup (1 ounce) freshly grated Parmesan cheese
1½ cups Basic Chicken Stock (page 29) or reduced-sodium chicken broth	2½ cups cubed cooked chicken breast
½ cup half-and-half or milk	Basic Crêpes (facing page)

Preheat the oven to 350°F. In a medium saucepan over medium heat, melt the butter. Add the onions and mushrooms and sauté until tender, about 5 minutes. Add the flour and stir until bubbly. Add the stock, half-and-half, salt, and pepper to taste and stir constantly until thickened, 2 to 3 minutes. Add the wine and Parmesan and blend. Set aside.

To assemble, fill each crêpe down the middle with some chicken and about ¼ cup of sauce, including some mushrooms. Roll up and place seam-side down in a lightly sprayed or oiled 7-by-11-inch glass baking dish. Pour the remaining sauce over the rolled crêpes. Bake, uncovered, until heated through and bubbly, about 25 minutes.

Makes 5 servings of 2 crepes each

BASIC CRÊPES

Don't be afraid to try making crêpes; they are easy and quick to make. Cooking times may vary, depending on the stove.

  2 large eggs
1¼ cups whole milk
  1 cup all-purpose flour
  1 tablespoon butter, melted
¼ teaspoon salt

Blender method: Place all the ingredients in a blender and pulse several times. Scrape down the sides with a spatula, then blend for 30 seconds. Transfer to a pitcher. Let stand for 1 hour or longer before cooking.

Bowl method: In a medium bowl, using an electric mixer, beat the eggs with the milk. Add the flour, butter, and salt and beat until well blended. Let stand for 1 hour or longer before cooking.

To cook: Preheat an 8-inch nonstick skillet over medium heat and lightly spray or oil it. Pour 3 tablespoons of the batter into the skillet. Quickly lift the pan off the burner and tilt it all around until the batter covers the bottom of the skillet. Cook until the top is dry and the underside is lightly browned, about 1 minute. Turn over carefully with a rubber spatula and cook for about 30 seconds longer. Remove from the pan and stack the crêpes on a plate between squares of parchment paper, unless using immediately. Repeat with the remaining batter.

Makes 10 crêpes

CASSEROLES

"Casserole" refers to both the baking dish and the ingredients it contains. Casserole recipes are convenient to make because they are cooked and served in the same dish—from the oven to the table—with very little cleanup. Many can be made ahead and baked later or frozen.

This chapter offers a large selection of casseroles for family and friends for any occasion. Chicken casseroles consist of pieces of chicken combined with complementary ingredients such as vegetables, beans, rice, pasta, and other meats, baked in a flavorful sauce or broth and often topped with cheese or crumbs.

Choose from such recipes as Cashew Chicken and Brown Rice; Chicken, Broccoli, and Artichoke Casserole; Chicken, Vegetable, and Pasta Casserole; Chicken, Ham, and Fennel Casserole; Chicken with Chile-Cheese Rice; Fiesta Casserole; and Chicken and Chile Egg Puff.

CHICKEN, MUSHROOM, AND RICE CASSEROLE WITH PARMESAN CHEESE SAUCE

This make-ahead casserole is for the cook who likes to entertain without last-minute preparations. Serve with steamed asparagus and a tossed green salad.

2 cups Basic Chicken Stock (page 29) or reduced-sodium chicken broth
1 cup uncooked long-grain white rice
2 to 3 tablespoons butter
8 ounces mushrooms, sliced
½ red bell pepper, chopped
¼ cup slivered almonds

2 tablespoons chopped yellow onion
¼ cup chopped fresh parsley
1 tablespoon chopped fresh basil or ¾ teaspoon dried basil
3 to 4 cups cubed cooked chicken
Parmesan Cheese Sauce (facing page)
Salt and freshly ground pepper

In a medium saucepan over high heat, bring the stock to a boil. Add the rice, reduce the temperature to low, and cook, covered, until the liquid is absorbed, about 20 minutes. Spread out in a lightly sprayed or oiled 2-quart casserole.

Preheat the oven to 350°F. In a medium skillet over medium heat, melt the butter. Add the mushrooms, bell pepper, almonds, and onions and sauté until the vegetables are tender, about 5 minutes. Stir in the parsley and basil. Add the mixture to the rice in the casserole along with the chicken. Stir in the Parmesan Cheese Sauce and mix well. Season with salt and pepper to taste. Bake, covered, until bubbly, about 30 minutes.

Makes 6 servings

PARMESAN CHEESE SAUCE

3   tablespoons butter
3   tablespoons all-purpose flour
¼   teaspoon salt
¼   teaspoon white pepper
¾   cup Basic Chicken Stock (page 29) or
    reduced-sodium chicken broth
1   cup whole milk
¼   cup (1 ounce) freshly grated Parmesan cheese
2   tablespoons dry white wine
½   cup sour cream

In a saucepan over medium-high heat, melt the butter. Add the flour, salt, and pepper and stir until bubbly. Add the stock and stir until thickened, about 2 minutes. Add the milk, cheese, and wine and stir until smooth and the flavors are blended, about 2 minutes longer. Remove from the heat and whisk in the sour cream.

Makes about 2 cups

CHICKEN, RICE, MUSHROOM, AND TOMATO CASSEROLE

This casserole has it all—starch, vegetables, and protein. Make it when you have leftover rotisserie chicken. It can be made ahead and baked later. Bring to room temperature before baking.

2	tablespoons vegetable oil
1	cup chopped yellow onion
½	red bell pepper, chopped
1	celery stalk, chopped
8	ounces mushrooms, sliced
½	cup uncooked long-grain white rice
1	can (14½ ounces) whole tomatoes including juice, chopped
1	cup Basic Chicken Stock (page 29) or reduced-sodium chicken broth
½	teaspoon dried thyme
½	teaspoon dried marjoram
½	teaspoon salt
	Freshly ground pepper
1½	cups cubed cooked chicken

Preheat the oven to 350°F. In a large skillet over medium heat, warm the oil. Add the onions, bell pepper, celery, and mushrooms and sauté until tender, 6 to 7 minutes. Stir in the rice. Add the tomatoes, stock, thyme, marjoram, salt, and pepper to taste and simmer, uncovered, for 5 minutes. Add the chicken and mix well.

Transfer to a lightly sprayed or oiled 2-quart casserole. Cover and bake until the liquid is absorbed and the rice is tender, about 45 minutes. Let stand for 5 to 10 minutes before serving.

Makes 4 servings

SPINACH-RICE CASSEROLE WITH CHICKEN

This recipe is adapted from my "Famous Spinach-Rice Casserole" that appeared in one of my earlier cookbooks. It has been so popular that I have added chicken to make it a complete entrée.

3 large eggs
⅔ cup whole milk
½ cup finely chopped yellow onion
2 tablespoons butter, melted
2 tablespoons chopped fresh parsley
1 teaspoon dried thyme
1 teaspoon salt
¼ teaspoon Worcestershire sauce

2 packages (10 ounces each) frozen chopped spinach, thawed and squeezed dry
2 cups chopped cooked chicken breast
3 cups (12 ounces) shredded Cheddar cheese, divided
1 cup long-grain white or brown rice, cooked according to package directions (3 cups cooked)

Preheat the oven to 350°F. In a large bowl, whisk the eggs until blended. Add the milk, onions, butter, parsley, thyme, salt, and Worcestershire sauce and mix well. Stir in the spinach, chicken, 2 cups of the cheese, and the rice. Turn the mixture into a lightly sprayed or oiled 3-quart casserole or baking dish.

Bake, uncovered, until bubbly, about 45 minutes. Sprinkle the remaining 1 cup cheese over the top and bake, uncovered, until the cheese melts, about 5 minutes longer.

Makes 4 to 6 servings

SUPER BOWL CASSEROLE

This combination of chicken, tomato sauce, creamy cheeses, and noodles is a perfect dish to serve for a tailgate party or TV game–watching at home. Pass assorted breads and crudités.

6 ounces egg noodles (about 4 cups), cooked according to package directions, drained
1 can (15 ounces) tomato sauce
½ cup chopped red bell pepper
1 teaspoon salt
½ teaspoon dried basil
¼ teaspoon dried thyme
Freshly ground pepper

1 cup cottage cheese
4 ounces cream cheese
½ cup sour cream
2 cups cubed cooked chicken
8 green onions including some tender green tops, sliced
2 cups (8 ounces) shredded Cheddar cheese

Preheat the oven to 350°F. Put the noodles in a lightly sprayed or oiled 2-quart casserole. In a medium saucepan over medium heat, combine the tomato sauce, bell pepper, salt, basil, thyme, and pepper to taste, and simmer for 5 minutes.

In a food processor, puree the cottage cheese, cream cheese, and sour cream until smooth. Add the cheese mixture and the tomato mixture to the noodles and mix well. Fold in the chicken and onions. Sprinkle the Cheddar cheese on top. Bake, covered, for 30 minutes. Uncover and bake until bubbly, about 10 minutes longer. Let stand for 5 to 10 minutes before serving.

Makes 6 servings

CHICKEN, VEGETABLE, AND PASTA CASSEROLE

This combination makes a complete oven meal when you have leftover chicken. Serve with a salad of baby greens with a vinaigrette.

2   medium zucchini, halved lengthwise and cut into ½-inch slices (about 3 cups)
8   ounces medium mushrooms, quartered
½   red bell pepper, cut into large bite-sized pieces
6   green onions including some tender green tops, sliced
½   teaspoon salt
    Freshly ground pepper
2   cups Tomato Sauce (page 247)
8   ounces (2¼ cups) ziti, cooked according to package directions, drained
1½ cups cubed cooked chicken
1   cup (4 ounces) shredded mozzarella cheese

Preheat the oven to 350°F. In a medium saucepan over medium heat, bring salted water to a boil. Simmer the zucchini, mushrooms, bell pepper, and onions, covered, until tender-crisp, 3 to 4 minutes. Drain well, return to the pan, and season with the salt and pepper to taste. Mix in the tomato sauce.

Put the pasta in a lightly sprayed or oiled 2-quart casserole. Add the vegetable mixture and chicken and mix well. Bake, covered, until bubbly, about 30 minutes. Stir and sprinkle with the cheese and bake, uncovered, 10 minutes longer.

Makes 6 to 8 servings

CHICKEN, BROCCOLI, AND RICE CASSEROLE

In this "all-in-one" casserole, chicken pieces and chopped broccoli are combined with seasoned rice and bound together with a creamy sauce. This is a dish your family will enjoy.

1 cup uncooked long-grain white rice

2¼ cups Basic Chicken Stock (page 29) or reduced-sodium chicken broth

½ teaspoon dried oregano

½ teaspoon dried basil

1 teaspoon salt

Freshly ground pepper

2 tablespoons vegetable oil, divided

4 boned and skinned chicken breast halves (about 2 pounds)

½ cup chopped yellow onion

2 garlic cloves, minced

2 tablespoons all-purpose flour

2¼ cups whole milk

3 ounces cream cheese, cut up

½ cup (2 ounces) freshly grated Parmesan cheese

1 cup chopped frozen broccoli, thawed

½ cup chopped walnuts

Preheat the oven to 350°F. In a medium saucepan over medium-high heat, cook the rice with the stock, oregano, basil, salt, and pepper to taste, covered, until the rice is tender and the liquid is absorbed, about 20 minutes. Transfer to a lightly sprayed or oiled 9-by-13-inch glass baking dish.

In a large skillet over medium heat, warm 1 tablespoon of the oil. Add the chicken and cook until lightly browned, about 5 minutes on each side. Arrange the chicken on top of the rice. In the same skillet, add the remaining 1 tablespoon oil and sauté the onions and garlic until tender, about 5 minutes. Add the flour and stir until bubbly, about 1 minute. Add the milk and stir until slightly thickened, about 2 minutes. Add the cream cheese and Parmesan and stir until smooth. Add the broccoli and mix well. Spoon the mixture over the chicken and sprinkle with the walnuts. Bake, covered, until the chicken is cooked through and the casserole is bubbly, 25 to 30 minutes.

Makes 4 to 6 servings

CASHEW CHICKEN AND BROWN RICE

Unexpected company dropped by just before dinnertime to deliver a lemon pie because I had been ill. Luckily, this casserole was in the oven and waiting to be shared with good friends. I added more greens to the tossed salad and warmed some garlic bread, and we all enjoyed the lemon meringue pie.

3 tablespoons butter, divided
1 pound chicken tenders, cut into 1½-inch pieces
  Salt and freshly ground pepper
1 cup chopped yellow onion
1 red bell pepper, cut into 1-inch pieces
4 ounces mushrooms, sliced
2 garlic cloves, minced

½ teaspoon dried thyme
1 cup uncooked brown rice
2 cups Basic Chicken Stock (page 29) or reduced-sodium chicken broth
1 cup whole unsalted cashews
3 to 4 tablespoons soy sauce, plus additional for serving

Preheat the oven to 350°F. In a large skillet over medium heat, melt 2 tablespoons of the butter. Add the chicken and sauté until lightly browned, about 5 minutes. Season with salt and pepper to taste. Add the onions, bell pepper, mushrooms, garlic, and thyme and sauté until the vegetables are tender, about 5 minutes longer. Move the vegetables to the outer edges of the pan. Add the remaining 1 tablespoon butter and the rice, stirring until coated. Add the stock, cashews, and soy sauce and mix the vegetables in well. Transfer to a lightly sprayed or oiled 2-quart casserole. Cover and bake until the liquid is absorbed, about 1 hour and 15 minutes. Serve with extra soy sauce.

Makes 4 servings

CHICKEN LASAGNA

Lasagna doesn't always have to be made with beef. Using chicken and mushrooms makes a lighter dish, but with the same great taste and appeal. This is a good casserole to serve for a casual supper with a Caesar salad and garlic bread.

1 tablespoon olive oil	Freshly ground pepper
½ cup chopped yellow onion	2 cups cottage cheese
6 ounces mushrooms, sliced	2 cups (8 ounces) shredded, packed mozzarella cheese, divided
1 garlic clove, minced	
1 can (14½ ounces) whole tomatoes including juice, puréed in a food processor	½ cup sour cream
	1 cup (4 ounces) freshly grated Parmesan cheese, divided
1 can (15 ounces) tomato sauce	
¾ teaspoon dried basil	¼ cup chopped fresh flat-leaf parsley
½ teaspoon dried oregano	9 lasagna noodles, cooked according to package directions, drained
¼ teaspoon sugar	
½ teaspoon salt	3 cups chopped cooked chicken breast

In a medium skillet over medium heat, warm the oil. Add the onions, mushrooms, and garlic and sauté until tender, about 5 minutes. Stir in the tomatoes, tomato sauce, basil, oregano, sugar, salt, and pepper to taste. Bring to a boil, reduce the heat to low, and simmer, uncovered, until the flavors are blended, about 10 minutes.

In a medium bowl, mix together the cottage cheese, 1 cup of the mozzarella, the sour cream, ½ cup of the Parmesan, and the parsley.

Preheat the oven to 350°F. Spread about ¼ cup of the mushroom-tomato sauce on the bottom of a lightly sprayed or oiled 9-by-13-inch glass baking dish. Layer 3 noodles, one third of the cheese mixture (it will not completely cover), one third of the chicken, and one third of the mushroom-tomato sauce. Repeat the layers 2 more times, ending with sauce. Sprinkle the remaining 1 cup mozzarella and ½ cup Parmesan on top. Bake, covered, for 30 minutes. Uncover, and bake until bubbly, about 20 minutes longer. Let stand for 5 to 10 minutes before serving. Cut the lasagna into squares to serve.

Makes 8 servings

CHICKEN, MUSHROOM, AND NOODLE CASSEROLE

If you like the old favorite tuna noodle casserole, this one with chicken is even better. Forget the canned cream of mushroom soup and make this simple sauce to bind the chicken and noodles together. This is an easy main-course supper dish to serve with green beans.

¼ cup (½ stick) butter
1 cup chopped yellow onion
4 ounces mushrooms, coarsely chopped
½ cup chopped celery
¼ cup all-purpose flour
1¼ cups Basic Chicken Stock (page 29) or reduced-sodium chicken broth
½ cup whole milk

½ teaspoon dried thyme
¾ teaspoon salt
Freshly ground pepper
8 ounces (about 4 cups) egg noodles, cooked according to package directions, drained
1½ cups cooked shredded chicken breast
1 cup (4 ounces) shredded Cheddar cheese

Preheat the oven to 350°F. In a medium saucepan over medium-high heat, melt the butter. Add the onions, mushrooms, and celery and sauté until tender, about 5 minutes. Add the flour and stir until bubbly. Add the stock, milk, thyme, salt, and pepper to taste, and stir until thickened, about 2 minutes.

Put the noodles and chicken in a lightly sprayed or oiled 2-quart casserole. Add the mushroom sauce and mix well. Top with the cheese. Bake, uncovered, until bubbly, 25 to 30 minutes. Let stand for 5 to 10 minutes before serving.

Makes 6 servings

CHEESY SCALLOPED POTATOES WITH CHICKEN

Scalloped potatoes are always a favorite, and this one with chicken will bring the family to the table in a hurry.

½ cup sour cream

½ package (4 ounces) cream cheese, at room temperature, cut into small pieces

½ cup Basic Chicken Stock (page 29) or reduced-sodium chicken broth

½ teaspoon salt

Freshly ground pepper

6 red potatoes (about 2 pounds), unpeeled, scrubbed, and thinly sliced

1 cup cubed cooked chicken breast

1½ cups (6 ounces) shredded Cheddar cheese, divided

Preheat the oven to 350°F. In a medium bowl, whisk together the sour cream, cream cheese, stock, salt, and pepper to taste. In a lightly sprayed or oiled 8-by-8-inch glass baking dish, layer half of the potatoes, all of the chicken, and half of the Cheddar. Pour half of the cream cheese mixture over the top. Layer on the remaining potatoes and pour on the rest of the cream cheese mixture. Sprinkle the remaining Cheddar on top. Bake, uncovered, until the potatoes are tender, about 1 hour. Let stand for 5 to 10 minutes before serving.

Makes 4 servings

CHICKEN AND ARTICHOKE GRATIN

This elegant combination of chicken breasts and artichoke hearts is baked in individual gratin dishes and topped with a delicious hollandaise sauce and crumbs. Hollandaise sauce is a smooth, rich, creamy sauce made with butter, eggs, and lemon juice. It is well known in classic eggs Benedict and is also used to enhance some vegetable dishes. The sauce can be prepared ahead and reheated (see Note).

1 can (14 ounces) quartered artichoke hearts, drained
4 skinned and boned chicken breast halves (about 2 pounds), poached (see page 25) and cut into bite-size pieces
  Salt and freshly ground pepper
  Hollandaise Sauce (recipe follows)
  Paprika for sprinkling on top
  Dried fine bread crumbs for sprinkling on top

Preheat the oven to 350°F. In 4 lightly sprayed or oiled ¾-cup gratin dishes, put equal portions of the artichoke hearts and chicken. Season to taste with salt and pepper. Spoon 4 to 5 tablespoons of the hollandaise sauce over the top of each and sprinkle with paprika. Sprinkle about 1 teaspoon of crumbs on top of each dish. Bake, uncovered, until bubbly, about 20 minutes. Let stand for 5 to 10 minutes before serving.

Makes 4 servings

HOLLANDAISE SAUCE

This method of making hollandaise sauce is safe from possible salmonella because the egg yolks are cooked. Use a blender for best results.

4 egg yolks
3 tablespoons fresh lemon juice
1 tablespoon water
¼ teaspoon salt
  Dash cayenne
1 cup (2 sticks) butter, melted (no substitute)

In a small, heavy saucepan over medium-low heat, combine the yolks, lemon juice, water, salt, and cayenne. Whisk constantly until the mixture bubbles and begins to thicken, 2 to 3 minutes. Transfer to a blender using a spatula. With the motor running, add the butter in a slow, steady stream and blend until all the butter is used and the sauce is thickened, about 30 seconds.

Makes about 1½ cups

NOTE: To reheat hollandaise sauce, warm in a pan over hot water. Whisk again before using.

CHICKEN POT PIE WITH FRESH VEGETABLES

Chicken pot pie has been a longtime favorite of many families. In this updated version, fresh vegetables are used for more color and flavor. Cover with a flaky homemade pie crust (recipe follows) or purchased.

1½ cups Basic Chicken Stock (page 29) or reduced-sodium chicken broth, divided
2 or 3 carrots, thinly sliced
2 celery stalks, cut into ½-inch slices
½ cup chopped yellow onion
1 cup corn kernels, fresh or frozen
1 cup peas, fresh or frozen
2 cups diced cooked chicken breast

3 tablespoons butter
3 tablespoons all-purpose flour
½ cup whole milk
¾ teaspoon salt
Freshly ground pepper
¼ cup chopped fresh parsley
Food Processor Pie Crust (facing page)

In a medium saucepan over medium heat, bring ½ cup of the stock to a boil. Cook the carrots, celery, and onions in the stock, covered, until tender, about 10 minutes. Drain the vegetables, reserving the stock.

Preheat the oven to 350°F. Place the carrots, celery, onions, corn, peas, and chicken in a 10-inch round, deep-dish pie plate.

In a medium saucepan over medium heat, melt the butter. Add the flour and stir until bubbly. Add the remaining 1 cup stock, milk, salt, and pepper to taste. Bring to a boil, stirring constantly, until thickened, about 2 minutes. Pour over the vegetables and mix well. Sprinkle with the parsley.

Place the crust over the vegetables, fold the edges under, and crimp them. Make several slits in the crust to prevent puffing. Bake until the vegetables are bubbly and the pastry is golden on top, about 35 minutes. Let stand for 5 to 10 minutes before serving.

Makes 6 servings

FOOD PROCESSOR PIE CRUST

1¼   cups all-purpose flour
  6   tablespoons (¾ stick) chilled butter, cut into
      small pieces
  3   tablespoons chilled vegetable shortening
  ½   teaspoon salt
2 to 3   tablespoons ice water

Place all the ingredients except the water in a food processor. With on/off pulses, process until the mixture resembles coarse meal, about 30 pulses. With the motor running, slowly add the water, 1 tablespoon at a time, until the dough sticks together. Stop just before a ball forms (you may not need all the water). Turn the dough onto a sheet of waxed paper and flatten it into a 6-inch disk. Wrap with waxed paper and refrigerate for 30 minutes.

On a lightly floured surface and with a floured rolling pin, roll the dough from the center to the edges into a 12-inch circle.

Makes 1 pie crust

CHICKEN, HAM, AND FENNEL CASSEROLE

Fennel is an aromatic plant, sometimes referred to as "sweet anise." It adds a distinctive light licorice flavor that complements the ham and chicken. Serve with a butter lettuce salad tossed with a lemony dressing.

2 tablespoons olive oil, divided
4 boned and skinned chicken breast halves (about 2 pounds), cut into bite-size pieces
Salt and freshly ground pepper
2 cups cubed cooked ham
1 small fennel bulb, stems and fronds removed, bulb sliced lengthwise, then chopped
½ cup chopped green onion including some tender green tops
2 garlic cloves, minced
1 cup uncooked long-grain white rice
2¼ cups Basic Chicken Stock (page 29) or reduced-sodium chicken broth

Preheat the oven to 350°F. In a large skillet over medium-high heat, warm 1 tablespoon of the oil. Add the chicken and sauté until the chicken turns white. Season with salt and pepper to taste. Transfer the chicken to a lightly sprayed or oiled 2-quart casserole. Reduce the heat under the skillet to medium. Add the remaining 1 tablespoon oil to the skillet and sauté the ham, fennel, onions, and garlic until the vegetables are tender, about 5 minutes. Stir in the rice, then add the stock. Transfer the mixture to the casserole holding the chicken and mix well. Bake, covered, until the rice is tender and the liquid is absorbed, about 45 minutes. Let stand for 5 to 10 minutes before serving.

Makes 4 to 6 servings

CHICKEN, BROCCOLI, AND ARTICHOKE CASSEROLE

Layers of tender chicken breasts, artichokes, and crisp broccoli meld together in a creamy cheese sauce. This is a great casserole to serve if you are hosting a meeting at your house. It can be made ahead and baked as the meeting is in progress.

4 cups fresh broccoli florets
4 tablespoons (½ stick) butter, divided
8 ounces mushrooms, sliced
¼ cup all-purpose flour
2½ cups Basic Chicken Stock (page 29) or reduced-sodium chicken broth
1 teaspoon Dijon mustard
½ teaspoon dried thyme
½ teaspoon salt

Freshly ground pepper
1 cup (4 ounces) shredded Cheddar cheese
4 boned and skinned chicken breast halves (about 2 pounds), poached (see page 25) and cut into large pieces
1 can (14 ounces) quartered water-packed artichoke hearts, drained
Freshly grated Parmesan cheese for sprinkling on top

Preheat the oven to 350°F. In a small saucepan over medium-high heat, bring water to a boil. Simmer the broccoli until tender-crisp, 4 to 5 minutes. Drain and set aside.

In a medium skillet over medium heat, melt 2 tablespoons of the butter. Add the mushrooms and sauté until almost tender, about 5 minutes. With a slotted spoon, transfer them to a plate. Add the remaining 2 tablespoons butter and the flour to the skillet and stir until bubbly. Add the stock, mustard, and seasonings and whisk until the sauce thickens, about 2 minutes. Add the Cheddar cheese and stir until smooth.

In a 3-quart casserole lightly coated with cooking spray or oil, layer the chicken, broccoli, mushrooms, and artichokes. Pour the sauce over them all. Cover and bake until bubbly, about 40 minutes. Stir and sprinkle the Parmesan cheese on top. Bake, uncovered, until the cheese melts, 5 to 10 minutes longer. Let stand for 5 to 10 minutes before serving.

Makes 8 servings

CHICKEN DIVAN

Cream of chicken soup was originally called for in this classic dish, but in this updated version, the chicken and broccoli are topped with a rich, well-seasoned white sauce for more flavor and less sodium. Red bell pepper is added for color and taste.

4   cups fresh broccoli florets

4   boned and skinned chicken breast halves (about 2 pounds), poached (see page 25) and cut into large bite-sized pieces

¼   cup (½ stick) butter

8   ounces mushrooms, sliced

2   shallots, chopped, or 8 green onions including some tender green tops, sliced

¼   cup chopped red bell pepper

3   tablespoons all-purpose flour

2   cups Basic Chicken Stock (page 29) or reduced-sodium chicken broth

½   cup half-and-half

¼   cup dry white wine

½   cup (2 ounces) freshly grated Parmesan cheese, divided

1   teaspoon fresh lemon juice

½   teaspoon salt

    Freshly ground pepper

Preheat the oven to 350°F. In a medium saucepan with gently boiling water, cook the broccoli until tender-crisp, about 5 minutes. Drain and arrange them in a single layer in a lightly sprayed or oiled 7-by-11-inch glass baking dish. Lay the chicken pieces on top.

In a medium saucepan over medium heat, melt the butter. Add the mushrooms, shallots, and bell pepper and sauté until tender, about 5 minutes. Add the flour and stir until bubbly. Add the stock, half-and-half, wine, ¼ cup of the Parmesan, the lemon juice, salt, and pepper to taste and stir until thickened, about 2 minutes. Pour the sauce over the chicken and broccoli. Sprinkle with the remaining ¼ cup Parmesan. Bake, uncovered, until bubbly, 20 to 25 minutes. Let stand for 5 to 10 minutes before serving.

Makes 4 to 6 servings

MEXICAN CHICKEN TORTILLA CASSEROLE

This casserole of chicken, tortillas, cheese, and chiles baked in a creamy tomato sauce is great for a Mexican-theme dinner party. If you cook the chicken ahead, the casserole goes together fast. Serve with a salad of orange and avocado slices and jicama sticks. Offer additional salsa and sour cream for toppings.

1 cup light sour cream, plus additional for serving

1 can (8 ounces) tomato sauce

½ cup Fresh Tomato Salsa (page 35) or purchased salsa, plus extra for serving

1 can (4 ounces) diced green chiles, drained

½ cup chopped green onions including some tender green tops

2 garlic cloves, minced

½ teaspoon paprika

¼ teaspoon ground cumin

¼ teaspoon salt

9 corn tortillas (6-inch), softened (see page 128)

4 cups cubed cooked chicken breast

4 cups (1 pound) shredded Monterey Jack cheese or part Jack and part Cheddar

Preheat the oven to 350°F. In a bowl, mix together the sour cream, tomato sauce, salsa, chiles, onions, garlic, paprika, cumin, and salt. In a lightly sprayed or oiled 9-by-13-inch glass baking dish, place 3 tortillas, slightly overlapping. Add one third of the chicken, one third of the sour cream mixture (it will not cover completely), and one third of the cheese. Repeat 2 more times, beginning with tortillas and ending with cheese.

Bake, covered, for 35 minutes. Uncover, and bake until bubbly, about 15 minutes longer. Let stand for 5 to 10 minutes before serving.

Makes 6 servings

CHICKEN, BLACK BEAN, AND CORN CASSEROLE

Layers of your favorite Mexican ingredients are combined in this one-dish casserole. Two of my grandkids ate the whole thing, so don't count on it serving six hearty eaters! Serve with toppings.

2 teaspoons vegetable oil	Freshly ground pepper
1 cup chopped yellow onion	2 or 3 cups cubed cooked chicken breast
½ cup chopped red or green bell pepper	2 cans (15 ounces each) black beans, drained and rinsed
2 garlic cloves, minced	1 cup corn, fresh or frozen
1 can (14½ ounces) whole tomatoes including juice, slightly puréed in a food processor	8 corn tortillas (6-inch)
½ cup Fresh Tomato Salsa (page 35) or purchased salsa	4 cups (1 pound) shredded Cheddar cheese, divided
½ teaspoon dried oregano	Toppings: Guacamole (page 126) or purchased guacamole, sour cream, sliced green onions, additional salsa
½ teaspoon chili powder	
½ teaspoon ground cumin	
¼ teaspoon salt	

Preheat the oven to 350°F. In a large skillet over medium heat, warm the oil. Add the onions, bell pepper, and garlic and sauté until tender, about 5 minutes. Add the tomatoes, salsa, oregano, chili powder, cumin, salt, and pepper to taste. Stir in the chicken, beans, and corn.

In a lightly sprayed or oiled 9-by-13-inch glass baking dish, spread one third of the chicken mixture evenly over the bottom of the dish. Lay 4 tortillas on top, slightly overlapping. Add another one third of the chicken mixture and 2 cups cheese. Add 4 more tortillas and the remaining chicken mixture. Cover with foil and bake for 30 minutes. Sprinkle on the remaining 2 cups cheese and bake, uncovered, until the cheese is melted, about 10 minutes longer. Let stand for 5 to 10 minutes before serving. Pass the toppings in bowls.

Makes 6 to 8 servings

CHICKEN WITH CHILE-CHEESE RICE

Chicken gains a distinctive flavor from the chiles and cilantro in this tasty casserole. If you're not a fan of cilantro, you can substitute parsley.

1 tablespoon olive oil
1 pound chicken tenders, cut into large pieces
1 cup chopped yellow onion
1 cup chopped green bell pepper
2 garlic cloves, minced
¾ teaspoon salt
 Freshly ground pepper
1 cup uncooked long-grain white rice

2 cups Basic Chicken Stock (page 29) or reduced-fat chicken broth
1 can (7 ounces) whole green chiles, drained, split, seeded, and cut into large pieces
1½ cups (6 ounces) shredded Monterey Jack cheese, divided
1 cup chopped fresh cilantro leaves or parsley

Preheat the oven to 350°F. In a large skillet over medium heat, warm the oil. Add the tenders, onions, bell pepper, and garlic and sauté until the chicken is no longer pink and the vegetables are tender, 6 to 7 minutes. Season with salt and pepper to taste. Stir in the rice. Add the stock and bring to a boil. Transfer the mixture to a lightly sprayed or oiled 2-quart casserole dish. Stir in the chiles and ¾ cup of the cheese. Cover and bake until the liquid is absorbed and the rice is tender, about 45 minutes. Uncover, stir in the cilantro, and sprinkle the remaining ¾ cup cheese on top. Bake, uncovered, until the cheese melts, about 5 minutes longer. Let stand for 5 to 10 minutes before serving.

Makes 4 servings

POLLO VERDE

Our friends introduced us to this chicken dish when we visited them in San Antonio, Texas. Chicken rolls are filled with green chiles (the "verde") and cheese and baked in a flavorful green salsa. Serve a side dish of rice to absorb the delicious sauce. Pass the Black Bean Salsa for a complementary relish.

6   boned and skinned chicken breast halves (about 3 pounds)
    Salt and freshly ground pepper
1   can (8 ounces) whole green chiles, drained, split, seeded, and dried with a paper towel
12 ounces Monterey Jack cheese, cut into six 1-by-2-inch strips and the remainder shredded (about 2 cups)

2   tablespoons vegetable oil
    Sauce Verde (facing page)
½   cup chopped fresh cilantro
2   avocados, peeled, pitted, and sliced
    Black Bean Salsa (facing page)

Preheat the oven to 350°F. Place the chicken breasts between 2 pieces of plastic wrap and pound with the flat side of a meat mallet to ⅜ inch thick. Season with salt and pepper to taste. Place a chile on each chicken breast half and top with a strip of cheese. Roll up from the small end and secure with a toothpick.

In a large skillet over medium heat, warm the oil. Sauté the chicken rolls until lightly browned on all sides, about 10 minutes. Transfer them to a lightly sprayed or oiled 7-by-11-inch glass baking dish or decorative Mexican casserole. Pour the Sauce Verde over the top and sprinkle the top with the cilantro and the shredded cheese. Bake, uncovered, until bubbly and the chicken is no longer pink in the center, about 35 minutes. Let stand for 5 to 10 minutes before serving. Transfer the chicken rolls to a warmed platter and remove the toothpicks. Garnish with the avocado slices and pass the salsa.

Makes 4 to 6 servings

SAUCE VERDE

1 cup sour cream
1 can (7 ounces) salsa verde
¼ teaspoon salt
¼ teaspoon ground cumin

In a medium bowl, whisk together all the ingredients.

Makes about 2 cups

BLACK BEAN SALSA

This is also a good filling for Quesadillas (page 34).

1 can (15 ounces) black beans, drained and rinsed
1 cup seeded chopped tomatoes, drained
½ cup diced red onion
¼ cup minced fresh cilantro
1 small jalapeño, seeded and minced
2 tablespoons fresh lime juice
1 tablespoon olive oil
Salt and freshly ground pepper

In a medium bowl, mix together all the ingredients. Refrigerate until ready to serve.

Makes about 2½ cups

CHICKEN ENCHILADAS WITH CREAMY SALSA

This casserole is one of our family favorites, combining traditional Mexican ingredients with a creamy sauce of salsa and sour cream. This is a great dish for a casual company dinner.

3 tablespoons butter
½ cup diced yellow onion
3 tablespoons all-purpose flour
1½ cups Basic Chicken Stock (page 29) or reduced-sodium chicken broth
¼ teaspoon salt
 Freshly ground pepper
1 cup sour cream, plus extra for serving
½ cup Fresh Tomato Salsa (page 35) or purchased salsa, plus extra for serving

8 corn tortillas (9-inch), warmed (see page 128)
3 cups diced cooked chicken
6 green onions including some tender green tops, sliced
3 cups (12 ounces) shredded Monterey Jack cheese
 Pitted black olives for garnish

Preheat the oven to 350°F. In a medium saucepan over medium heat, melt the butter. Add the yellow onions and sauté until tender, about 5 minutes. Add the flour and stir until bubbly. Add the stock, salt, and pepper to taste and stir until the mixture boils and thickens, about 2 minutes. Stir in the sour cream and salsa and mix well. Cover the bottom of a 9-by-13-inch glass baking dish with one third of the sauce.

Lay a tortilla on a flat surface. Add about 2 tablespoons chicken, 1 tablespoon sauce, and a few green onions down the center of the tortilla. Sprinkle with about 1 tablespoon cheese. Roll up and place, seam-side down, in the baking dish on top of the sauce. Repeat with the remaining tortillas. Pour the remaining sauce over them all. Sprinkle with the remaining cheese.

Cover and bake for 30 minutes. Uncover and bake until bubbly, about 10 minutes longer. Let stand for 5 to 10 minutes before serving. Garnish with the olives. Pass additional salsa and sour cream in separate bowls.

Makes 6 servings

SOUR CREAM–LIME CHICKEN ENCHILADAS

Here's a dish to satisfy your craving for Mexican food. These chicken-filled enchiladas have a creamy, refreshing lime sauce instead of the traditional tomato sauce. This could be your winter's best party casserole.

2 cups (16 ounces) sour cream
½ cup whole milk
1 teaspoon grated lime zest
Juice of 1 large lime
⅛ teaspoon ground cayenne
3 cups shredded cooked chicken

9 corn tortillas (6-inch), warmed (see page 128)
2 cups (8 ounces) shredded Monterey Jack cheese, divided
Cilantro sprigs for garnish
Fresh Tomato Salsa (page 35) or purchased salsa, for serving

Preheat the oven to 400°F. In a medium bowl, stir together the sour cream, milk, zest, lime juice, and cayenne. Fill each tortilla with ⅓ cup chicken, 1 tablespoon cheese, and 1 tablespoon sour cream sauce. Roll the tortillas and place them seam-side down in a lightly sprayed or oiled 9-by-13-inch glass baking dish and top with the remaining sour cream sauce. Sprinkle with the remaining cheese. Bake, uncovered, until bubbly, about 30 minutes. Let stand for 5 to 10 minutes before serving. Garnish with cilantro and serve with salsa.

Makes 6 to 8 servings

SPICY CHICKEN ENCHILADA CASSEROLE

Layers of chicken, tortillas, cheeses, and enchilada sauce make up this classic dish. Ground chicken is used in this casserole instead of chicken pieces, adding a different texture. For convenience, canned enchilada sauce is called for. This makes a large quantity and is great to serve at a post-game party or potluck. I like to make it in a large, oval, decorative Mexican pottery dish.

1   teaspoon vegetable oil
1¼ pounds ground chicken
1   cup chopped yellow onion
½   teaspoon salt
      Freshly ground pepper
2   cans (10 ounces each) mild enchilada sauce
1   can (8 ounces) tomato sauce
¼   teaspoon chili powder or more to taste
1   cup lowfat cottage cheese
1   large egg, beaten
9   corn tortillas (6-inch)
2   cups (8 ounces) shredded Monterey Jack cheese
2   cups (8 ounces) shredded Cheddar cheese
      Light sour cream for passing

In a large skillet over medium heat, warm the oil. Sauté the chicken and onions until the chicken is no longer pink and the onions are tender, about 5 minutes. Season with the salt and pepper to taste. Add the enchilada and tomato sauces and chili powder and stir until blended.

In a small bowl, mix together the cottage cheese and egg and set aside.

Preheat the oven to 375°F. In a lightly sprayed or oiled 9-by-13-inch glass baking dish, make 3 layers, starting with one third of the sauce, 3 tortillas (they will overlap), one third of the Jack cheese, and all of the egg–cottage cheese mixture. Repeat 2 more times, ending with the sauce. Sprinkle the Cheddar cheese on top. Bake, uncovered, until bubbly, about 45 minutes. Let stand for 5 to 10 minutes before serving. Pass the sour cream.

Makes 8 to 10 servings

FIESTA CASSEROLE

A great company casserole to make ahead and bake just before the guests arrive. Serve with side dishes of spicy black beans and Spanish rice.

1 tablespoon vegetable oil

1½ cups chopped yellow onion

½ cup chopped green or red bell pepper

3 garlic cloves, minced

1 teaspoon finely chopped jalapeño or more to taste

1 can (15 ounces) tomato sauce

1 cup Basic Chicken Stock (page 29) or reduced-sodium chicken broth

1 teaspoon sugar

1 teaspoon chili powder

¾ teaspoon dried oregano

½ teaspoon salt

¼ teaspoon ground cumin

9 corn tortillas (6-inch), softened (see page 128)

4 cups cubed cooked chicken breast

4 cups (about 1 pound) shredded Cheddar cheese

1 cup pitted black olives, sliced

Sour cream for serving

In a large saucepan over medium heat, warm the oil. Add the onions, bell pepper, garlic, and jalapeño and sauté until tender, about 5 minutes. Add the tomato sauce, stock, sugar, and seasonings. Bring to a boil, reduce the temperature to low, and simmer, uncovered, until the flavors are blended, 8 to 10 minutes.

Preheat the oven to 375°F. In a 9-by-13-inch glass baking dish sprayed with cooking spray or oil, spread a thin coating of sauce. Add 3 tortillas, overlapping slightly. Add one third of the chicken, one third of the sauce, one third of the cheese, and all of the olives. Repeat the layers 2 more times, ending with cheese.

Bake, covered, for 30 minutes. Uncover and bake until bubbly, about 10 minutes longer. Let stand for 5 to 10 minutes before serving. Pass the sour cream.

Makes 6 to 8 servings

CHICKEN TAMALE PIE

The traditional Mexican tamale is a combination of various fillings such as meat and vegetables and masa (dough), wrapped in a corn husk and steamed. In this Americanized version, the chicken and vegetables are baked with a cornmeal topping in a casserole.

1   tablespoon vegetable oil
1   cup chopped yellow onion
½   cup chopped green bell pepper
1   garlic clove, minced
1   can (15 ounces) kidney beans, drained and rinsed
1   can (14½ ounces) Mexican-style tomatoes including juice, cut up

1   cup corn kernels, fresh or frozen
1   teaspoon chili powder
½   teaspoon dried oregano
½   teaspoon salt
    Freshly ground pepper
2   cups cubed cooked chicken
    Cornmeal Topping (recipe follows)
2   cups (8 ounces) shredded Cheddar cheese

Preheat the oven to 350°F. In a large skillet over medium heat, warm the oil. Add the onions, bell pepper, and garlic and sauté until the vegetables are tender, about 5 minutes. Add the beans, tomatoes, corn, and seasonings and simmer, uncovered, until the flavors are blended, about 10 minutes. Stir in the chicken. Pour the chicken mixture into a lightly sprayed or oiled 9-by-13-inch glass baking dish. Spread the cornmeal topping evenly on top and sprinkle the cheese over it.

Bake, uncovered, until bubbly, about 30 minutes. Let stand for 5 to 10 minutes before serving.

Makes 8 servings

CORNMEAL TOPPING

1   cup yellow cornmeal
3½   cups water
½   teaspoon salt

In a medium bowl, mix the cornmeal with 1 cup of the water. In a deep saucepan over high heat, bring the remaining 2½ cups water and the salt to a boil. Slowly stir the cornmeal mixture into the boiling water. Reduce the heat to low and simmer, uncovered, stirring constantly, until the cornmeal mixture is thick and smooth, about 5 minutes. Remove from the heat and set aside.

Makes about 4 cups

CHICKEN, BLACK BEAN, AND RICE CASSEROLE

Beans and rice are typical Mexican staples. Here they are combined with chicken, corn, and tomatoes in a casserole and baked. Serve with jicama strips and tomato slices. Jicama is a Mexican root vegetable that is crisp and refreshing. By omitting the chicken, this makes a good side dish to serve with other Mexican food.

1 tablespoon vegetable oil
½ cup chopped yellow onion
½ cup chopped green pepper
2 garlic cloves, minced
1 can (14½ ounces) Mexican-style tomatoes, chopped
1 can (4 ounces) diced green chiles, drained
1 teaspoon chili powder
½ teaspoon ground cumin
½ teaspoon paprika

½ teaspoon salt
Freshly ground pepper
1 can (15 ounces) black beans, drained and rinsed
1½ cups tomato juice
1½ cups diced cooked chicken
1 cup corn kernels, fresh or frozen, thawed
⅔ cup uncooked long-grain white rice
½ cup chopped fresh cilantro or parsley
Sour cream for serving

Preheat the oven to 350°F. In a large skillet over medium heat, warm the oil. Add the onions, bell pepper, and garlic and sauté until the vegetables are tender, about 5 minutes. Add the tomatoes, chiles, and seasonings and mix well. Combine the beans, tomato juice, chicken, corn, and rice in a lightly sprayed or oiled 2-quart casserole. Pour the tomato mixture over the top and mix well. Cover and bake until the rice is tender and the liquid is absorbed, about 45 minutes. Stir in the cilantro just before serving. Let stand for 5 to 10 minutes before serving. Pass the sour cream in a bowl.

Makes 6 to 8 servings

BAKED CHICKEN AND MUSHROOM RISOTTO

Risotto is a creamy, delectable Italian rice dish using a short-grain rice such as Arborio. It is usually made by gradually adding warm stock or broth, half a cup at a time, into the rice and stirring constantly until the liquid is absorbed after each addition. In this short-cut method, it is started on top of the stove, then finished in the oven with the same good results. The addition of chicken makes it an entrée.

2½ cups Basic Chicken Stock (page 29) or reduced-sodium chicken broth
2 tablespoons vegetable oil
1 cup chopped yellow onion
6 ounces mushrooms, sliced
1 garlic clove, minced

¾ cup uncooked Arborio rice
½ teaspoon salt
Freshly ground pepper
1 cup cubed cooked chicken
⅓ cup chopped fresh parsley

Preheat the oven to 350°F. In a medium saucepan over medium heat, warm the stock and keep it warm.

In a large skillet over medium heat, warm the oil. Add the onions, mushrooms, and garlic and sauté until tender, about 5 minutes. Add the rice and stir to coat. Season with salt and pepper to taste. Add ½ cup of the warm stock and stir until the liquid is absorbed, 2 to 3 minutes. Add the remaining stock all at once and bring to a boil. Stir in the chicken.

Transfer to a lightly sprayed or oiled 2-quart casserole dish. Cover and bake until all of the stock is absorbed, about 50 minutes, stirring several times. Stir in the parsley and cook, uncovered, until the rice is tender and creamy, about 10 minutes longer. Let stand for 5 to 10 minutes before serving.

Makes 4 to 6 servings

CHICKEN FLORENTINE

This nutritious casserole can be conveniently made ahead and baked later, or frozen for a busy weeknight meal. Serve with a fresh fruit salad.

2 tablespoons butter

2 boned and skinned chicken breast halves (about 1 pound), cut into 1-inch pieces

½ cup chopped yellow onion

¾ cup uncooked long-grain white rice

1¾ cups Basic Chicken Stock (page 29) or reduced-sodium chicken broth

½ package (5 ounces) frozen spinach, thawed and squeezed dry

½ teaspoon dried oregano

¼ teaspoon salt

Freshly ground pepper

Dash ground nutmeg

¼ cup (1 ounce) freshly grated Parmesan cheese

Preheat the oven to 350°F. In a large skillet over medium heat, melt the butter. Add the chicken and onions and sauté until the chicken is no longer pink and the onions are tender, about 5 minutes. Stir in the rice. Add the stock, spinach, oregano, salt, pepper to taste, and nutmeg and mix well. Transfer to a lightly sprayed or oiled 2-quart casserole and sprinkle with the Parmesan. Cover and bake until the liquid is absorbed and the rice is tender, about 45 minutes. Let stand for 5 to 10 minutes before serving.

Makes 4 servings

CHICKEN TETRAZZINI

This dish is named after the famous Italian opera singer Luisa Tetrazzini. Use leftover rotisserie chicken or any cooked chicken for this rich baked dish of chicken and mushrooms in a cheese sauce. Peas are added for color and flavor.

4 tablespoons (½ stick) butter, divided
½ cup chopped yellow onion
8 ounces mushrooms, sliced
2 garlic cloves, minced
¼ cup all-purpose flour
1½ cups half-and-half or whole milk
1 cup Basic Chicken Stock (page 29) or reduced-sodium chicken broth
¾ cup (3 ounces) freshly grated Parmesan cheese, divided

3 tablespoons sherry or dry white wine
½ teaspoon dried thyme
¾ teaspoon salt
⅛ teaspoon ground white pepper
3 to 4 cups cubed cooked chicken
8 ounces spaghetti, broken into thirds, cooked according to package directions, drained
2 cups peas, fresh or frozen

Preheat the oven to 350°F. In a saucepan over medium heat, melt 2 tablespoons of the butter. Sauté the onions, mushrooms, and garlic until tender, about 5 minutes. Remove the vegetables to a plate with a slotted spoon. Add the remaining 2 tablespoons butter to the saucepan. Add the flour and stir until bubbly, about 1 minute. Add the half-and-half, stock, ½ cup of the cheese, the sherry, thyme, salt, and pepper. Stir until smooth and thickened, about 2 minutes. Return the vegetables to the pan and mix.

In a lightly sprayed or oiled 9-by-13-inch glass baking dish, combine the chicken, sauce and vegetables, and spaghetti and mix well.

Cover and bake for 30 minutes. Stir in the peas and sprinkle with the remaining ¼ cup cheese. Bake, uncovered, until bubbly and the top is golden, about 10 minutes longer. Let stand for 5 to 10 minutes before serving.

Makes 6 to 8 servings

OVEN PASTA WITH CHICKEN, MUSHROOMS, AND CHEESE, ITALIAN STYLE

If you're looking for a casserole to take to a potluck or to serve for an informal gathering, this one fills the bill. It is easy to assemble and the seasonings lend a tantalizing aroma as it bakes in the oven.

2 tablespoons vegetable oil

1 cup chopped yellow onion

8 ounces mushrooms, sliced

2 large garlic cloves, minced

1 can (15 ounces) Italian-style tomatoes including juices, chopped

½ cup chopped fresh parsley

1 teaspoon dried basil

1 teaspoon dried oregano

¼ teaspoon salt

Freshly ground pepper to taste

6 ounces (2 cups) fusilli, cooked according to package directions, drained

1½ cups diced cooked chicken

1 cup (4 ounces) freshly grated Parmesan cheese

Preheat the oven to 350°F. In a large skillet over medium heat, warm the oil. Add the onions, mushrooms, and garlic and sauté until tender, about 5 minutes. Add the tomatoes, parsley, and seasonings and simmer for 5 minutes. Place the pasta in a lightly sprayed or oiled 2-quart casserole. Add the tomato-mushroom sauce and chicken and mix well. Sprinkle with the Parmesan cheese. Bake, uncovered, until bubbly, about 30 minutes. Let stand for 5 to 10 minutes before serving.

Makes 6 servings

CHICKEN AND MUSHROOM MANICOTTI

Italian dishes are popular any season and are always a good casserole dinner choice. In this manicotti, the shells are filled with a mixture of chicken and mushrooms and topped with a creamy béchamel sauce, a pleasing change from the usual heavy meat and tomato sauce. It has make-ahead ease and can be baked just before serving for a company dinner.

FILLING

1½ tablespoons vegetable oil

4 ounces mushrooms, chopped

½ cup chopped red bell pepper

1 garlic clove, minced

½ teaspoon dried thyme

½ teaspoon salt
Freshly ground pepper

2 cups diced cooked chicken

2 cups (8 ounces) shredded mozzarella cheese, divided

1 cup ricotta or cottage cheese

¾ cup (3 ounces) freshly grated Parmesan cheese

¼ cup sliced green onions including some tender green tops

1 large egg, beaten

12 manicotti shells, cooked according to package directions, drained
Béchamel Sauce (facing page)

To make the filling, in a medium skillet over medium heat, warm the oil. Add the mushrooms, bell pepper, and garlic and sauté until tender, about 5 minutes. Add the thyme, salt, and pepper to taste. In a large bowl, mix together the chicken, 1 cup of the mozzarella, the ricotta, Parmesan, onions, and egg. Add the sautéed vegetables and mix well.

Preheat the oven to 350°F. In a lightly sprayed or oiled 9-by-13-inch glass baking dish, spread ½ cup of the béchamel sauce. With a spoon, fill the manicotti with the chicken-mushroom mixture and place on top of the sauce (place the shells on a clean kitchen towel while assembling). Pour the remaining sauce over the manicotti and sprinkle with the remaining 1 cup mozzarella. Bake, uncovered, until the cheese is golden and the sauce is bubbly, about 30 minutes. Let stand for 5 to 10 minutes before serving.

Makes 6 servings

BÉCHAMEL SAUCE

3	tablespoons butter
¼	cup all-purpose flour
2½	cups whole milk
1	teaspoon salt
¼	teaspoon ground white pepper

In a large saucepan over medium heat, melt the butter. Add the flour and stir until bubbly, about 1 minute. Add the milk, salt, and pepper and whisk until thickened, about 2 minutes. Set aside to cool.

Makes about 3½ cups

CHICKEN CASSEROLE, ITALIAN STYLE

Bring this rustic, bubbly dish of saucy chicken and beans to the table for a colorful one-pot meal. Serve with artisan olive bread.

1   tablespoon olive oil

1   cup chopped yellow onion

½   red bell pepper, sliced lengthwise into narrow strips

2   garlic cloves, chopped

1   can (14½ ounces) Italian-style tomatoes including juice, cut up

¼   cup dry red wine

1   teaspoon salt

½   teaspoon dried thyme

½   teaspoon dried basil

¼   teaspoon dried oregano
    Freshly ground pepper

2   cans (15 ounces each) cannellini (white kidney beans), drained and rinsed

2   cups diced cooked chicken

3   tablespoons chopped fresh parsley
    Freshly grated Parmesan cheese for sprinkling on top

1   cup pitted black olives

Preheat the oven to 350°F. In a medium skillet over medium heat, warm the oil. Add the onions, bell pepper, and garlic and sauté until the vegetables are slightly tender, about 5 minutes. Add the tomatoes, wine, and seasonings and simmer for 2 to 3 minutes. Transfer the sauce to a lightly sprayed or oiled 2-quart casserole dish. Add the beans, chicken, and parsley and mix well.

Cover and bake until bubbly, about 35 minutes. Sprinkle with the Parmesan and dot with the olives and bake, uncovered, 10 minutes longer. Let stand for 5 to 10 minutes before serving.

Makes 6 to 8 servings

GREEK CHICKEN AND RICE

This Greek-inspired dish of chicken, rice, and vegetables with a light lemon flavor is a good change of pace and will add variety to your menu. Warm pita bread is a typical accompaniment, along with sliced tomatoes and cucumbers.

1 tablespoon olive oil	½ cup pitted kalamata olives
1 cup chopped yellow onion	Juice of 1 lemon
1 cup chopped red bell pepper	¾ teaspoon dried oregano
1 garlic clove, minced	½ teaspoon salt
1 cup uncooked long-grain white rice	Freshly ground pepper
2½ cups cubed cooked chicken	½ cup crumbled feta cheese
2¼ cups Basic Chicken Stock (page 29) or reduced-sodium chicken broth	

Preheat the oven to 350°F. In a large skillet over medium heat, warm the oil. Add the onions, bell pepper, and garlic and sauté until tender, about 5 minutes. Stir in the rice. Transfer to a lightly sprayed or oiled 2-quart casserole. Add the chicken, stock, olives, lemon juice, oregano, salt, and pepper to taste and mix well. Cover and bake until the rice is tender and the liquid is absorbed, about 50 minutes. Sprinkle with the feta cheese. Let stand for 5 to 10 minutes before serving.

Makes 4 to 6 servings

FRIDAY NIGHT SUPPER

Parents' night out? Make this casserole ahead and let the kids pop it in the oven. Have plenty of ice cream and chocolate sauce on hand to keep everyone happy.

8 ounces (2 cups) large elbow macaroni, cooked according to package directions, drained
1 tablespoon vegetable oil, plus more to taste
1 pound ground chicken
½ cup chopped yellow onion
½ cup chopped red bell pepper

1 can (15 ounces) tomato sauce
½ teaspoon dried basil
¼ teaspoon salt
Freshly ground pepper
1 cup (4 ounces) shredded Cheddar cheese

Preheat the oven to 350°F. Place the macaroni in a lightly sprayed or oiled 2-quart casserole. In a large skillet over medium heat, warm the oil. Add the chicken and sauté, breaking it up with a spoon, until the chicken is no longer pink, about 5 minutes. Transfer the chicken to the casserole. Add the onions and bell pepper to the skillet and sauté until tender, 5 minutes. Add more oil, if needed. Stir in the tomato sauce, basil, salt, and pepper to taste. Add them to the casserole and mix well. Bake, covered, for 35 minutes. Uncover and stir. Sprinkle with the cheese and bake, uncovered, until bubbly and the cheese is melted, about 10 minutes longer. Let stand for 5 to 10 minutes before serving.

Makes 6 servings

BLUEBERRY-SOY CHICKEN BREASTS

You will be surprised at the unique taste of blueberries when combined with chicken. The blueberry-soy sauce makes a good balance of salty and sweet that complement the chicken.

4   boned and skinned chicken breast halves (about 2 pounds)
    Olive oil for brushing on chicken
    Salt and freshly ground pepper
    Blueberry-Soy Sauce (recipe follows)

Preheat the oven to 350°F. Place the chicken breasts in a lightly sprayed or oiled 7-by-11-inch glass baking dish. Brush with oil and season with salt and pepper to taste. Bake, uncovered, for 10 minutes. Pour the sauce over the chicken. Bake until the chicken is cooked through, about 25 minutes longer. Let stand for 5 to 10 minutes before serving.

Makes 4 to 6 servings

BLUEBERRY-SOY SAUCE

2   cups blueberries, fresh or frozen
¼   cup sugar
2   tablespoons soy sauce
2   tablespoons water
2   teaspoons cornstarch
½   teaspoon grated lemon zest
⅛   teaspoon ground cloves

In a saucepan over medium heat, combine all the ingredients. Cook, stirring constantly, until thickened, 1 to 2 minutes.

Makes about 2½ cups

CHICKEN BRUNCH CASSEROLE

This all-purpose casserole can be served for brunch, lunch, or supper. Avoid a last-minute rush by preparing it ahead and baking later. Fresh fruit sorbet is a light, refreshing accompaniment.

3   tablespoons butter
12 ounces medium mushrooms, sliced
6   green onions including some tender green tops, sliced
2   cups small-curd cottage cheese
2   cups sour cream
8   large eggs
1   cup (4 ounces) freshly grated Parmesan cheese

½   cup all-purpose flour
½   teaspoon salt
    Dash ground white pepper
3   cups (12 ounces) shredded Monterey Jack cheese
2   cups chopped cooked chicken

Preheat the oven to 350°F. In a medium skillet over medium heat, melt the butter. Add the mushrooms and onions and sauté until tender, about 5 minutes. Set aside.

In a food processor or blender, blend the cottage cheese, sour cream, eggs, Parmesan, flour, salt, and pepper. Transfer to a large bowl. Fold in the Monterey Jack, chicken, and sautéed vegetables. Pour the mixture into a lightly sprayed or oiled 9-by-13-inch glass baking dish. Bake until the casserole is puffed up and golden, about 45 minutes. Let stand for 5 to 10 minutes before serving. Cut into squares to serve.

Makes 8 servings

CHICKEN AND CHILE EGG PUFF

This is a popular brunch dish, with chicken added for substance and flavor. This recipe can easily be doubled for a crowd. Serve with buttermilk biscuits and homemade jam.

5 large eggs
2 tablespoons all-purpose flour
½ teaspoon baking powder
¼ teaspoon salt
Freshly ground pepper
1½ cups (6 ounces) shredded Cheddar cheese
1 cup cottage cheese

1 cup diced cooked chicken
½ can (2 ounces) diced green chiles or more to taste, drained
⅓ cup Fresh Tomato Salsa (page 35) or purchased salsa
Toppings: Sour cream and avocado slices

Preheat the oven to 350°F. In a medium bowl, whisk together the eggs, flour, baking powder, salt, and pepper to taste. Fold in the cheeses, chicken, chiles, and salsa. Pour into a lightly sprayed or oiled 8-by-8-inch glass baking dish. Bake until the eggs are set, about 45 minutes. Let stand for 5 to 10 minutes before serving. Serve the toppings in bowls.

Makes 4 servings

CHICKEN
ON THE GRILL

Grilling is one of the easiest ways to cook chicken. It can be done any time of the year, but is especially popular in the summer months for outdoor eating. It is generally considered a healthy method because little or no fat is required. Grilling produces a light smoky flavor and aesthetic grill marks. All forms of chicken—whole or parts—lend themselves well to grilling. Any type barbecue can be used, whether charcoal, gas, or electric. A covered grill is needed for a whole chicken.

GOOD NEIGHBOR CHICKEN

Call the neighbors over for an impromptu barbecue with this delicious chicken, and serve it with corn on the cob and sliced summer tomatoes with a fresh basil vinaigrette. Sometimes "spur of the moment" dinners are the most fun.

MARINADE

½ cup ketchup

¼ cup soy sauce

¼ cup dry white wine

1 tablespoon honey

1 tablespoon vegetable oil

2 garlic cloves, minced

1 teaspoon Worcestershire sauce

1 chicken (3½ to 4 pounds), cut into serving pieces, excess fat and skin trimmed

To make the marinade, in a small bowl, mix together all the ingredients. Place the chicken in a 9-by-13-inch glass baking dish, pour the marinade over it, and turn to coat. Cover and marinate for several hours in the refrigerator, turning once. Bring to room temperature before grilling.

Prepare a grill for cooking over medium indirect heat. Remove the chicken from the marinade and boil the marinade in a small pan for 1 minute. Place the chicken on a sprayed or oiled grate. Grill until it is no longer pink in the center or a meat thermometer inserted in a thigh registers 180°F, about 1 hour, turning several times and basting with the marinade.

Makes 4 servings

MUSTARD CHICKEN WITH SESAME SEEDS

You'll love the flavor and texture of this chicken marinated in a zesty combination of beer, mustard, and seasonings and covered with a crunchy coating of sesame seeds. Serve with roasted new potatoes.

MUSTARD MARINADE

½ cup flat beer
¼ cup prepared mustard
¼ cup sesame seeds, divided
1 tablespoon vegetable oil
1 garlic clove, minced
½ teaspoon salt
½ teaspoon paprika
⅛ teaspoon freshly ground pepper

1 chicken (3½ to 4 pounds), cut into serving pieces, excess fat and skin trimmed

To make the marinade, in a small bowl, stir together all the ingredients except 2 tablespoons of the sesame seeds. Place the chicken in a 9-by-13-inch glass baking dish. Pour the marinade over it. Cover and marinate for several hours in the refrigerator, turning once. Bring to room temperature before grilling.

Prepare a grill for cooking over medium indirect heat. Remove the chicken from the marinade and boil the marinade in a small pan for 1 minute. Place the chicken on a sprayed or oiled grate. Grill, turning occasionally and basting with the marinade, for about 45 minutes. Using the back of a spoon, pat the remaining 2 tablespoons sesame seeds onto the chicken pieces, coating evenly. Grill until the chicken is no longer pink in the center or a meat thermometer inserted in a thigh registers 180°F and the sesame seeds are toasted, about 15 minutes longer, turning once.

Makes 4 servings

GRILLED CHICKEN WITH FAVORITE BARBECUE SAUCE

Everyone likes a summer barbecue, especially with this grilled chicken in a zesty barbecue sauce. The sweet tomato-based sauce burns easily, so it is added halfway through the grilling period. Serve with fresh summer vegetables and grilled sourdough bread slices on the side.

1 chicken (3½ to 4 pounds), cut into serving pieces, excess fat and skin trimmed
Vegetable oil for brushing
Favorite Barbecue Sauce (recipe follows)

Prepare a grill for cooking over medium indirect heat. Brush the chicken with oil and place on a sprayed or oiled grate. Grill for about 30 minutes, turning several times. Brush with the sauce and continue to grill, brushing often with sauce and turning several times, until the chicken is no longer pink in the center or a meat thermometer inserted in a thigh registers 180°F, about 30 minutes longer.

Makes 4 servings

FAVORITE BARBECUE SAUCE

¼ cup ketchup
¼ cup chili sauce
  Juice of 1 lemon (about 3 tablespoons)
1 tablespoon vegetable oil
1 tablespoon prepared horseradish
1 tablespoon brown sugar
1 teaspoon prepared mustard

1 teaspoon Worcestershire sauce
½ teaspoon salt
⅛ teaspoon freshly ground pepper

In a medium bowl, whisk together all the ingredients.

Makes about ⅔ cup

CHICKEN CHARDONNAY

Wine and herbs add a complex flavor to this sophisticated chicken.
Serve with chilled Chardonnay for a complementary drink.

1   chicken (3½ to 4 pounds), cut into serving
pieces, excess fat and skin trimmed
1   cup Chardonnay or other dry white wine
2   tablespoons Dijon mustard
2   tablespoons vegetable oil
½   teaspoon dried basil
½   teaspoon salt
¼   teaspoon dried oregano
¼   teaspoon dried rosemary
Freshly ground pepper

Place the chicken in a 9-by-13-inch glass baking dish. In a small bowl, whisk together the remaining ingredients and pour them over the chicken. Cover and marinate in the refrigerator for several hours, turning once. Bring to room temperature before grilling.

Prepare a grill for cooking over medium indirect heat. Remove the chicken from the marinade and discard the marinade. Place the chicken on a sprayed or oiled grate. Grill until it is no longer pink in the center or a meat thermometer inserted in a thigh registers 180°F, about 1 hour, turning several times.

Makes 4 servings

PICNIC CHICKEN IN A TANGY BEER MARINADE

Pack up a picnic basket with this chicken that is equally good hot or cold. Include artisan bread, assorted cheeses, and fresh fruit for a lunch in the country.

TANGY BEER MARINADE

1 cup flat beer
¼ cup soy sauce
1 tablespoon vegetable oil
2 garlic cloves, minced
1 teaspoon ground mustard

1 chicken (3½ to 4 pounds) cut into serving pieces, excess fat and skin trimmed

To make the marinade, in a large bowl, combine all the ingredients. Add the chicken pieces and mix well. Cover and refrigerate several hours or overnight, turning once. Bring to room temperature before grilling.

Prepare a grill for cooking over medium indirect heat. Remove the chicken from the marinade and boil the marinade in a small pan for 1 minute. Place the chicken on a sprayed or oiled grate. Grill, turning occasionally and basting with the marinade, until no longer pink in the center or a meat thermometer inserted in a thigh registers 180°F, about 1 hour. Serve immediately or, if transporting, cover and chill thoroughly in the refrigerator and pack in an insulated container to transport.

Makes 4 servings

BUTTERMILK HERBED CHICKEN ON THE GRILL

A mixture of buttermilk and herbs gives this chicken a great, old-fashioned fried flavor. Serve hot or cold at your next picnic or potluck.

BUTTERMILK MARINADE

1   cup well-shaken buttermilk
½   teaspoon dried thyme
½   teaspoon ground sage
½   teaspoon dried marjoram
½   teaspoon dried rosemary
½   teaspoon freshly ground pepper
½   teaspoon salt

1   chicken (3½ to 4 pounds), cut into serving pieces, excess fat and skin trimmed

To make the marinade, in a large bowl, mix together all the ingredients. Add the chicken and turn to coat. Cover and marinate in the refrigerator for several hours, turning once. Bring to room temperature before grilling.

Prepare a grill for cooking over medium indirect heat. Remove the chicken from the marinade and discard the marinade. Place the chicken on a sprayed or oiled grate. Grill until the chicken is no longer pink in the center or a meat thermometer inserted in a thigh registers 180°F, about 1 hour, turning several times.

Makes 4 servings

GRILLED CHICKEN BREASTS WITH CITRUS MARINADE

When grilling chicken breasts, care must be taken not to overcook, as they dry out easily and become tough. Citrus flavors liven up this chicken and impart a refreshing taste for something different to serve for your next barbecue. Pair with a pasta salad.

MARINADE

2	tablespoons fresh lemon juice
2	tablespoons fresh lime juice
2	tablespoons olive oil
1	tablespoon honey
2	garlic cloves, minced
1	teaspoon grated lime zest
1	teaspoon dried oregano
¼	teaspoon salt
2 or 3	drops Tabasco sauce

4   boned and skinned chicken breast halves (about 2 pounds)

To make the marinade, in a medium bowl, mix together all the ingredients. Put the chicken in a sprayed or oiled 8-by-8-inch glass baking dish and pour the marinade over it. Cover and marinate in the refrigerator for several hours, turning once.

Prepare a grill for cooking over medium indirect heat. Remove the chicken from the marinade and discard the marinade. Place the chicken on a sprayed or oiled grate and grill until it is cooked through or a meat thermometer inserted in the middle registers 170°F, 10 to 12 minutes, turning once.

Makes 4 servings

GRILLED LEMON-SOY-HONEY CHICKEN BREASTS

A sweet-tart marinade adds a lot of flavor to these chicken breasts. Allow several hours for them to marinate. Serve with rice or Chinese noodles and pass additional soy sauce.

¼ cup soy sauce
  Juice of 1 lemon
1 tablespoon vegetable oil
1 tablespoon honey
1 garlic clove, minced
1 teaspoon grated lemon zest
4 boned and skinned chicken breast halves (about 2 pounds)

In a 7-by-11-inch glass baking dish, whisk together the soy sauce, lemon juice, oil, honey, garlic, and zest. Add the chicken breasts and turn to coat. Cover and marinate in the refrigerator for several hours, turning once. Bring to room temperature before grilling.

Prepare a grill for cooking over medium indirect heat. Remove the chicken from the marinade and discard the marinade. Place the chicken on a sprayed or oiled grate, and grill until it is cooked through or a meat thermometer inserted in the middle registers 170°F, 10 to 12 minutes, turning once.

Makes 4 servings

GRILLED CHICKEN BREASTS WITH ONIONS AND BACON

This delicious grill combination was developed by my husband, Reed, who loves onions and bacon. The chicken, onions, and bacon are placed in a hinged grill rack, and as they cook on the grill, the bacon drippings flavor the chicken and onions and add a smoky taste. Let the man of the house show off his grilling expertise with this one.

8   slices bacon
1   yellow onion, thinly sliced
4   boned and skinned chicken breast halves (about 2 pounds)
    Salt and freshly ground pepper

Prepare a grill for cooking over medium-high direct heat. Using a hinged grill rack, place 4 bacon slices on 1 side of the rack, then a layer of onion slices on top of the bacon. Add the chicken breasts and season with salt and pepper to taste. Add another layer of onion slices and bacon slices. Close the rack and grill until the bacon is crisp and the chicken is cooked through or a meat thermometer inserted in the middle registers 170°F, 10 to 12 minutes, turning several times. Watch carefully and, if the drippings flare up, turn the grill rack over quickly and move it to the cooler side.

Makes 4 servings

GRILLED CHICKEN WITH ORANGE-APRICOT BARBECUE SAUCE

When you want something different, this fruity, sweet barbecue sauce will add a new dimension to grilled chicken breasts. The marmalade and preserves can be purchased at most supermarkets. Serve with coleslaw.

ORANGE-APRICOT BARBECUE SAUCE

2   tablespoons vegetable oil, divided
½   cup minced yellow onion
1   garlic clove, minced
¼   cup orange marmalade
¼   cup apricot preserves
¼   cup ketchup
2   teaspoons prepared mustard
1   teaspoon Worcestershire sauce
¼   teaspoon salt
    Freshly ground pepper

6   boned and skinned chicken breast
    halves (about 3 pounds)

To make the sauce, in a medium saucepan over medium heat, warm 1 tablespoon of the oil. Add the onion and garlic and sauté until tender, about 5 minutes. Add the remaining ingredients and mix well. Set aside.

Prepare a grill for cooking over medium indirect heat. Brush the chicken with the remaining 1 tablespoon oil. Place it on the grate. Brush both sides with sauce and close the grill cover. Grill until the chicken is cooked through or a meat thermometer inserted in the middle registers 170°F, 10 to 12 minutes longer, turning once.

Makes 4 to 6 servings

GRILLED CHICKEN BREASTS AND VEGETABLES WITH WINE-SOY MARINADE

Chicken and vegetables cook here alongside each other on the grill for a complete entrée. A grill basket is a good way to grill vegetables. Take a trip to the farmer's market for a selection of fresh vegetables.

WINE-SOY MARINADE:

⅓ cup dry white wine

⅓ cup soy sauce

2 tablespoons fresh lemon juice

1 tablespoon honey

1 tablespoon vegetable oil

1 teaspoon Worcestershire sauce

1 garlic clove, minced

¼ teaspoon salt

Freshly ground pepper

4 boned and skinned chicken breast halves (about 2 pounds)

1 zucchini, ends trimmed, cut in half lengthwise

1 small red bell pepper, quartered lengthwise

1 small green or yellow bell pepper, quartered lengthwise

1 red onion, cut into ¾-inch slices

To make the marinade, in a small bowl or cup, mix together all the ingredients. Place the chicken in an 8-by-8-inch glass baking dish and pour half of the marinade over it. Set aside the remaining marinade. Cover and marinate the chicken in the refrigerator for several hours, turning once. Bring to room temperature before grilling.

Prepare a grill for cooking over medium indirect heat. Place the vegetables in a lightly sprayed or oiled grill basket and brush with the reserved marinade. Grill for 5 minutes, turning once. Remove the chicken from the marinade and discard the marinade. Place the chicken on a sprayed or oiled grate along with the vegetable basket. Grill until the chicken is cooked through or a meat thermometer inserted in the middle registers 170°F and the vegetables are tender-crisp, 10 to 12 minutes longer, brushing with the reserved marinade and turning once.

Makes 4 servings

CHICKEN BREASTS WITH MUSTARD GLAZE

Topped with this zesty glaze of two mustards and horseradish, you'll never think these chicken breasts are boring. A macaroni salad makes a good side dish.

GLAZE

¼ cup Dijon mustard

¼ cup prepared mustard

2 tablespoons red wine vinegar

1 tablespoon prepared horseradish sauce

1 tablespoon vegetable oil

1 tablespoon light molasses

1 teaspoon Worcestershire sauce

6 boned and skinned chicken breast halves (about 3 pounds)

To make the glaze, in a small bowl, stir together all the ingredients. Place the chicken in a 7-by-11-inch glass baking dish and spread half of the mixture on the chicken. Set the remaining mixture aside. Cover and marinate the chicken in the refrigerator for several hours, turning once. Bring to room temperature before grilling.

Prepare a grill for cooking over medium indirect heat. Place the chicken on a sprayed or oiled grate and grill, brushing with the remaining glaze, until it is cooked through or a meat thermometer inserted in the middle registers 170°F, 10 to 12 minutes, turning once.

Makes 6 servings

GRILLED CASHEW CHICKEN BREASTS

These juicy chicken breasts are flavored with just a hint of orange and topped with chopped cashew nuts for extra crunch. This makes a tasty dish to serve for a spring dinner with young, tender asparagus.

MARINADE

¼ cup fresh orange juice
¼ cup soy sauce
¼ cup dry white wine
1 tablespoon vegetable oil
1 garlic clove, minced
1 teaspoon grated orange zest
½ teaspoon salt
¼ teaspoon dried thyme
   Freshly ground pepper

6 boned and skinned chicken breast halves (about 3 pounds)
½ cup coarsely chopped unsalted cashew nuts
   Orange slices for garnish
   Flat-leaf parsley sprigs for garnish

To make the marinade, in a medium bowl, mix together all the marinade ingredients. Place the chicken in a 7-by-11-inch glass baking dish. Pour the marinade over the chicken. Cover and marinate in the refrigerator for several hours, turning occasionally. Bring to room temperature before grilling.

Prepare a grill for cooking over medium indirect heat. Remove the chicken from the marinade and discard the marinade. Place the chicken on a sprayed or oiled grate and grill until it is cooked through or a meat thermometer inserted in the middle registers 170°F, about 10 minutes, turning once. Sprinkle the cashews on top of the chicken and grill, covered, until the nuts are toasted, 2 to 3 minutes longer. Transfer the chicken to a platter and garnish with orange slices and parsley sprigs.

Makes 6 servings

TANDOORI-STYLE CHICKEN BREASTS

Originating in India, tandoori dishes refer to food marinated in a tangy sauce of yogurt and spices and roasted in a hot brick and clay oven called a tandoor. Tandoori is also the name of the dish. A grill is the next best thing to a tandoor to bring out the authentic, exotic flavors of this dish. Serve with sliced cucumbers, flatbread, and lime slices.

TANDOORI MARINADE

1 cup nonfat plain yogurt
  Juice of 1 lime
4 garlic cloves, minced
1 tablespoon peeled, grated fresh ginger
1 teaspoon grated lime zest
1 teaspoon paprika
1 teaspoon turmeric
1 teaspoon ground cumin
1 teaspoon ground coriander
1 teaspoon salt
¼ teaspoon cayenne
¼ teaspoon ground cloves

6 boned and skinned chicken breast halves (about 3 pounds)
  Lime wedges for garnish

To make the marinade, in a large bowl, combine the marinade ingredients. Add the chicken breasts and coat well. Cover and marinate in the refrigerator for 6 to 8 hours, turning once. Bring to room temperature before grilling.

Prepare a grill for cooking over medium indirect heat. Remove the chicken from the marinade and discard the marinade. Place the chicken on a sprayed or oiled grate and grill until it is cooked through or a meat thermometer inserted in the middle registers 170°F, 10 to 12 minutes, turning once. Transfer to a plate and garnish with lime wedges.

Makes 6 servings

RUM CHICKEN ON THE GRILL

To dress up your everyday menu, grill these breasts with a refreshing marinade of rum, lime juice, and soy sauce.

LIME MARINADE

½ cup white rum

3 tablespoons soy sauce

2 limes, 1 juiced and 1 cut into wedges
   for garnish

1 tablespoon honey

2 garlic cloves, minced

6 boned and skinned chicken breast
   halves (about 3 pounds)

To make the marinade, in a small bowl, mix together the rum, soy sauce, lime juice, honey, and garlic. Place the chicken in a deep-dish glass pie plate and pour the mixture over it. Cover and marinate in the refrigerator for several hours, turning once. Bring to room temperature before grilling.

Prepare a grill for cooking over medium indirect heat. Remove the chicken from the marinade and discard the marinade. Place the chicken on a sprayed or oiled grate and grill until it is cooked through or a meat thermometer inserted in the middle registers 170°F, 10 to 12 minutes, turning once. Garnish with the lime wedges.

Makes 6 servings

ASIAN-STYLE GRILLED CHICKEN BREASTS

For a mellow flavor, a sweet hoisin glaze is brushed on these chicken breasts while they grill. Serve with rice or noodles and offer chopsticks for a fun dinner.

4   boned and skinned chicken breast halves (about 2 pounds)
    Vegetable oil for brushing
    Salt and freshly ground pepper
    Hoisin Glaze (recipe follows)
¼   cup chopped green onions, including some tender green tops

Prepare a grill for cooking over medium indirect heat. Brush the chicken breasts lightly with oil. Season with salt and pepper to taste. Place them on a sprayed or oiled grate, brush with the glaze, and grill for about 5 minutes. Turn the chicken over, brush with the glaze, and grill until the chicken is no longer pink in the center or a meat thermometer inserted in the middle registers 170°F, 5 to 6 minutes longer. Transfer to a plate and sprinkle with the green onions.

Makes 4 servings

HOISIN GLAZE

¼   cup hoisin sauce
3   tablespoons ketchup
2   tablespoons white wine vinegar
1   tablespoon soy sauce
¼   teaspoon ground ginger

To make the glaze, in a medium bowl, mix together all the ingredients.

Makes about ½ cup

GRILLED INDIAN-SPICED CHICKEN BREASTS

Experience a new taste sensation with this spicy yogurt marinade that contributes to the moist, tender chicken. In keeping with the theme, serve with a side dish of basmati rice or couscous along with a platter of exotic fruit such as papaya, kiwi, and mango.

MARINADE

1	cup nonfat plain yogurt
¼	small red onion, cut up
2 or 3	sprigs fresh cilantro, torn
2	garlic cloves, cut up
½	teaspoon curry powder
½	teaspoon ground cumin
½	teaspoon ground coriander
½	teaspoon salt
¼	teaspoon turmeric

6 boned and skinned chicken breast halves (about 3 pounds)
Cilantro sprigs for garnish

To make the marinade, place all the marinade ingredients in a food processor and process until smooth. Put the chicken in a 7-by-11-inch glass baking dish and pour the marinade over it. Cover and marinate in the refrigerator for several hours, turning once. Bring to room temperature before grilling.

Prepare a grill for cooking over medium indirect heat. Remove the chicken breasts from the marinade and discard the marinade. Place the chicken on a sprayed or oiled grate and grill until it is cooked through or a meat thermometer inserted in the middle registers 170°F, 10 to 12 minutes, turning once. Transfer to a plate and garnish with cilantro.

Makes 6 servings

SPICED ORANGE CHICKEN POCKETS

Boned and skinned chicken breast pieces marinated in orange juice and spices make a flavorful filling for pocket bread (pita) sandwiches. Serve with sliced cucumbers.

MARINADE

¾ cup fresh orange juice

1 tablespoon honey

2 teaspoons grated orange zest

1 garlic clove, minced

½ teaspoon ground cumin

½ teaspoon ground ginger

¼ teaspoon cayenne

¼ teaspoon ground coriander

Dash ground cinnamon

4 boned and skinned chicken breast halves (about 2 pounds)

6 pocket breads (7-inch), halved and warmed (see Note, facing page)

2 bunches green onions including some tender green tops, chopped

Yogurt Sauce (facing page)

To make the marinade, in a medium bowl, mix together all the ingredients. Set aside ¼ cup marinade. Add the chicken to the remaining marinade and refrigerate for several hours, turning once. Bring to room temperature before grilling.

Prepare a grill for cooking over medium indirect heat. Remove the chicken from the marinade and discard the marinade. Place the chicken on a lightly sprayed or oiled grate and grill until it is cooked through or a meat thermometer inserted in the middle registers 170°F, 10 to 12 minutes, brushing with reserved marinade, and turning once. Cut into bite-sized pieces and slide the chicken into the pocket bread halves. Add onions and a dollop of Yogurt Sauce.

Makes 4 servings

NOTE: To warm pocket bread, wrap it in foil and warm in a 350°F oven for 10 minutes.

YOGURT SAUCE

1 cup nonfat plain yogurt
1 tablespoon honey
Juice of 1 lime
½ teaspoon ground cumin
¼ teaspoon salt

In a small bowl, whisk together all the ingredients.

Makes about 1 cup

GRILLED TERIYAKI DRUMSTICKS

These drumsticks are glazed with a flavorful combination of soy, rice vinegar, and honey. Make ahead and let them marinate for several hours to develop flavor. This marinade is good on all chicken parts.

MARINADE

- ½ cup soy sauce
- ½ cup rice vinegar
- 3 tablespoons honey
- 1 tablespoon vegetable oil
- 2 garlic cloves, minced

- 16 chicken drumsticks (about 4 pounds), excess skin and fat trimmed

To make the marinade, in a large bowl, mix together all the ingredients. Pour half of the marinade over the chicken. Set aside the remaining marinade for basting. Cover and marinate the chicken in the refrigerator for 2 to 3 hours, turning once. Bring to room temperature before grilling.

Prepare a grill for cooking over medium indirect heat. Remove the chicken from the marinade and boil the marinade in a small pan for 1 minute. Place the chicken on a sprayed or oiled grate. Grill until the drumsticks are lightly browned and crispy on the outside and no longer pink in the center or a meat thermometer inserted in a drumstick registers 180°F, about 45 minutes, turning and basting with the marinade several times.

Makes 6 to 8 servings

ISLAND CHICKEN KABOBS WITH FRESH PINEAPPLE AND PAPAYA

Kabobs are fun to make and are an impressive presentation. Here the fruit is grilled along with the chicken to bring out its natural sweetness and flavor.

1 container (12 ounces) fresh pineapple chunks, drained and juice reserved	1 firm papaya, peeled, seeded, and cut into 1½-inch pieces
¼ cup soy sauce	1 red onion, cut into 1-inch wedges and separated
1 tablespoon packed brown sugar	2 boned and skinned chicken breast halves (about 1 pound), cut into 1½-inch pieces
1 teaspoon ground ginger	
¼ teaspoon ground mustard	
¼ teaspoon salt	Mint leaves for garnish
Freshly ground pepper	
2 to 3 drops Tabasco sauce	

In a medium bowl, mix together the reserved pineapple juice, soy sauce, sugar, ginger, mustard, salt, pepper to taste, and Tabasco. Add the pineapple and papaya chunks and toss to coat with the mixture. Remove the fruit with a slotted spoon, cover, and refrigerate it.

Add the chicken to the marinade and mix well. Cover and marinate in the refrigerator for several hours, turning once. Bring to room temperature before grilling.

Prepare a grill for cooking over medium indirect heat. Remove the chicken from the marinade and discard the marinade. Thread the chicken on skewers, alternating with the pineapple and papaya chunks and the onions. Place the kabobs on a sprayed or oiled grate and grill until the chicken is cooked through and the pineapple and papaya are warmed, about 10 minutes, turning several times. Transfer the skewers to a platter and garnish with mint leaves.

Makes 4 servings

NOTE: If using wooden skewers, soak in water for 30 minutes prior to using.

CHICKEN WITH BOURBON SAUCE

This dramatic grilled chicken recipe, featuring a distinctive bourbon sauce, makes a bold statement. Serve with a fresh tomato and watercress salad with feta cheese.

SAUCE

1 cup ketchup
¼ cup light molasses
¼ cup bourbon
2 tablespoons Dijon mustard
1 tablespoon Worcestershire sauce
1 garlic clove, minced
1 teaspoon paprika
1 teaspoon salt
   Dash Tabasco sauce

4 bone-in chicken thighs (about 1½ pounds), excess fat and skin trimmed
4 chicken drumsticks (about 1 pound), excess fat and skin trimmed
2 boned and skinned chicken breast halves (about 1 pound), cut in half

To make the sauce, in a medium saucepan over medium-high heat, combine all the ingredients and bring to a boil. Reduce the heat to low and simmer, uncovered, until the flavors are blended, about 5 minutes.

Prepare a grill for cooking over medium indirect heat. Place the chicken on a sprayed or oiled grate and brush it with the sauce. Grill with the lid closed, brushing with sauce and turning several times, until the chicken is no longer pink in the center, or a meat thermometer inserted in a thigh registers 180°F, about 30 minutes for the breasts and 45 minutes for the thighs and drumsticks.

Makes 6 to 8 servings

GRILLED THAI CHICKEN

For a departure from the usual grilled chicken, here is a combination of Thai ingredients for an interesting topping. Lemongrass is often used in Thai cooking; however, it is not always available and, as an alternative, lemon zest can be used. Keep in mind that boneless thighs do not take as long to cook as thighs with bones.

THAI TOPPING

2	shallots, cut up
2	garlic cloves, cut up
3 or 4	sprigs fresh cilantro
1	tablespoon sugar
1	teaspoon turmeric
1	teaspoon ground cumin
2 to 3	tablespoons chopped fresh lemongrass or 1 teaspoon grated lemon zest
¼	cup soy sauce, divided
6 or 8	boned and skinned chicken thighs (about 1½ pounds)

To make the topping, place all the ingredients in a food processor except 2 tablespoons of the soy sauce, and process until chunky; set aside. Place the remaining 2 tablespoons soy sauce in a 7-by-11-inch glass baking dish. Add the chicken and turn to coat. Cover and marinate in the refrigerator for several hours, turning once. Bring to room temperature before grilling.

Prepare a grill for cooking over medium indirect heat. Remove the chicken from the marinade and discard the marinade. Place the chicken on a sprayed or oiled grate. Grill for 10 minutes, and then spread on the topping. Grill until the chicken is no longer pink in the center or a meat thermometer inserted in a thigh registers 180°F, and the topping is warm, about 10 minutes longer.

Makes 4 servings

GRILLED WHOLE CHICKEN, GREEK STYLE

Serve this delicious Greek-inspired lemony chicken with a side dish of orzo, a Greek salad, and pita bread.

GREEK MARINADE

½ cup dry white wine
    Juice of 1 lemon
1   lemon, cut in half, 1 half sliced, 1 half
    left whole
1   tablespoon olive oil
3   garlic cloves, minced
2   teaspoons grated lemon zest
1   teaspoon dried oregano
1   teaspoon salt
¼   teaspoon freshly ground pepper

1   chicken (3½ to 4 pounds), giblets removed,
    excess fat and skin trimmed

To make the marinade, in a medium bowl, mix together the wine, lemon juice, oil, garlic, and seasonings. Pour half of the marinade over the chicken. Reserve the remaining marinade for basting. Cover the chicken and refrigerate for 2 to 3 hours. Spoon the marinade over it several times. Bring to room temperature before grilling.

Prepare a grill for cooking over medium indirect heat. Remove the chicken from the marinade and discard the marinade. Place the chicken on a rotisserie attachment and follow the manufacturer's directions, or place it in a lightly sprayed or oiled foil pan. Put the lemon half in the cavity. Grill the chicken, basting with the reserved marinade several times, until it is no longer pink in the center or a thermometer inserted in the thigh registers 180°F, about 1½ hours. Transfer to a platter and let it stand 5 to 10 minutes before carving. Arrange the lemon slices on top of the chicken.

Makes 4 servings

CALIFORNIA GRAPEFRUIT CHICKEN

When friends came for a visit from California, they brought sacks and sacks of beautiful grapefruit from their yard. We gave a lot away, but developed this recipe with chicken to showcase the grapefruit flavor.

1 chicken (3½ to 4 pounds), quartered, excess fat and skin trimmed
Grapefruit Marinade (recipe follows)

1 fresh grapefruit, peeled and divided into segments
Fresh mint leaves for garnish

Place the chicken quarters in a 9-by-13-inch glass baking dish and pour the marinade over them. Cover and marinate in the refrigerator for several hours, turning once. Bring to room temperature before grilling.

Prepare a grill for cooking over medium indirect heat. Remove the chicken from the marinade and boil the marinade in a small pan for 1 minute. Place the chicken on a sprayed or oiled grate. Grill until no longer pink in the center or a meat thermometer inserted in a thigh registers 180°F, about 1 hour, turning and brushing with marinade several times. Arrange on a platter and garnish with the grapefruit segments and mint leaves. Serve immediately.

Makes 4 servings

GRAPEFRUIT MARINADE

½ cup fresh grapefruit juice
¼ cup soy sauce
1 tablespoon vegetable oil
1 tablespoon honey
2 garlic cloves, minced
¼ teaspoon ground ginger

In a small bowl, stir together all the ingredients.

Makes about ¾ cup

CHICKEN AND SAUSAGE KABOBS, NEW ORLEANS STYLE

Serve these impressive Cajun-style kabobs on a bed of fluffy white rice. Cajun seasoning is a blend of bold spices used in Louisiana cooking. It's available at most supermarkets or you can make your own with the following recipe. Andouille sausage is a spicy, heavily smoked sausage, popular in Cajun cooking.

¼ cup vegetable oil

2 teaspoons Cajun Seasoning (facing page) or purchased

1 zucchini, cut into 1-inch pieces

½ green bell pepper, cut into 1-inch pieces

½ red bell pepper, cut into 1-inch pieces

½ yellow onion, cut into wedges

2 boned and skinned chicken breast halves (about 1 pound), cut into 1-inch pieces

8 ounces fully cooked andouille sausage, cut diagonally into ¾-inch pieces

In a large bowl, stir together the oil and Cajun Seasoning. Add the vegetables and stir to coat. With a slotted spoon, remove the vegetables to another bowl. Add the chicken to the remaining marinade and turn to coat. Cover and marinate in the refrigerator for several hours, turning once. Bring to room temperature before grilling.

Prepare a grill for cooking over medium indirect heat. Remove the chicken from the marinade and discard the marinade. Thread the chicken on skewers, alternating with the vegetables and sausage. Lay the skewers on a sprayed or oiled grate. Grill until the chicken is cooked through, the sausage is lightly browned, and the vegetables are tender-crisp, about 10 minutes, turning several times.

Makes 4 servings

NOTE: If using wooden skewers, soak in water for 30 minutes prior to using.

CAJUN SEASONING

You may vary the spices to adjust the amount of heat.

1   teaspoon garlic powder

1   teaspoon onion powder

1   teaspoon dried basil

1   teaspoon dried thyme

1   teaspoon paprika

½   teaspoon salt

½   teaspoon finely ground black pepper

¼   teaspoon ground cayenne

¼   teaspoon dried oregano

In a small bowl, mix together all the ingredients. Store leftovers in a tightly covered jar.

Makes about 3 tablespoons

CHILI-LIME DRUMSTICKS AND THIGHS

These drumsticks and thighs are brushed with a sweet-spicy baste and grilled to perfection. Talk about flavor! Make ahead a creamy potato salad and baked beans for a patio party.

CHILI-LIME SAUCE

- 1 tablespoon chili powder
- 1 teaspoon salt
  Freshly ground pepper
- 1 tablespoon honey
  Juice of 1 lime
- 1 tablespoon vegetable oil

- 4 chicken drumsticks (about 1 pound), excess fat and skin trimmed
- 4 bone-in chicken thighs (about 1½ pounds), excess fat and skin trimmed

To make the sauce, in a large bowl, stir together the ingredients. Add the chicken and turn to coat. Let stand for 10 minutes at room temperature.

Prepare a grill for cooking over medium indirect heat. Remove the chicken from the sauce and discard the sauce. Place the chicken on a sprayed or oiled grate. Grill until it is no longer pink in the center or a meat thermometer inserted in a thigh registers 180°F, about 45 minutes, turning several times.

Makes 4 servings

CHICKEN-VEGETABLE KABOBS

Enjoy the great aroma of these kabobs as they cook on the grill. Each person gets his own kabob of chicken and mixed vegetables. Serve with a pasta salad and fresh fruit for a carefree patio dinner.

KABOB MARINADE

¼ cup dry white wine

¼ cup soy sauce

1 tablespoon fresh lemon juice

1 tablespoon honey

1 tablespoon vegetable oil

1 garlic clove, minced

1 teaspoon Worcestershire sauce

¼ teaspoon salt

  Freshly ground pepper

3 boned and skinned chicken breast halves (about 1½ pounds), cut into 1½-inch pieces

1 red bell pepper, cut into 1-inch pieces

1 yellow onion, cut into 1-inch wedges and separated

1 zucchini, cut into ¾-inch pieces

3 plum tomatoes, quartered, or 12 cherry tomatoes

12 mushrooms, stemmed

To make the marinade, in a bowl large enough to hold the chicken, stir together all the marinade ingredients. Remove ¼ cup and set it aside for basting. Add the chicken to the bowl and mix well. Cover and marinate in the refrigerator for several hours, turning once. Bring to room temperature before grilling.

Prepare a grill for cooking over medium indirect heat. Remove the chicken from the marinade and discard the marinade. Thread the chicken on skewers, alternating with the vegetables. Place the kabobs on a sprayed or oiled grate and grill until the chicken is cooked through and the vegetables are tender-crisp, about 10 minutes, turning and brushing with the reserved marinade several times.

Makes 6 servings

NOTE: If using wooden skewers, soak in water for 30 minutes prior to using.

CHICKEN, SHRIMP, AND VEGETABLE KABOBS

Most grillers will love to impress their guests with these showy kabobs flavored with a lemon-wine-herb marinade. Cheesecake makes a complementary dessert.

3 or 4	boned and skinned chicken breast halves (1½ to 2 pounds), cut into 1-inch squares Lemon-Wine-Herb Marinade (facing page)
12	large shrimp, peeled and deveined
½	red bell pepper, cut into 1-inch pieces
½	green bell pepper, cut into 1-inch pieces

8	mushrooms, stems trimmed
1	small yellow onion, cut into 1-inch wedges and separated
	Parsley sprigs for garnish

In a medium bowl, toss the chicken with half of the marinade. Set aside the remaining marinade in a small bowl for basting. Cover and refrigerate the chicken for several hours, turning once. Bring to room temperature before grilling. Fifteen minutes before grilling, toss the shrimp in the marinade with the chicken.

Prepare a grill for cooking over medium indirect heat. Remove the chicken and shrimp from the marinade and discard the marinade. Thread the chicken and shrimp onto skewers, alternating with the vegetables. Place the skewers on a sprayed or oiled grate and grill until the chicken is cooked through, the vegetables are tender-crisp (see Note), and the shrimp is pink, about 10 minutes, turning once. Use the reserved marinade to baste the skewers during grilling. Serve on a platter, garnished with parsley.

Makes 4 servings

NOTE: Peppers take longer to cook than the other vegetables. They can be blanched in boiling water for 2 minutes before grilling, if desired.

If using wooden skewers, soak in water for 30 minutes prior to using.

LEMON-WINE-HERB MARINADE

1   teaspoon grated lemon zest
    Juice of 1 lemon
¼   cup dry white wine
2   tablespoons vegetable oil
1   garlic clove, minced
1   tablespoon chopped fresh basil or
    1 teaspoon dried basil
1   tablespoon chopped fresh rosemary or
    1 teaspoon dried rosemary
½   tablespoon chopped fresh thyme or
    ½ teaspoon dried thyme
½   teaspoon salt
    Freshly ground pepper

In a medium bowl, mix together all the ingredients.

Makes about ½ cup

VODKA-MARINATED CHICKEN QUARTERS

You can have some fun and good table conversation with these chicken quarters uniquely flavored by this smooth vodka marinade. Each diner gets one chicken quarter. Serve with a Caesar salad and a loaf of crusty bread.

MARINADE

½ cup vodka
   Juice of 1 lime
2 tablespoons chopped fresh mint leaves
2 tablespoons sugar
1 tablespoon vegetable oil
1 teaspoon grated lime zest
¼ teaspoon salt

1 chicken (3½ to 4 pounds), quartered,
   excess fat and skin trimmed
   Mint leaves for garnish

To make the marinade, in a 9-by-13-inch glass baking dish, mix together all the marinade ingredients and stir until the sugar is dissolved. Add the chicken and turn to coat. Cover and refrigerate for several hours, turning several times. Bring to room temperature before grilling.

Prepare a grill for cooking over medium indirect heat. Remove the chicken from the marinade and discard the marinade. Place the chicken on a sprayed or oiled grate and grill until lightly browned and it is no longer pink in the center or a meat thermometer inserted in a thigh registers 180°F, about 1 hour, turning several times. Serve on a platter garnished with mint leaves.

Makes 4 servings

WHOLE CHICKEN WITH COUNTRY BARBECUE SAUCE

Busy cooks will enjoy this method of cooking chicken on the grill because it needs little attention. Just brush on this spicy sauce and you will have a tender, moist bird every time. Use a rotisserie or a foil pan in a covered grill.

COUNTRY BARBECUE SAUCE

1 tablespoon vegetable oil
1 tablespoon finely chopped yellow onion
2 garlic cloves, minced
1 can (8 ounces) tomato sauce
3 tablespoons cider vinegar
2 tablespoons packed brown sugar
1 tablespoon Worcestershire sauce
1 teaspoon chili powder
¼ teaspoon ground ginger
¼ teaspoon ground allspice
¼ teaspoon celery salt
¼ teaspoon salt
Freshly ground pepper
2 or 3 drops Tabasco sauce

1 chicken (3½ to 4 pounds), excess fat and skin trimmed, giblets and wing tips removed
½ yellow onion
Vegetable oil for brushing on chicken

To make the sauce, in a medium saucepan over medium heat, warm the oil. Add the 1 tablespoon onions and the garlic and sauté until tender, about 5 minutes. Add the remaining sauce ingredients. Reduce heat to low and simmer until the flavors are blended, about 5 minutes longer. Set aside.

Prepare a grill for cooking over medium indirect heat. Rub the chicken on all sides with oil. Place the ½ onion in the cavity. Place the chicken on a rotisserie attachment and follow the manufacturer's directions, or place it in a lightly sprayed or oiled foil pan on the grate. Cover and grill until it is no longer pink in the center or a meat thermometer inserted in the thigh registers 180°F, about 1½ hours. Transfer to a platter and let it stand for 10 to 15 minutes before carving. Serve with the barbecue sauce.

Makes 4 servings

ROASTED WHOLE CHICKEN ON THE GRILL, ROTISSERIE STYLE

Whole chicken on the grill is one of the easiest and most satisfying ways to serve a crowd. Fully cooked, purchased rotisserie chickens have become very popular and are available in many supermarkets. They are highly seasoned with a spicy rub and cooked on a rotating spit, several at a time. The result is a tender, juicy bird every time. Some stores soak them in a brine first to tenderize and add flavor. You can make your own rotisserie chicken at home if you have a grill with a rotisserie attachment, or it can also be done in a foil pan in a covered grill. The brine is optional.

BASIC BRINE (OPTIONAL)

1 gallon water or enough water to cover chicken
1 cup coarse salt
¼ cup sugar
Other ingredients for extra flavor (optional):
2 bay leaves; 1 teaspoon dried thyme;
4 garlic cloves, split

To make the brine, in a large, nonreactive container, dissolve the salt and sugar in the water. Add other ingredients, if desired.

RUB

1 teaspoon paprika
1 teaspoon chili powder
1 teaspoon ground mustard
½ teaspoon dried thyme
½ teaspoon garlic powder
½ teaspoon onion powder
½ teaspoon salt (omit if brining)
¼ to ½ teaspoon ground cayenne
¼ teaspoon brown sugar

1 chicken (3½ to 4 pounds), excess fat and skin trimmed, giblets and wing tips removed

To make the rub, in a small bowl, mix together all ingredients.

Soak the chicken in brine, if using. Soak several hours or overnight in the refrigerator or in a large, clean ice chest. Rinse and dry with paper towels. Bring to room temperature before grilling.

Prepare a grill for cooking over medium indirect heat. Place the chicken on a rotisserie attachment and follow the manufacturer's directions, or place it in a lightly sprayed or oiled foil pan and put it on the grate. Cook until it is no longer pink in the center or a meat thermometer inserted in the thigh registers 180°F, about 1½ hours. Turn once, if grilling in a pan. Transfer to a platter and let it stand 10 to 15 minutes before carving.

Makes 4 servings

GRILLED CHICKEN UNDER A BRICK

This method appears in some upscale restaurants, but it can also be done at home. For equipment you will need a covered grill, a cast-iron skillet, and a brick or large heavy rock wrapped in foil.

SPICY PASTE

3   tablespoons olive oil
1   tablespoon garlic powder
1   tablespoon ground mustard
1   teaspoon chili powder
1   tablespoon brown sugar
1   teaspoon freshly ground pepper
1   tablespoon paprika

1   chicken (3½ to 4 pounds), excess fat and skin trimmed, butterflied (see page 22)

To make the paste, in a small bowl, mix together all the ingredients.

Prepare a grill for cooking over medium indirect heat. Brush the chicken all over with the paste. Place the chicken skin-side down on the grate. Spray the bottom of a large cast-iron skillet with vegetable spray. Put the skillet containing a brick or large rock wrapped in foil on top of one half of the chicken. Grill for 10 minutes. Move the skillet to the other chicken half and grill for 10 minutes. Turn the chicken and repeat, alternating once more on each half for 10 minutes. Continue grilling uncovered, until it is no longer pink in the center or a meat thermometer inserted in the thigh registers 180°F, about 30 minutes longer. Total grilling time will be about 50 minutes.

Makes 4 servings

BEER CAN CHICKEN ON THE GRILL

Everyone thinks this is a fun way to grill chicken—at least, it gives you something to talk about! Roasting a whole chicken vertically on a can half filled with steaming beer produces a moist, succulent, juicy bird. Add a rub of your choice for flavor. A covered barbecue must be used.

1 chicken (3½ to 4 pounds), excess fat and skin trimmed, giblets and wing tips removed
1 tablespoon vegetable oil

Basic Spice Rub (recipe follows) or purchased rub
1 can (12 ounces) beer

Prepare a grill for cooking over medium indirect heat. Brush the chicken with oil and add the rub inside and out. Open the beer can and pour off (or drink) half of the beer. Place the chicken upright over the can so it fits in the cavity. Transfer the chicken to a foil pan. Place the pan on the grate, keeping the chicken upright. Cover and grill until a meat thermometer inserted in the thigh registers 180°F and the juices run clear when cut with a sharp knife in the thickest part, 1¼ to 1½ hours. Carefully lift the chicken off the can and transfer it to a platter. (The beer will be very hot.) Let it stand for 10 to 15 minutes before carving.

Makes 4 to 6 servings

BASIC SPICE RUB

1 tablespoon sugar
1 teaspoon garlic powder
1 teaspoon onion powder
1 teaspoon ground mustard
1 teaspoon paprika
1 teaspoon cayenne
1 teaspoon salt

In a small bowl, mix together all the ingredients. Store in a covered jar.

Makes about ¼ cup

CHICKEN BURGERS WITH CHIPOTLE MAYONNAISE

When seasonings are added, ground chicken makes delicious, lowfat burgers. You won't believe how good these burgers are. The chipotle mayonnaise adds a fresh taste and makes them unique. Serve with chips and vegetable strips.

1¼ pounds ground chicken
½ cup finely chopped yellow onion
¼ cup fine dried bread crumbs
¼ teaspoon salt
   Freshly ground pepper
4 slices Monterey Jack cheese
   Chipotle Mayonnaise (facing page)
4 hamburger buns, warmed
½ red onion, thinly sliced
   Lettuce leaves
   Tomato slices (optional)

In a medium bowl, mix together the chicken, onion, crumbs, salt, and pepper to taste. Cover and refrigerate for 30 minutes for easier handling. Form the mixture into 4 patties and spray both sides with vegetable spray.

Prepare a grill for cooking over medium indirect heat. Place the patties on the grate and grill until they are cooked through or a meat thermometer inserted in the center registers 165°F, 10 to 12 minutes, turning once. Add the cheese slices and cook until the cheese melts, 1 to 2 minutes longer. Spread Chipotle Mayonnaise on both sides of the buns. Add a patty, onion slice, lettuce leaf, and tomato slice, if using, to each bun and put on the top.

Makes 4 servings

CHIPOTLE MAYONNAISE

½	cup mayonnaise
1 or 2	chipotle chiles in adobo sauce, mashed
1	tablespoon fresh lime juice
1	tablespoon chopped fresh cilantro
1	garlic clove, minced
	Freshly ground pepper

In a small bowl, mix together all the ingredients. Let stand for several hours to allow the flavors to develop.

Makes about ¾ cup

CHICKEN BURGERS WITH PESTO MAYONNAISE

When seasonings are added, ground chicken makes delicious, lowfat burgers. You won't believe how good these burgers are. The basil pesto mayonnaise adds a fresh taste and makes them unique. Serve with chips and vegetable strips.

1¼ pounds ground chicken
2 tablespoons finely chopped green onions including some tender green tops
1 teaspoon Worcestershire sauce
½ teaspoon salt
Freshly ground pepper

1 to 2 drops Tabasco sauce
Pesto Mayonnaise (recipe follows)
4 seeded hamburger buns, warmed
¼ red onion, thinly sliced
Lettuce leaves

In a medium bowl, mix together the chicken, onions, Worcestershire, salt, pepper to taste, and Tabasco. Cover and refrigerate for 30 minutes for easier handling. Form the mixture into 4 patties and spray both sides with vegetable spray.

Prepare a grill for cooking over medium indirect heat. Place the patties on the grate and grill until they are cooked through or a meat thermometer inserted in the center registers 165°F, 10 to 12 minutes, turning once. Spread Pesto Mayonnaise on both sides of the buns. Add a patty, onion slice, and lettuce leaves to each bun and put on the top.

Makes 4 servings

PESTO MAYONNAISE

½ cup mayonnaise
¼ cup Basil Pesto (page 99) or purchased pesto
1 teaspoon fresh lemon juice
¼ teaspoon salt

In a small bowl, mix together all the ingredients.

Makes about ¾ cup

SOUTHWESTERN CHICKEN BURGERS

Chopped cilantro adds a fresh, distinctive flavor to these burgers topped with spicy cheese and avocado slices. Serve with tortilla chips and vegetable strips.

1¼ pounds ground chicken
3 tablespoons finely chopped fresh cilantro
2 tablespoons finely chopped yellow onion
½ teaspoon salt
    Freshly ground pepper
4 slices pepper Jack cheese
¼ cup mayonnaise
1 tablespoon chili sauce
4 onion hamburger buns, warmed
1 avocado, peeled, pitted, and sliced

In a medium bowl, mix together the chicken, cilantro, onions, salt, and pepper to taste. Cover and refrigerate for 30 minutes for easier handling. Form the mixture into 4 patties and spray both sides with vegetable spray.

Prepare a grill for cooking over medium indirect heat. Place the patties on the grate and grill until they are cooked through or a meat thermometer inserted in the center registers 165°F, 10 to 12 minutes, turning once. Add the cheese slices and grill until the cheese is melted, 1 to 2 minutes longer. In a small bowl, mix together the mayonnaise and chili sauce. Spread the mixture on both sides of the buns. Add a patty and avocado slices to each bun and put on the top.

Makes 4 servings

INDEX

❊ ABOUT THE AUTHOR

Maryana Vollstedt is a native of Oregon and graduated from Oregon State University with a degree in Home Economics. In 1952 she and her husband, Reed, started Reed and Cross, a small nursery and garden center that grew into a retail complex including a landscape service, a florist, a gift shop, clothing, gourmet cookware, a wine shop, and a deli. This is where Maryana started her writing career in the mid-1960s, by authoring the first cookbook and manual for the Kamado barbecue. She continued to write, and self-published 15 other cookbooks on a variety of subjects.

The Vollstedts sold the store in 1979 to travel and pursue other interests. Since 1995, Maryana has written *Pacific Fresh, What's for Dinner?, The Big Book of Casseroles, The Big Book of Soups and Stews, The Big Book of Breakfast, The Big Book of Potluck, The Big Book of Easy Suppers,* and *Meatloaf,* all published by Chronicle Books. These books, with practical recipes and straightforward directions, appeal to the home cook, and all have been best-sellers.

Maryana has written a bimonthly food column called "What's for Dinner?" for her local newspaper, the *Eugene Register-Guard,* for more than twelve years. She is active in her community as the volunteer coordinator for a mentor program in middle schools. She has four grown children, seven grandchildren, and one great-grandchild. Maryana lives with Reed in Eugene, Oregon, where she continues to write cookbooks. She can be reached through her Web site at www.maryanavollstedt.com.